My Windows® Phone 8

Brien Posey

800 East 96th Street,
Indianapolis, Indiana 46240 USA

My Windows® Phone 8

Copyright © 2013 by Pearson Education, Inc.

ISBN-13: 978-0-7897-4853-9
ISBN-10: 0-7897-4853-3

Library of Congress Control Number: 2013935207

Printed in the United States of America

First Printing: May 2013

Trademarks

All terms mentioned in this book that are known to be trademarks or service marks have been appropriately capitalized. Que Publishing cannot attest to the accuracy of this information. Use of a term in this book should not be regarded as affecting the validity of any trademark or service mark.

Warning and Disclaimer

Every effort has been made to make this book as complete and as accurate as possible, but no warranty or fitness is implied. The information provided is on an "as is" basis. The author and the publisher shall have neither liability nor responsibility to any person or entity with respect to any loss or damages arising from the information contained in this.

Bulk Sales

Que Publishing offers excellent discounts on this book when ordered in quantity for bulk purchases or special sales. For more information, please contact

U.S. Corporate and Government Sales
1-800-382-3419
corpsales@pearsontechgroup.com

For sales outside of the U.S., please contact

International Sales
international@pearsoned.com

Editor-in-Chief
Greg Wiegand

Executive Editor
Loretta Yates

Development Editor
Todd Brakke

Managing Editor
Kristy Hart

Senior Project Editor
Lori Lyons

Copy Editor
Krista Hansing Editorial Services

Indexer
Erika Millen

Proofreader
Kathy Ruiz

Technical Editor
Troy Thompson

Editorial Assistant
Cindy Teeters

Book Designer
Anne Jones

Compositor
Trina Wurst, TnT Design, Inc.

Manufacturing Buyer
Dan Uhrig

Contents at a Glance

Table of Contents

3 Messaging   69

4 The Multimedia Experience 117

6   Microsoft Office Mobile   229

8 The Phone   **315**

About the Author

Brien Posey is a ten-time Microsoft MVP with two decades of IT experience. Prior to becoming a freelance technical writer, Brien served as CIO for a national chain of hospitals and healthcare facilities. He has also worked as a network administrator for some of the nation's largest insurance companies and for the Department of Defense at Fort Knox.

Since going freelance in 2001, Brien has become a prolific technical author. He has published many thousands of articles and numerous books on a wide variety of topics (primarily focusing on enterprise networking). In addition to his writing, Brien has provided consulting services to clients and speaks at IT events all over the world.

When Brien isn't busy writing, he enjoys traveling to exotic places around the world with his wife Taz. Together they have visited more than sixty different countries. In fact, portions of this book were written while visiting Panama, Guatemala, and Columbia.

Some of Brien's other personal interests include scuba diving, aviation, flying RC helicopters, and shredding waves in his Cigarette boat. Brien's most recent endeavor has been to pursue his lifelong aspiration of becoming an astronaut.

Dedication

Over the past twenty years or so I have had the privilege of writing and contributing to dozens of books. Most of those books have focused on technology in some way. As you can imagine, technology has changed a lot in the last two decades. The one thing that has never changed is that I have dedicated every book that I have ever written to my wife Taz, whom I love very much. She really is the best wife that I ever could have hoped for.

This time around, however, I want to dedicate my book in loving memory of my sister, Cara. Sadly, Cara passed away while I was working on the last chapter of this book. Even though Cara was not an IT professional and probably didn't understand a lot of what she was reading, she read many of my books during her three-year battle with cancer. She often told me that my writing was a great cure for insomnia. Reading two or three pages was usually more than enough to put her to sleep. ;-)

Well, Cara, this one is for you!

Acknowledgments

First and foremost, I would like to thank my wife Taz for her patience and understanding while I was writing this book. Writing a book is a time-consuming process that unfortunately results in friends, family, and household chores being neglected.

It was especially rough this time around because I was working on multiple books at the same time, while also doing a 30-city speaking tour (on top of my usual work). I feel fortunate to have a wife who has put up with my crazy writing schedule for the past eighteen years and understands when I have to dedicate extra time to my writing.

I would also like to thank Loretta Yates for allowing me to write this book and for providing me with many other writing opportunities over the years. It is always a pleasure to work with Loretta, and her easy-going attitude really helps to ease the stress involved in taking on a project like this one.

I also want to thank Troy Thompson for doing the technical editing for yet another one of my books. I first met Troy back in the late 90s when we both worked at Fort Knox (thanks again for helping me to pass my Exchange Server exam).

Even though I left Fort Knox in the late 90s, Troy has remained one of my closest friends in spite of the fact that we live 500 miles apart. Troy has helped me with numerous projects like this one. I sleep well at night knowing that he is hard at work trying to keep my mistakes from making it into print.

Finally, I want to thank Todd Brakke, Krista Hansing, and the rest of the editorial and production team who has been hard at work behind the scenes to make this book the best it can be.

We Want to Hear from You!

As the reader of this book, *you* are our most important critic and commentator. We value your opinion and want to know what we're doing right, what we could do better, what areas you'd like to see us publish in, and any other words of wisdom you're willing to pass our way.

We welcome your comments. You can email or write to let us know what you did or didn't like about this book—as well as what we can do to make our books better.

Please note that we cannot help you with technical problems related to the topic of this book.

When you write, please be sure to include this book's title and author as well as your name and email address. We will carefully review your comments and share them with the author and editors who worked on the book.

Email: feedback@quepublishing.com

Mail: Que Publishing
          ATTN: Reader Feedback
          800 East 96th Street
          Indianapolis, IN 46240 USA

Reader Services

Visit our website and register this book at quepublishing.com/register for convenient access to any updates, downloads, or errata that might be available for this book.

Learn how to efficiently make
use of the Windows Phone
unique tile-based layout.

In this chapter, you learn the basics of working with Windows Phone 8. Some of the topics discussed in this chapter include:

→ The phone's hardware
→ Preparing your phone for its first use
→ The basics of interacting with your phone

Getting Started with Windows Phone 8

First, you get an overview of the device's physical features. Then you learn how to prepare the phone for its first use and install the Windows Phone software on your computer or tablet. Finally, you walk through the basics of interacting with your phone.

Minimum Hardware Specifications

Microsoft requires all Windows Phone 8 manufacturers to adhere to certain minimum hardware specifications. As a result, all Windows Phone 8 devices contain a certain minimum amount of hardware, such as the main processor (a Qualcomm Snapdragon S4 dual core processor) and support for at least the 802.11 b/g wireless standard (802.11n support is optional).

However, some phone manufacturers equip Windows Phone 8 devices with higher-end hardware. For example, some Windows Phone 8 devices offer additional storage through the use of Micro SD cards. Likewise, Microsoft allows manufacturers to choose from one of three display resolutions, outlined in this table.

	WVGA	**HD**	**WXGA**
Resolution	480×800	720×1280	768×1280
Aspect ratio	15:9	16:9	15:9
Phones that use these resolutions	Nokia Lumina 820 Nokia Lumina 810 Nokia Lumina 822 HTC Windows Phone 8S	HTC Windows Phone 8X	Nokia Lumina 920

The Phone's External Features

Although Windows Phone 8 is designed to be used primarily through the touchscreen interface, the phone includes a few hardware buttons designed to make the phone easier to use.

A. **Power button:** The power button turns the phone or the phone's display on and off. If you want to completely power down the phone, you do so by holding down the power button.

B. **Start button:** Pressing the Start button takes you to the phone's Start screen. Virtually everything you do with your Windows Phone begins here, as you'll see in tasks throughout this book. You can also hold down the Start button to access the phone's speech-recognition functions.

C. **Back button:** Pressing the Back button takes you to the previous screen or to the Task Switcher.

D. **Search button:** The Search button takes you to an interface that helps you locate information quickly.

E. **Volume buttons:** The volume buttons enable you to adjust the device's volume.

F. **Camera button:** Pressing the Camera button activates the device's camera. After that, you can press the button halfway to focus the camera or all the way to snap a photo.

In addition to the phone's hardware buttons, you need to know about a few other external features.

A. USB port: The USB port is used for charging the device and connecting it to a PC or tablet.

B. Headphone jack: The headphone jack is used for listening to media through headphones or for hands-free phone conversations.

C. Rear-Facing Camera lens: Windows Phone 8 includes a camera that can take still photos and videos.

D. Battery cover: The battery and the SIM card are located beneath the battery cover.

E. Micro SD card slot: Some Windows Phone 8 models include a micro SD slot that you can use to expand the phone's storage capacity.

F. Flash: Windows Phone 8 devices include a flash for the rear-facing camera.

G. Near Field Communications sensor: The Near Field Communications (NFC) sensor is used to facilitate Tap and Send functionality, and is also used by the new Microsoft Wallet feature. Some manufacturers have also created wireless chargers that power the phone through the NFC sensor when the phone is placed on top of the charger.

H. Front camera: Some Windows Phone 8 devices include a forward-facing camera. No flash is provided for this camera.

I. Speaker: This is the speaker used for the phone's audio.

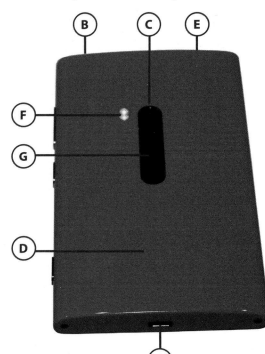

Getting Started with Your Phone

When you power up your Windows phone for the first time, you have to work through a short configuration wizard before you can use it. The phone gives you the choice of performing a setup with the recommended settings or using custom settings. The recommended settings are almost always acceptable, but both configurations are presented here.

Transferring Phone Numbers

In addition to the general set up, if you're upgrading from an existing phone, you may need to perform a procedure to transfer your old number to the new device. This procedure varies based on carrier and the device from which you're transferring, so you need to consult your phone provider for those directions.

Configuring the Phone Using the Recommended Settings

To configure the phone using the recommended settings, turn on your phone and follow these steps when the Welcome screen appears:

1. Tap Get Started.

2. Choose your language.

3. Tap Next, and then tap Accept when the Windows Phone Terms of Use screen appears.

4. Tap Recommended to set up the phone using the recommended settings.

5. Specify your home country or region.

6. Choose your time zone.

7. Choose whether you want to send your phone's location to Microsoft when the phone is activated.

8. Tap Next.

9. Tap Sign in Later on the Keep Your Life in Sync screen.

Microsoft Accounts

When prompted to sign in with a Microsoft account, you can use an existing account, create a new account, or choose the Sign In Later option. The remaining steps in this section are based on using the Sign In Later option; I cover Microsoft accounts in Chapter 3, "Messaging."

10. The phone takes a moment to set up any apps that the manufacturer preinstalled. When this process finishes, you see a message stating that all apps have finished installing. At this point, tap Next.

11. Tap Done.

CONFIGURING USING CUSTOM SETTINGS

Performing a custom setup (refer to Step 4) is similar to performing a recommended setup, except that you have the option of whether to allow the use of cellular data (as opposed to accessing data only over Wi-Fi). You also can choose whether you want to provide Microsoft with usage data. A few other settings control the phone's overall behavior, as shown here.

If you have a cellular plan that charges you based on the amount of data you use, you should perform a custom setup and deselect the option to send information to help improve Windows phones. This helps you avoid going over your data usage cap and incurring excess phone charges.

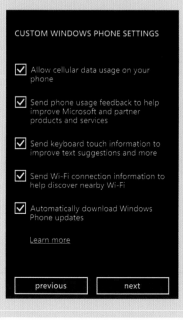

Installing the Windows Phone Software

Microsoft's Windows Phone app is an optional utility that can be used for copying data such as photos, music, or videos from a Windows 8 or RT device to your phone. The Windows Phone app is currently available only for devices running Windows 8 or Windows RT. You can install the Windows Phone app onto your computer or tablet by completing these steps:

1. Log into Windows 8 or Windows RT, and click on the Store tile.

2. Move the mouse to the right side of the screen, and click the Search icon.

3. Enter **Windows Phone 8** into the Search box. (Just start typing— the Search box automatically appears.)

4. Click Windows Phone Tools in the Search results.

5. Click Install.

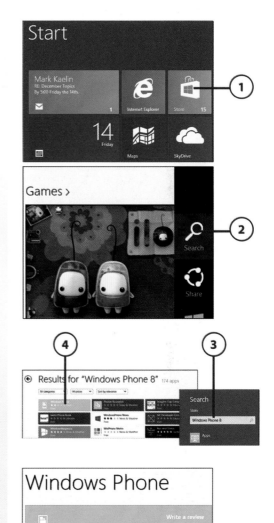

Do I Really Need the Software?

The Windows Phone software is not required for using your phone. You can use File Explorer (Windows 8) or Windows Explorer (Windows 7 and earlier) to drag and drop contents to and from the phone, as if the phone were a USB flash drive. However, if you have a Windows 8 PC or a Microsoft Surface tablet, the Windows Phone software can make it easier to manage photos, videos, music, and so on.

Setting Up the Windows Phone Software

The first time you use the Windows Phone software on your PC or tablet, you must perform a few steps that allow Windows to identify your phone. To do so, plug your phone into your Windows 8 PC or your tablet, and then complete these steps:

1. Launch the Windows Phone software by clicking the Windows Phone tile on the Start screen.

2. Provide a name for your phone. Windows uses this name to uniquely identify your phone from this point forward.

3. Decide whether you want your computer to automatically import your photos when you connect your phone. This behavior is enabled by default, but if you do not want photos automatically imported, you can deselect the Automatically Import My Photos When I Connect My Phone check box.

4. Click All Done.

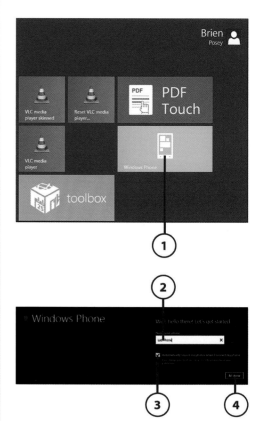

Updating the Phone

As is the case for the desktop Windows operating systems, such as Windows 7 and Windows 8, Microsoft periodically releases updates for Windows Phone 8. The phone can be configured to automatically download and install updates, but it is also possible to manually update the phone.

Accessing the Phone's Settings

The options for updating your phone are found on the phone's Settings screen. The Settings screen also contains dozens of other configuration options that are referenced throughout this book. You can access the Settings screen by completing these steps:

1. From the Start screen, flick the screen to the left to access the App List.

2. Scroll to the bottom of the App List and tap Settings.

Configuring How Windows Phone Updates

Your phone should be configured by default to automatically check for updates, but you can verify this behavior (and enable automatic updates, if necessary) by going to the phone's Settings screen and completing these steps:

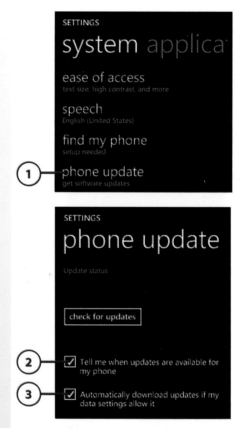

SETTINGS

system applica·

ease of access
text size, high contrast, and more

speech
English (United States)

find my phone
setup needed

① phone update
get software updates

SETTINGS

phone update

Update status

check for updates

② ☑ Tell me when updates are available for my phone

③ ☑ Automatically download updates if my data settings allow it

1. Tap Phone Update.

2. Select the Tell Me When Updates Are Available for My Phone check box.

3. You can optionally select the Automatically Download Updates If My Data Settings Allow It check box.

Manual Updates

If you don't want to use automatic updates, you can use this screen to manually update your phone by tapping the Check for Updates button.

It's Not All Good

It is generally recommended that you not use the cellular connection to check for updates. Some updates can be quite large, and you can consume a lot of air time and battery power if you download such updates over a cellular connection. You can download updates much more quickly using a Wi-Fi connection.

The Windows Phone 8 Interface

The Windows Phone 8 operating system makes use of the Modern interface (for a long time Microsoft called it Metro, but the had to abandon the term), which is also used in Windows 8 and Windows RT. This interface was designed specifically for use in touchscreen devices, which makes it ideal for use on Windows Phone 8 devices.

The Lock Screen

When you turn on a Windows Phone 8 device, the first thing you see is the lock screen. Although this screen initially looks like nothing more than a wallpaper screen, it provides several pieces of information.

A. **Cellular signal strength:** This indicator displays the signal strength as a series of bars. It also shows you when no cellular service is available. In the figure, this icon indicates that no service is available.

B. **Wireless connection type:** This icon displays the type of wireless connection. For example, the icon could indicate 4G or LTE connectivity.

C. **Wi-Fi indicator:** This icon shows you whether Wi-Fi is enabled, whether you're connected to a Wi-Fi network, and the network's signal strength.

D. **Battery strength:** The battery indicator shows how much battery power remains.

E. **Time:** This is the current time.

F. **Date:** This is today's date.

G. Message indicator: The bottom of the lock screen might contain icons indicating that you have missed messages. The icon in the figure indicates that a text message has been received, but you can also configure indicators to display missed calls or new e-mail messages.

You can get past the lock screen by touching the wallpaper and flicking it upward. If your phone has a lock screen password, you must enter that before you can continue to the Start screen.

Lock Screen Inconsistencies

Your Windows Phone 8's lock screen might differ slightly from the one shown here. Hardware manufacturers sometimes customize the lock screen by adding indicators or hiding default indicators. Windows Phone 8 also gives you the capability to customize some of the information shown on the lock screen.

Wireless Connection Types

The lock screen indicates the current wireless connection type via an icon at the top of the screen. Here is a list of the icons and their meanings:

- **G:** GPRS
- **E:** Edge
- **3G:** 3G

- **4G:** 4G
- **H:** HSDPA/HSUPA
- **1X:** RTT

- **DO:** EVDO
- **DV:** EVDV
- **LTE:** LTE

Other Common Indicators

As you saw in the previous section, Windows Phone 8 uses icons to convey the phone's status. A number of different icons can potentially appear on the phone's lock screen, or on the status bar displayed at the top of any of the phone's other screens. This section covers the icons that you might encounter and their meanings.

✈ Airplane mode

Battery charging

Battery charging complete

Battery remaining

Battery saver enabled

Bluetooth device connected

 Call forwarding enabled

 Cellular Connection is being shared

 Location information is being used by an app

 No signal

▲ Roaming

Signal strength

 Silent (ring and vibrate disabled)

 SIM locked

 SIM missing

Vibrate mode

Wi-Fi connected

Wi-Fi not connected

Customizing the Lock Screen

In the previous section, you saw that the Windows Phone 8 lock screen conveys device status information (such as the cellular signal strength and the date and time) even when the device is locked. Although this type of information can certainly be handy, you aren't limited to using the default lock screen. The lock screen is highly customizable. You can access the customization options by going to the Settings screen (see "Accessing the Phone's Settings," earlier in this chapter) and tapping the Lock Screen option.

Tap the Lock Screen option to customize the lock screen.

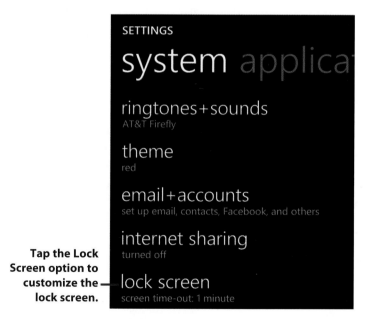

The next few sections take you through some of the customizations you can make from this screen.

Using a Photo as the Phone's Wallpaper

Just as you can configure desktop versions of Windows to display a personalized wallpaper image, you can change the wallpaper that Windows Phone 8 uses. To do so, go to the Lock Screen Settings screen and perform the following steps:

1. Tap Choose Background.

2. Tap Photo.

3. Tap Change Photo.

4. Tap either Camera Roll or Backgrounds. If you prefer, you can also select to have your photos shown by Date or Favorites. See Chapter 5, "Windows Phone 8 Apps."

5. Choose the photo that you want to use for the phone's wallpaper.

6. Position the photo on the screen, if necessary, by dragging it within the crop area.

7. Tap the Crop icon to complete the process.

Where's My Wallpaper?

The wallpaper that you choose is displayed only on the phone's Lock screen.

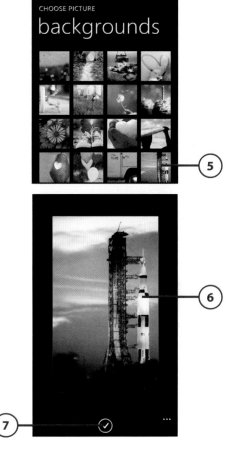

USING BING AS THE PHONE'S WALLPAPER

If you prefer, you can use Bing's daily photo as your desktop instead of using a photo of your own. This provides a degree of variety because the Bing desktop is regularly rotated. To configure Windows Phone 8 to use the Bing desktop, go to the Lock Screen Settings screen and, after you tap Choose Background, choose Bing instead of Photo.

>>>Go Further

Enabling Notifications

Windows Phone 8 enables you to choose one app from which to show detailed status information on the phone's lock screen. For example, you might choose to see notification information from your calendar, or you might opt to see text messages. You can configure notifications by going to the Lock Screen Settings screen and completing these steps:

1. Locate the Notifications section and then tap the Choose an App to Show Detailed Status box.

2. Tap the app for which you want to enable notifications.

Enabling Quick Status Indicators

Often you might not need detailed notifications on your lock screen. An indication of how many calls you have missed or how many e-mail messages you have received might be sufficient. Windows Phone 8 provides a mechanism for adding quick status indicators to the lock screen. To do so, go to the Lock Screen Settings screen and completing these steps:

1. Locate the Notifications section. The Quick Status icons indicate which quick status notifications are currently enabled.

2. To add a new notification, tap on one of the plus sign icons.

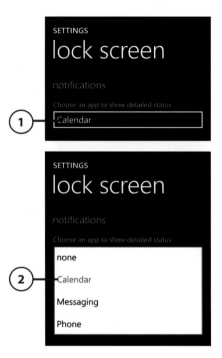

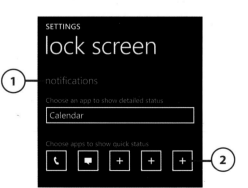

3. Choose the app for which you want to add a quick status notification. The chosen app's icon appears in place of the plus icon on the Lock Screen Settings screen.

CHOOSE AN APP

(3) Games

Messaging

Phone

Removing a Quick Status Notification

If you later decide to remove or replace a quick status notification, you can do so by going to the Lock Screen Settings screen and tapping the icon for that app. From there, you can choose to replace it with a different one or eliminate the notification icon altogether by selecting None.

Artist Information

Although music and related options are covered in Chapter 4, "The Multimedia Experience," you can do a bit of music-related customization from the Lock Screen Settings screen. Windows Phone 8 gives you the capability to display artist information on the phone's lock screen whenever music is playing. To do so, go to the Lock Screen Settings screen and complete these steps:

1. Locate the Show Artist when Playing Music option.

2. Set the slide bar to On.

SETTINGS

lock screen

(1) Show artist when playing music
Off   (2)

notifications

Choose an app to show detailed status

Calendar

The Start Screen

The Start screen (which you can access by pressing the Start button) contains a series of tiles, which Microsoft refers to as Live Tiles. Live Tiles serve two purposes. First, you can access commonly used apps and tools by tapping the appropriate Live Tile. Second, Live Tiles are often dynamically updated to provide important information through the tile itself. For instance, Live Tiles can tell you how many e-mail messages you have waiting or how many calls you missed.

Each device manufacturer can choose the Live Tiles that appear on the device's Start screen. Manufacturers typically use a combination of default Microsoft Live Tiles and custom Live Tiles. Of course, you can customize the Start screen by adding, removing, resizing, or rearranging Live Tiles using both the apps that came with your phone and apps you might download later from the App Store.

The Live Tiles that are present on the Start screen by default (excluding vendor-specific tiles) include these:

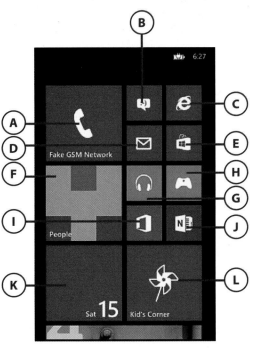

A. **Phone:** The Phone tile provides one-touch access to the dialing pad. The tile also displays the current number of missed calls.

B. **Messaging:** The Messaging tile displays the number of unread SMS text messages. You can tap the tile to access the messaging app.

C. **Internet Explorer:** The Internet Explorer tile provides access to Internet Explorer.

D. **Mail:** The Mail tile provides one-touch access to your e-mail. You can create multiple mail tiles if you have more than one mailbox. You can also configure Windows Phone 8 to display all your mail through a single mail tile.

E. **Store:** This tile provides access to the App Store.

F.   People: The People tile provides access to your contact list (known as the People Hub). The tile displays thumbnails of the profile photos used within your contacts.

G.   Music: The Music tile provides access to your music collection.

H.   Games: The Games tile provides access to your collection of games and to XBOX Live.

I.   Office: Tapping the Office tile takes you to the Microsoft Office hub.

J.   OneNote: Tapping the OneNote tile opens Microsoft OneNote.

K.   Calendar: The Calendar tile displays your next appointment and provides one-touch access to the device's calendar.

L.   Kids Corner: The Kids Corner tile provides access to the Kids Corner feature, which locks down your phone so that a child can access only the apps and features that you approve.

Too Many Default Tiles

The Start screen often contains too many default tiles to display them all at once. You can access additional default tiles by flicking the Start screen upward.

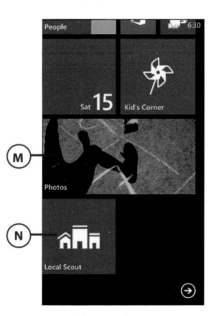

M.   Photos: The Photos tile provides access to your photo collection. The tile itself displays one of your photos.

N.   Local Scout: This tile provides access to information about your current geographic location. For instance, Local Scout can find nearby restaurants, shopping, and attractions.

Extra Tiles

Some phone manufacturers include extra tiles on the Start screen. For example, AT&T includes a tile for AT&T U-verse Mobile. Any extra tiles that are present on the Start screen by default are manufacturer specific and are not a part of the core Windows Phone 8 operating system.

As noted earlier, Windows Phone 8 does not require you to use the default tile layout. You can add, remove, rearrange, and resize the tiles to meet your own individual preferences.

Windows Phone 8 also enables you to control the size of the tiles on the Start screen. Tiles can be three different sizes, as shown here. In the case of Live Tiles, the size of the tile reflects the amount of information displayed on the tile.

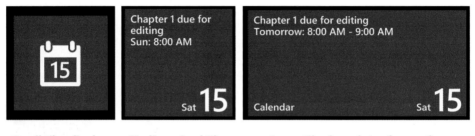

Small tiles display a minimal amount of information.

Medium sized tiles can display a bit more information.

Large tiles have lots of space for displaying data.

Moving a Tile

To rearrange the tiles on the Start screen, follow these steps:

1. Tap and hold the tile that you want to move. When the tile's appearance changes, drag the tile to the desired location. When the tile is in its new location, lift your finger and then tap the tile one last time.

Tile Arrangement

As you can see here, tile arrangement can vary greatly based on the size of the tiles. You can group together small tiles or mix and match them with medium or large tiles. It's entirely up to you!

Resizing a Tile

You can change the size of a tile by going to the Start screen and completing these steps:

1. Tap and hold the tile that you want to resize.

2. Tap the resize icon repeatedly until the tile reaches the desired size.

3. Tap the tile to accept the new size.

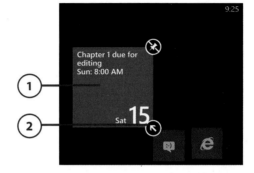

Removing a Tile

To remove a tile from the Start screen, complete these steps:

1. Tap and hold the tile until its appearance changes.

2. Tap the unpin button that is displayed in the upper-right corner of the tile.

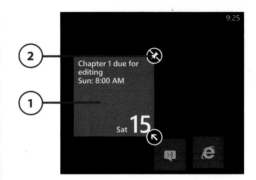

Adding a Tile

Virtually any object can be pinned to the Start screen. For example, you can pin an application to the Start screen, or you can pin an individual person from your contacts to the Start screen. That way, you can access that person's contact information and social networking updates with a single touch. To pin an object to the Start screen, follow these steps:

1. Tap and hold the object. In this example, I've selected the Calculator app in the Apps List (swipe left on the Start screen).

2. When the object's menu appears, tap the Pin to Start option.

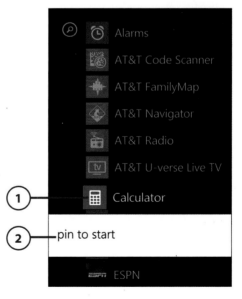

You Don't Have to Settle for the Defaults

The object is added to the bottom of the Start screen, but you can move it to any position.

Touch Gestures

Windows Phone 8 uses a multitouch display that supports six distinct touch gestures:

 Tap: In the Windows Phone 8 OS, a tap works exactly like it did in previous versions of Windows Mobile. You simply tap your finger on an object to select it.

 Double-tap: Windows Phone 8 enables you to open files and applications by double-tapping them.

Drag: Dragging enables you to scroll the device's screen. You simply press your finger onto the device screen and then move your finger in the direction you want to pan. The main Windows Phone 8 screen contains too many tiles to fit all of them onto the screen at once, so you must pan the screen to access some of the tiles.

Flicking

A variation on dragging is flicking, which enables you to scroll rapidly through a long list of items. Flicking is similar to panning, except that after you have pressed your finger onto the screen, you slide it quickly and then remove your finger.

 Touch and hold: The touch-and-hold gesture is used similarly to right-clicking your mouse in Windows 7. You simply press an object on the screen and then hold your finger in the same position until any available options are displayed. For example, you can use the touch-and-hold gesture to pin an item to the Start screen.

 Pinch: Use a pinch motion with two fingers to zoom in on a screen. To pinch, spread two fingers apart, and then put them on the screen and slide your fingers until they come together.

 Unpinch: Unpinching is the opposite of pinching and is used to zoom out on a screen. Place two fingers together on the screen, and then slide those fingers apart.

Using the Phone's Hardware Buttons

As you saw at the beginning of the chapter, in the section "The Phone's External Features," the front of the phone contains three hardware buttons. These buttons perform a variety of functions, depending on whether they are pressed or held.

The Back Button

Pressing the Back button returns you to the previous screen. In some cases, this can be a bit disorientating. If your previous screen was the Start screen, the phone usually skips it and instead takes you to the screen that you were viewing before the Start screen.

If you hold down the Back button, Windows displays the Task Switcher, which is new to Windows Phone 8. The Task Switcher displays a series of recently visited screens so that you can pick the screen you want to return to without having to repeatedly press the Back button.

The Start Button

Pressing the Start button from anywhere in the operating system takes you to the phone's Start screen. Holding down the Start button takes you to the voice command screen. I cover voice control in Chapter 9, "Search," along with verbal searches.

The Search Button

Pressing the Search button takes you to Bing so that you can perform a web search. I discuss searches at length in Chapter 9.

The Power Button

Pressing the power button turns off the phone's display. You can turn the display back on by pressing the power button again. When you turn off the display, the phone is still active—it can still receive phone calls and text messages, for example.

If you need to completely shut down the phone, you do so by pressing and holding the power button. After several seconds, the phone displays a shutdown screen that requires you to swipe the screen downward to truly shut down the phone. You can power the phone back up by pressing the power button.

The Volume Buttons

Windows Phone 8 devices include an up volume button and a down volume button. These buttons function differently, depending on how the phone is currently being used. For example, the volume buttons can change the ringer volume, call volume, or music volume.

The Camera Button

The Camera button accesses the Camera app. It is also used as a shutter button for taking still pictures or as a record button for filming video.

>>>Go Further

SCREEN CAPTURES

If you want to take a screen capture, you can do so by pressing the Start button and the Power button simultaneously. The screen quickly flickers, indicating that a screen capture has been taken. The screen capture is stored in the device's `Pictures\Screenshots` folder.

In an odd way, having the capability to take screen captures is one of my favorite new features in Windows Phone 8. When Windows Phone 7 was released, I wrote a book similar to this one, called *My Windows Phone 7*. Windows Phone 7 did not have the capability to capture screen shots, so every image in the book had to be shot with a digital camera. Issues such as camera focus, reflections, fingerprints on the touch screen, and the need to keep the phone and the camera completely level made the process of acquiring the necessary screen captures extremely tedious. Needless to say, being able to natively capture screens in Windows Phone 8 is a welcome new feature.

The Soft Keyboard

The primary method of entering text into Windows Phone 8 is through a soft (onscreen) keyboard. Instead of providing you with a generic soft keyboard, Windows Phone 8 uses one of six different soft keyboards, depending on the activity you are performing. These soft keyboards include the following:

Default: A standard QWERTY keyboard layout

Text: A standard QWERTY layout, plus emoticons

E-mail Address: QWERTY layout plus a .com key and an @ key

Phone number: A 12-key phone layout

Web address: The QWERTY layout plus a .com key and a custom Enter key

SMS address: A QWERTY layout with access to the phone layout

You might occasionally discover that the soft keyboard is missing some of the keys you need to use. When this happens, look for either a left or a right arrow key. Tapping this key reveals additional keys on the soft keyboard. You can sometimes also access additional keys by tapping and holding keys. For example, tapping and holding the period key displays other punctuation keys (comma, question mark, and so on).

Typing with the soft keyboard can take some getting used to. The soft keyboard lacks the tactical feel of a hardware keyboard, and the screen's size limits the size of the keys. As such, typing can be tricky. Fortunately, you can do a few things to make typing easier.

One suggestion is to turn the phone sideways. When you do, the display changes to landscape orientation. This makes the keys on the soft keyboard wider, which makes typing easier.

Q	W	E	R	T	Y	U	I	O	P
	A	S	D	F	G	H	J	K	L
↑	Z	X	C	V	B	N	M	⟨×⟩
&123	☺	,			space			.	↵

As you type, Windows suggests words based on the letters you have entered. You can tap on a suggested word instead of having to type the entire word.

The soft keyboard does not contain a Caps Lock key. To activate the caps lock, simply tap and hold the Shift key for a few seconds. (You can also quickly tap the Shift key twice.) Repeat the process to release the caps lock.

Keyboard Configuration

Windows Phone 8 enables you to configure the behavior of the keyboard, including whether suggestions are displayed as you type. I cover the various keyboard configuration options in Chapter 2, "Configuring Basic Device Settings."

Resetting Your Phone

It is possible to reset your phone to its factory settings. Keep in mind that resetting your phone erases all data and apps. Apps that the manufacturer built into the phone are automatically reinstalled when the phone is reset.

Restoring Factory Settings

To reset your phone, go to the Settings screen and follow these steps:

1. Scroll to the bottom of the screen and tap About.

2. Scroll to the bottom of the screen and tap Reset Your Phone.

3. Read the warning message, and then tap Yes.

The System Settings page provides access to many of the device's configuration options.

SETTINGS

system applica

ringtones+sounds
Pure

theme
red

email+accounts
set up email, contacts, Facebook, and others

lock screen
screen time-out: never

Tap an item to see its configuration options.

Wi-Fi
turned off

Bluetooth
turned off

tap+send
turned on

In this chapter, you will learn how to configure the basic device settings. Some of the topics covered in this chapter include:

→ Accessing basic device settings
→ Controlling the on-screen keyboard
→ Backing up your phone
→ Configuring the battery saver

Configuring Basic Device Settings

In the previous chapter, you learned that it is possible to customize Windows Phone 8's Start screen. However, you can personalize your phone in many other ways as well. In this chapter, you learn how to apply themes to your phone and perform a variety of other personalizations. In addition, this chapter walks you through the various settings that are available.

Accessing the Device Settings Screen

This chapter explains how to configure most of the Windows Phone 8 settings, although some of the settings are covered in later chapters. The goal of this chapter is to cover the basics. Settings corresponding to major device features are covered in the chapters that discuss those features. For example, E-mail related features are discussed in Chapter 3, "Messaging."

Most of the procedures outlined in this chapter involve using the phone's Settings screen, which is accessible from the Start screen. Simply swipe left on the Start screen to access the App List, and then tap the Settings icon, as shown here.

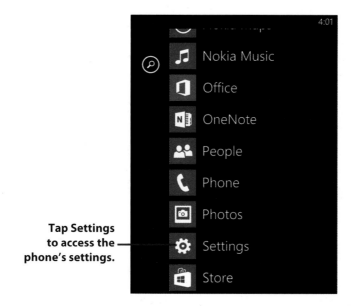

Tap Settings to access the phone's settings.

Changing the Device Theme

Although most Windows Phone 8 devices use red as the primary color for Live Tiles and some configuration options, you can alter the device's primary color by changing the device's theme. Go to the Settings screen and follow these steps:

1. Tap Theme.

2. Set the background to either Dark or Light.

3. Choose an Accent color.

Wi-Fi Networking

Even though Windows Phone 8 is designed to access the Internet through a cellular connection, the phone also supports Wi-Fi connectivity. Wi-Fi connections allow for faster Internet connectivity than what is possible through a cellular link, and using Wi-Fi has the added benefit of not incurring any data charges on your cellular bill. All Windows Phone 8 devices include support for 802.11b and 802.11g; some phones also offer 802.11n support.

Enabling or Disabling Wi-Fi

You can enable or disable Wi-Fi on a Windows Phone 8 device by going to the Settings screen and following these steps:

1. Tap Wi-Fi.

2. Use the slide bar to enable or disable Wi-Fi.

theme
red

email+accounts
set up email, contacts, Facebook, and others

lock screen
screen time-out: never

Wi-Fi
turned off

Bluetooth
turned off

SETTINGS
Wi-Fi

Wi-Fi networking
On

Connecting to a Wi-Fi Network

To connect a Windows Phone 8 device to a Wi-Fi network, go to the Settings screen and complete these steps:

1. Tap Wi-Fi.

2. Verify that Wi-Fi Networking is enabled.

3. Tap the Wi-Fi network that you want to connect to.

4. If the network is secured, it prompts you to enter the network password. If you have trouble entering the password blindly, you can select the Show Password check box to make the password visible. Remember that most wireless access points use case-sensitive passwords.

5. Tap Done. You see a message indicating that you are connected to the wireless network.

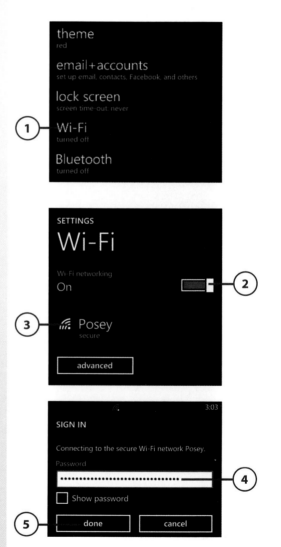

SUPPORT FOR HIDDEN WIRELESS NETWORKS

Some organizations disable SSID broadcasts to hide their wireless networks. Windows Phone 8 fully supports connecting to a hidden Wi-Fi network, as long as you know its name. If you need to connect to a hidden Wi-Fi network, go to the Wi-Fi settings screen and tap the Advanced button. Then tap the Add icon at the bottom of the screen and enter the name of the network you want to connect to. It is worth noting, however, that connecting to a hidden wireless network decreases the phone's battery life.

Removing Known Networks

Windows Phone 8 is designed to remember the settings for every Wi-Fi network you connect to. If you intend to connect your phone to a lot of public Wi-Fi hotspots, you will eventually accumulate a long list of known networks. Some of these networks might be Wi-Fi hotspots that you will never connect to again. Fortunately, there is an easy way to delete references to unwanted wireless networks. To remove these networks, go to the Settings screen and follow these steps:

1. Tap Wi-Fi.
2. Tap the Advanced button.

3. Tap the Select icon.

4. Select the check boxes for each network you want to remove.

5. Tap the Delete icon.

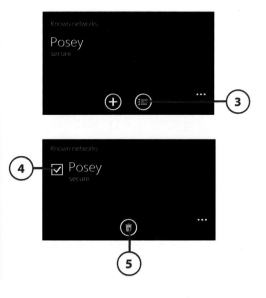

Passwords and Screen Timeouts

Few electronic devices contain as much sensitive information as a smartphone. If someone stole your cellphone, the thief could potentially use the information stored in your phone to determine the following details:

- Where you live

- When you will be away from home (by looking at the information in your calendar)

- The names and contact information of your friends, family, and business associates

As if that were not enough, someone who is in possession of your phone could send e-mail messages posing as you, or could run up your phone bill by placing a bunch of international calls. As such, you need to protect your Windows Phone 8 device just as you would protect a laptop loaded with personal information.

Setting the Screen Timeout

In an effort to preserve battery life and improve security, Windows Phone 8 is designed to time out after a period of inactivity. When the timeout threshold is reached, the device's screen automatically turns off, forcing you to re-enter your phone's password to regain access. You can adjust the timeout threshold period by going to the Settings screen and following these steps:

1. Tap Lock Screen.

2. Scroll to the bottom of the Lock Screen Settings screen and tap the Screen Times Out After box.

3. Choose the screen timeout period. You can choose 30 Seconds, 1 Minute, 3 Minutes, 5 Minutes, 15 Minutes, 30 Minutes, or Never. (The available options vary depending on device make and model.)

Saving Changes

The Lock and Wallpaper screen does not have any kind of button that you can press to make Windows accept the changes you have made. If you change the screen timeout period, your change goes into effect as soon as you select it. It is also worth noting that some device manufacturers do not offer the Never option.

Enabling a Password

The single most important thing that you can do to protect your phone is to configure it to require a password for access. To enable the password requirement, return to the lock screen and complete the following steps:

1. Scroll to the bottom of the screen and set the Password slide bar to On.

2. When prompted, enter a numeric password. You can use the Show Password check box to make the password visible as you type it, if necessary.

3. Tap Confirm Password and re-enter your password.

4. Tap Done.

Don't Forget Your Password

If you use a password with your Windows Phone 8 device, be careful not to forget it. There is no way to retrieve a lost password. If you forget your password, you will be forced to reset the device to its factory defaults, which means losing your data and having to redownload your apps.

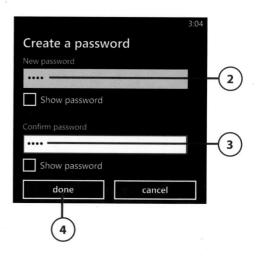

Changing Your Password

Most security professionals agree that changing your password on a regular basis is a good idea. You can change your password by returning to the phone's Lock Screen settings and completing these steps:

1. Tap Change Password.

2. Enter your previous password in the Current Password box.

3. Tap New Password and enter a new password.

4. Re-enter your new password in the Confirm Password box.

5. Tap Done.

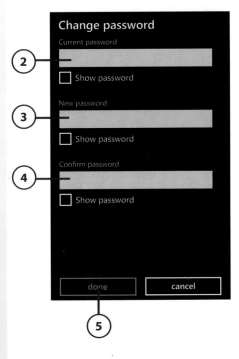

Disabling a Password

Although it is not necessarily recommended, you can disable your device's password so that you are no longer required to enter a password to access the device. To disable a password, return to the Lock Screen settings and complete these steps:

1. Set the Password slide bar to Off.

2. When prompted, enter your password.

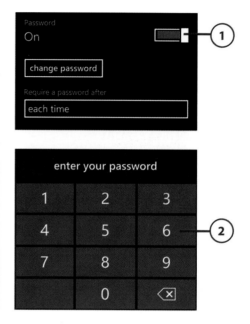

Date and Time

Although it might seem trivial, it is important to ensure that the phone's date and time are set correctly. Some of the phone's functions might not work properly unless they're both accurate.

Windows Phone 8 provides two methods for setting the date and time. You can manually set the date and time, or you can have the phone to do it automatically. In either case, you can access the date and time settings by going to the Settings screen and tapping Date+Time.

Setting the Date and Time

Windows Phone 8's default behavior is to set the date and time automatically. If you prefer to set the date and time manually, you can easily accomplish this by going to the Settings screen, tapping Date+Time, and following these steps:

1. Set the Set Automatically slide bar to Off.

Setting for Automatic

You can always return to setting date and time automatically by setting this slider back to On.

2. Tap Date.

3. Set the date by tapping each number and dragging up and down to pick the correct day, month, and year.

4. Tap the Done icon.

5. Tap Time.

6. Set the time by tapping each part of the time and selecting the correct hour and minute; be sure to specify whether it's a.m. or p.m.

7. Tap the Done icon when you are finished.

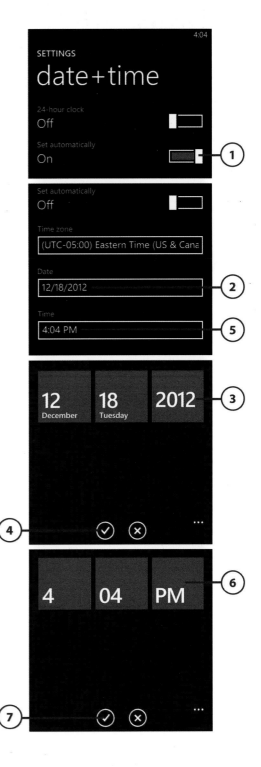

Changing Time Zones

If you can receive a cell signal, most cellular providers automatically adjust the time zone for you. But for that to work, you need to have a signal and have the time configured to be set automatically. If you manually set your phone's time and date, you also need to set your current time zone by going to the Settings screen, tapping Date+Time, and completing these steps:

1. Set the Set Automatically slide bar to Off.

2. Tap Time Zone.

3. Choose your desired time zone.

Time Zones and Your Calendar

When you change time zones, whether manually or automatically, any appointments that are stored in your calendar shift to reflect the local time. For example, if you start in Eastern Standard Time and enter a 2:30 appointment, and then fly to the West Coast, the calendar will display the appointment as occurring at 11:30, in response to the time zone change.

Using Military Time

Those who have served in the Armed Forces or who operate on a 24-hour clock might prefer to configure the phone to use military time. To enable military time, go to the Settings screen, tap Date+Time, and complete the following step:

1. Slide the 24-Hour Clock slide bar to On.

SETTINGS

date+time

24-hour clock
Off

Set automatically
Off   —①

Time zone
(UTC-05:00) Eastern Time (US & Cana   —②

Guadalajara, Mexico City, Monterrey
(UTC-06:00)

Saskatchewan
(UTC-06:00)

Bogota, Lima, Quito
(UTC-05:00)

Eastern Time (US & Canada)   —③
(UTC-05:00)

The time switches to 24 hour format

16:06

SETTINGS

date+time

24-hour clock
On   —①

Set automatically
On

Screen Brightness

Windows Phone 8 enables you to adjust the brightness of the screen either automatically (in response to the current lighting conditions) or manually to a level of your choosing.

Automatically Adjusting the Screen Brightness

Windows Phone 8 can automatically adjust the screen's brightness based on the current lighting conditions. If you want the phone to adjust the screen's brightness automatically, go to the Settings screen and perform these steps:

1. Scroll through the list of settings and tap Brightness.

2. Set the Automatically Adjust slide bar to On.

SETTINGS

system applica

turned off, 100% battery left

phone storage
26.88 GB free

backup
save stuff to the cloud

date+time
(UTC-05:00) Eastern Time (US & Canada)

brightness
automatic

SETTINGS

brightness

Automatically adjust

On

Level

high

Manually Adjusting the Screen Brightness

Manually adjusting the screen's brightness enables you to maintain a certain level of brightness, regardless of the current lighting conditions. For example, Windows Phone 8 is designed to automatically dim the screen when you are using the phone in a dark area and to brighten the screen when you are in a bright area. If you prefer to use a consistent level of brightness, go to the Settings screen and follow these steps:

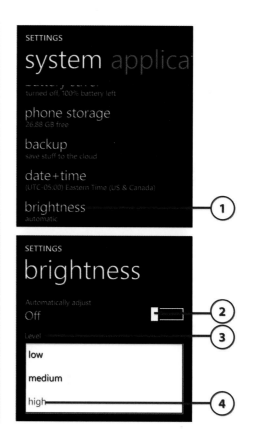

1. Scroll through the list of settings and Tap Brightness.

2. Set the Automatically Adjust slide bar to Off.

3. Tap Level.

4. Choose your desired brightness level.

Controlling the Keyboard's Behavior

In Chapter 1, "Getting Started with Windows Phone 8," you saw how Windows Phone 8 automatically suggests words as you type. However, you can control this and other behaviors through the phone's keyboard configuration settings.

For example, Microsoft provides different language selections for the Windows Phone 8 keyboard. The language that you choose affects the appearance of the soft keyboard, as well as the words that are suggested as you type. You can also remove languages from your phone, switch between installed languages, and more.

Setting the Keyboard Language

The keyboard defaults to using the language that you specified when you initially set up the phone, but you can add support for additional languages. You can also change the keyboard's language. You can configure the keyboard language by going to the Settings screen and completing these steps:

1. Scroll to and then tap the Keyboard option.

2. Tap Add Keyboards.

3. Tap the check boxes for the languages that you want to add.

4. Tap the Done icon.

Switching Between Multiple Keyboard Languages

When multiple keyboard languages are enabled, the onscreen keyboard defaults to using the language that you specified first. However, you can toggle between keyboard languages on the fly by tapping the language key.

Removing a Keyboard Language

After adding a keyboard language, you might later discover that you no longer want to use one of the languages that have been configured. To remove support for a language, go to the Settings screen, tap Keyboards, and then follow these steps:

1. Tap and hold the listing for the language that you want to remove.

2. Tap Remove.

Clearing Custom Suggestions

As you compose e-mail and text messages, you will occasionally use words that are not built into the phone's dictionary. Windows Phone 8 pays attention to the words that you use frequently and adds those words to the list of suggestions that are displayed as you type. The down side to this behavior is that if you frequently misspell words and don't correct them, your phone may begin to suggest those misspellings. As such, Microsoft gives you a way to clear the phone's cache of custom suggestions. To clear the custom suggestion list, go to the Settings screen, tap Keyboards, and follow these steps:

1. Tap the Advanced button.

2. Tap the Reset Suggestions button. When prompted, tap the Reset button.

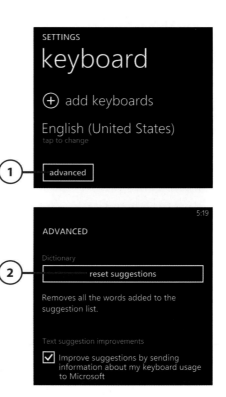

It's Not All Good

Windows Phone 8 has an autocorrect option that is enabled by default to automatically correct misspelled words. Unfortunately, this option sometimes changes words that are correct but unrecognized into something incorrect. For example, my wife's nickname is Taz, but whenever I try to type her name, AutoCorrect changes it to Tax.

AutoCorrect has been known to be problematic on mobile platforms other than Windows Phone 8. A friend of mine recently embarrassed herself by posting to Facebook without noticing what AutoCorrect had done to her typing. The post was supposed to have said, "Screw the gym, tonight I am getting Pringles." By the time Auto Correct got done with her post, it said, "Screen the gym, tonight I am getting pregnant." Thankfully, the Windows Phone 8 dictionary recognizes the word Pringles, so this particular mistake shouldn't happen to anyone who is using a Windows Phone 8 device! Even so, you have to be careful when using AutoCorrect.

Customizing the Keyboard's Behavior

Windows Phone 8 lets you fully customize the onscreen keyboard's behavior. For instance, you can disable the Auto Correct option or automatic capitalization. To customize the keyboard's behavior, go to the Settings page, tap Keyboard, and complete these steps:

1. Tap your preferred language.

2. Deselect the options that you want to disable. The keyboard behavior options that are available for American English keyboards include these:

Suggest Text: Causes the phone to display a list of words as you type. You can tap these suggestions as a shortcut instead of having to type the entire word.

Highlight Misspelled Words: When this option is enabled, misspelled words are underlined.

Correct Misspelled Words: When enabled, this option causes Windows to automatically correct misspelled words.

Insert a Space After Selecting a Suggestion: This option causes a space to be inserted when you select block of text.

Insert a Period After Double Tapping the Spacebar: If you double-tap the spacebar at the end of a sentence, this option inserts a period before the spaces.

Capitalize the First Letter of a Sentence: This option causes the first letter of a sentence to be automatically capitalized.

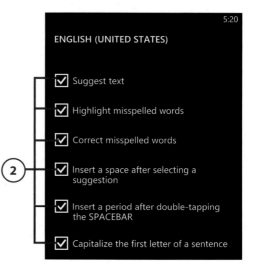

Configuring Regions and Languages

Windows Phone 8 supports custom localizations for more than just the keyboard. You can also configure device-wide settings that control things such as the preferred language and the preferred currency. You can adjust these global localization settings by going to the Settings screen and following these steps:

1. Tap Language+Region.

2. Tap the regional setting that you want to adjust. The options available include the following:

    Phone Language: The primary language that should be used on the device.

    Country/Region: The primary country where the device will be used.

    Region Format: The way various region specific parameters are displayed (such as currency). Unlike previous versions of Windows Phone, you cannot adjust the currency, date, and time formats outside the regional format.

    Browser and Search Language: The language that you want to use for Internet Explorer and Bing.

3. When you select the Regional Format box, you must then choose your preferred localization option.

SETTINGS

system applica

save start to the cloud

date+time
(UTC-05:00) Eastern Time (US & Canada)

brightness
high

keyboard
English

language+region
English (United States)

— (1)

5:21

SETTINGS

language+regi

Phone language

English (United States)

Country/Region

United States

Regional format

United States (English)

Regional format example:
Date: Tuesday, December 18, 2012
Time: 5:20 PM
Currency: $

Browser & search language

English (United States)

— (2)

United Kingdom (English)

United Kingdom (Scottish Gaelic)

United Kingdom (Welsh)

United States (Cherokee)

United States (English)

— (3)

Accessibility

Windows Phone's Ease of Access settings enable you to enable or disable various features designed to make it easier for people with disabilities to use the device. You can access these settings by going to the Settings screen and tapping Ease of Access.

Accessibility options are located under Ease of Access.

Adjusting the Text Size

You can adjust the text size as a way of making information displayed on the phone easier to read. To change the text size, go to the Ease of Access screen and perform the following steps:

1. Drag the Text Size slide bar to adjust the text size. Dragging the bar to the right makes the text larger; dragging it to the left makes the text smaller.

2. Use the Sample box to preview your selected text size.

Enabling High Contrast

A normal Windows Phone 8 display (using the default theme) displays some text in white and other text in gray. You can make the text earlier to read by using a high-contrast display. This causes all text to display in white. You can enable the high-contrast display by going to the Settings screen, tapping Ease of Access, and follow this step:

1. Drag the High Contrast slide bar to the On position.

SETTINGS

ease of access

Text size

Sample

Changes the text size in phone, People, email, messaging, and lock screen.

High contrast
On ———————— ①

Changes the colors for some features, and hides some of their background images.

High contrast displays use only black and white, not gray.

Enabling the Screen Magnifier

Enabling the magnifier option gives you the capability to zoom the screen on demand to make text and graphics larger or smaller. To enable the screen magnifier, go to the Settings screen, tap Ease of Access, and then complete the following step:

1. Drag the Screen Magnifier slide bar to the On position.

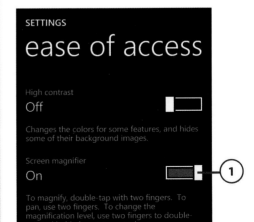

SETTINGS

ease of access

High contrast
Off

Changes the colors for some features, and hides some of their background images.

Screen magnifier
On ———————— ①

To magnify, double-tap with two fingers. To pan, use two fingers. To change the magnification level, use two fingers to double-tap and hold, then pan up or down.

>>>Go Further

USING THE MAGNIFIER

Enabling the magnifier does not automatically magnify the screen; it only *enables* you to magnify the screen. Magnification is controlled through a series of gestures:

- **Enable magnification:** Double-tap with two fingers.
- **Pan:** Move the screen using two fingers.
- **Change the magnification level:** Using two fingers, double-tap, hold, and then pan up or down.

It's Not All Good

The finger gestures used to control the magnify feature are not exactly intuitive. It stands to reason that Microsoft would have used a pinching motion to control the level of magnification, yet they opted for an obscure finger gesture instead.

Using Speech for Phone Accessibility

Even though the accessibility features are primarily intended for use by disabled persons, the Speech for Phone Accessibility feature is one of my favorite phone features. This feature enables talking caller ID. When the phone rings, it rings at normal volume once and then verbally announces the caller while playing a somewhat muffled ring tone. To enable this feature, go to the Settings screen, tap Ease of Access, and then follow these steps:

1. Scroll the display upward to reveal the Speech for Phone Accessibility section.

2. Slide the Speech for Phone Accessibility slide bar to the On position.

SETTINGS

ease of access

To magnify, double-tap with two fingers. To pan, use two fingers. To change the magnification level, use two fingers to double-tap and hold, then pan up or down.

(1)

Speech for phone accessibility
Off

(2)

Use Speech for speed dial, call forwarding, and announcing caller ID

Find My Phone

If your Windows Phone 8 device is ever lost or stolen, you can use the Find My Phone feature to locate it. This feature enables you to locate your phone by forcing it to ring (even if it is on silent or vibrate mode) or by displaying the phone's location on a map. You also have the option of locking the phone or erasing its contents.

Prerequisite Requirement

To use the Find My Phone feature, your phone must be linked to a Microsoft account.

Although anyone with cellular service can use the Find My Phone feature, it is a good idea to review your phone's configuration. Options exist that can help to improve your phone's location accuracy in case you ever need to track down your phone. You can access these configuration options by going to the Settings screen and tapping Find My Phone.

It's easier to locate your phone if you enable this option.

The Find My Phone screen contains two options. The first option is Send Apps to My Phone Using Push Notifications (Not SMS). You don't normally have to enable this option unless instructed to do so by Microsoft support.

The other option is Save My Phone's Location Periodically and Before the Battery Runs Out to Make It Easier to Find. Using this option might help you locate a lost phone more quickly, but enabling this feature can have an impact on battery life because the phone is required to periodically transmit location information.

Finding Your Phone

You have a few different options for finding your phone. You can force the phone to ring, or you can display its location on a map. You also have the option to lock your phone or remotely erase its contents. To access these features:

1. From your computer, go to www. windowsphone.com and log in using your Microsoft account.

2. Click the Windows Phone drop-down list.

3. Click the Find My Phone link.

4. Click Find My Phone.

5. When prompted, verify your phone number and select the check box authorizing Microsoft to find your phone.

6. Click Done.

7. Click Find My Phone again. After you do so, your phone's location is displayed on a map.

Your Experience May Differ

The steps listed here were based on using the Nokia 920, but users of some other makes and models of phones have reported a slightly different experience.

A LITTLE MORE DETAIL PLEASE!

As you look at the screen capture shown here, you might be concerned about how helpful the Find My Phone feature really is. After all, the map indicates that my phone is somewhere in the state of South Carolina. A little more detail would be nice! In actuality, I have the map zoomed all the way out, as a way of protecting my privacy. You can easily zoom in to determine the phone's exact whereabouts.

It is also worth mentioning that the Find My Phone interface contains links for refreshing the display, printing the map, and centering your phone on the map.

Other Location Options

Although mapping your phone's location is the primary method for finding your phone, it isn't the only option available. The other options on the Find My Phone screen include these:

Ring: Force the phone to ring nonstop for 1 minute, even if the phone is on silent or vibrate modes. To silence the ring, turn the phone's display off and back on.

Lock: Use this option to lock your phone. You can even use this option to put a Please Return message on the phone's lock screen. You can also add a PIN to the phone, even if you hadn't previously created one. There is even an option to ring the phone as you lock it.

Erase: Reset the phone to its factory settings. You'll lose any data you have on the phone, but you also prevent anyone else from accessing it.

Windows Phone 8 gives you other options for finding your phone.

About Your Phone

The About option is designed primarily for people who need technical assistance. The About screen provides virtually everything you need when seeking help, including detailed information about the phone's hardware and firmware and contact information for the technical support department. The About screen also provides links to the phone's Terms of Use policy and privacy policy. You can access the About screen by going to the Settings screen and tapping About.

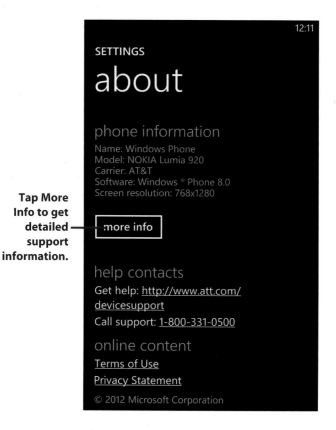

Tap More Info to get detailed support information.

Avoid the Reset Button!

The bottom of the About screen contains a button labeled Reset Your Phone (as discussed in the previous chapter). Tapping this button permanently erases your data and your apps (although your phone asks for a final confirmation before doing so). It's exceedingly unlikely that you'll need to use this option, except perhaps if you're giving your phone to someone else and want your data off it.

TECHNICAL SUPPORT

If you ever have to call technical support about a problem with your phone, you might find that the support technician needs more detailed information about your phone's hardware and firmware versions than what is displayed on the About screen. If so, go to the About screen and tap the More Info button. This causes the phone to reveal much more detailed version information.

Providing Feedback

The Feedback option enables you to control whether user experience information is sent to Microsoft. The information that is collected is used to improve Windows Phone. If you choose to enable the Feedback feature, feedback information is sent only over Wi-Fi connections; your cellular connection is never used. To configure feedback, go to the Settings screen and perform the following steps:

1. Tap Feedback.

2. Use the slide bar to turn feedback either on or off.

Protecting Your Privacy

Because your phone likely contains a lot of personal information, it is important to take steps to protect your privacy. As such, I recommend that you read Microsoft's privacy statement before enabling the Feedback feature. It is also worth noting that feedback information is sent only over a Wi-Fi connection. Even so, you should be aware that the phone might send as much as 10MB of feedback data every seven days.

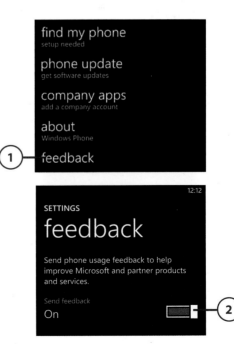

Backing Up Your Phone

As is the case with any computing device, it is a good idea to back up your Windows Phone 8 device, to prevent data from being lost if your phone is ever lost or destroyed. After all, you wouldn't want to lose irreplaceable pictures, videos, or application data. Fortunately, Windows Phone 8 contains a mechanism for backing up the phone to the cloud. You can access the backup settings by going to the Settings page, scrolling down, and tapping Backup.

You can back up three types of data:

- App list and settings

- Text messages

- Photos and video

Windows Phone 8 can be configured to back up any combination of these data types.

You have three options for backing up your phone.

Backing Up App Lists and Settings

When you back up your app lists and settings, you are really backing up your Internet Explorer favorites, a list of all the apps that were installed on the phone, and the configuration settings for your apps. You can back up your app list and settings by completing these steps:

1. Tap App List+Settings.

2. Set the Backup slide bar to the On position.

An Immediate Backup

If you want to perform an immediate backup, go to the App List+Settings screen and tap the Back Up Now button.

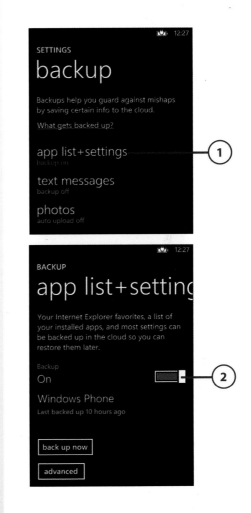

Removing Your Backup

If you want to erase your App List+Settings backup from cloud storage, you can do so by going to the Backup screen and following these steps:

1. Tap App List+Settings.

2. Tap Advanced.

3. Tap the Delete button.

It's Not All Good

Be careful not to press the Delete button by accident. Windows Phone 8 does not prompt you for confirmation before deleting your App List+Settings backup.

Backing Up Text Messages

Windows Phone 8 makes it possible to back up your text messages. The interesting point about the way Microsoft implemented this feature is that there are separate settings for regular text messages and group text messages. This enables you to back up only personal messages, without having to back up group texts. Of course, you can back up group texts, too, if you want. To back up all your text messages, go to the Backup screen and perform the following steps:

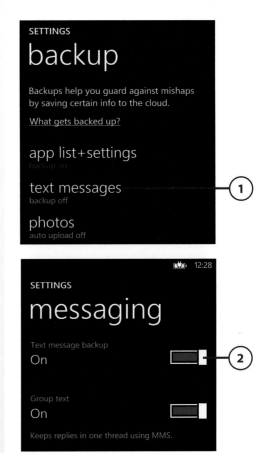

1. Tap Text Messages.

2. Set the Text Message Backup slide bar to the On position.

Unlike App List+Settings backups, there is no Backup Now option for text messages.

Determining Backup Quality for Your Photos and Videos

If you have photos or video on your phone that you really don't want to lose, it is extremely important to back them up. Windows Phone 8 uses the Photos backup function to back up both photos and video, although you can control photo and video backups separately.

As you plan your backups, you must determine how important the quality of your photos and videos is. Microsoft gives you three options for photo and video backups:

- **Don't Upload:** Data is not backed up.

- **Good Quality:** The backup copy of your photos and videos might not be as good as the quality of the original. You can make good-quality photo backups over the phone's cellular connection. Good-quality video backups require Wi-Fi.

- **Best Quality:** The quality of the backup is as good as the quality of the photo and video files stored in your phone. Best-quality backups require Wi-Fi for both photos and videos.

Backing Up Your Photos and Videos

To back up your photos and videos, go to the Backup screen and perform the following steps:

1. Tap Photos.

2. Choose the quality of backup that you want to use for your photos.

3. Choose the quality of backup that you want to use for your videos.

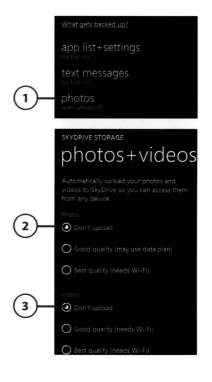

Its Not All Good

Unlike App List+Settings backups, no Backup Now option exists for backing up photos or videos.

Restoring Your Backups

Microsoft does not provide direct access to your backups. You can access your backups only if you are setting up your phone for the first time (you can reset your existing phone or replace it with a new phone). During the initial configuration process, Windows Phone 8 asks if you want to connect to a Microsoft account. Assuming that you use the same Microsoft account that you were previously using, you can restore your backup by following these steps:

1. The phone asks whether you want to start fresh or restore your backup. Tap your backup.

2. Tap Next.

3. Tap Next on the Preparing to Restore screen, which tells you how the restore process works.

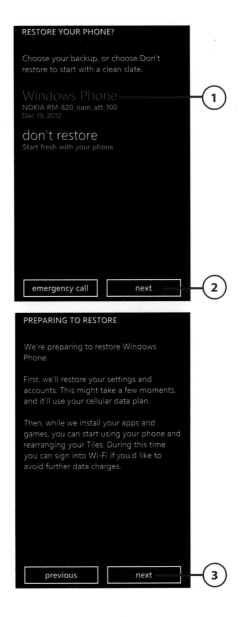

RESTORE YOUR PHONE?

Choose your backup, or choose Don't restore to start with a clean slate.

Windows Phone
NOKIA RM-820_nam_att_100
Dec 19, 2012

don't restore
Start fresh with your phone

emergency call   next

PREPARING TO RESTORE

We're preparing to restore Windows Phone.

First, we'll restore your settings and accounts. This might take a few moments, and it'll use your cellular data plan.

Then, while we install your apps and games, you can start using your phone and rearranging your Tiles. During this time you can sign into Wi-Fi if you'd like to avoid further data charges.

previous   next

4. Wait for the initial restoration to complete and then tap Next. From there, you can continue with the remainder of the phone Setup process as described in Chapter 1.

Enable Wi-Fi Immediately!

When you restore a backup, your Wi-Fi connectivity is not restored as part of the App List+Settings restoration. You must manually configure your Wi-Fi connectivity—and you should do so quickly, to avoid excessive data charges.

RESTORING YOUR PHONE

We're restoring your phone's settings. It may take a few moments.

Downloading 4%

emergency call   next

Battery Saver

The Battery Saver is a feature that can disable some of the phone's functions when the battery gets low, as a way of saving power. When the Battery Saver is enabled, the phone still receives calls and texts, but apps run only when you open them and e-mail must be synchronized manually. You can enable the Battery Saver by going to the Settings screen and following these steps:

1. Tap Battery Saver.

SETTINGS

system applica

cellular
no network found

location
turned on

kid's corner
turned off

battery saver
turned off, 100% battery left

2. Move the Battery Saver slide bar to the On position.

3. Tap the Advanced button.

4. Choose when the Battery Saver should be enabled.

5. When enabled, whenever Battery Saver is engaged, you see a heart symbol over the battery life indicator whenever it's visible at the top of your screen.

Avoid Using the Always Option

Using the Always option is not recommended because it is disruptive to apps running in the background and it requires you to manually check for e-mail updates.

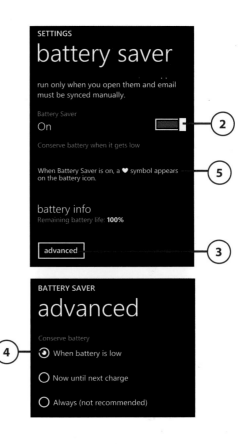

Phone Storage

Windows Phone 8 enables you to save content such as music, videos, and pictures directly to the phone's internal storage. With the Phone Storage feature, you can see how much storage space is currently being used and redirect the storage of new content to an SD card (if available). You can access the Phone Storage settings by going to the Settings page and then scrolling to and tapping Phone Storage.

SETTINGS

system applica

location
turned on

kid's corner
turned off

battery saver
turned off, 100% battery left

Tap Phone Storage. ── ## phone storage
26.12 GB free

backup
save stuff to the cloud

The Phone Storage screen shows the amount of storage being used (and the amount of free storage) on the phone and on the currently inserted SD card (if your phone supports the use of SD cards).

>>>Go Further   STORAGE REDIRECTION

By default, music, videos, and pictures are saved to the phone's internal storage. If you want to redirect the storage to an SD card, you can do so by going to the Phone Storage screen, tapping either Store New Music+Videos On or Store New Photos On and then choosing your preferred storage medium.

Note that you can change the preferred storage medium only if your phone supports the use of SD cards and you have an SD card installed in the phone. This is different from the SIM cards that some cellular providers use. Not all Windows Phone 8 devices allow for the use of SD cards.

Configure
your phone
to access all
of your email
accounts.

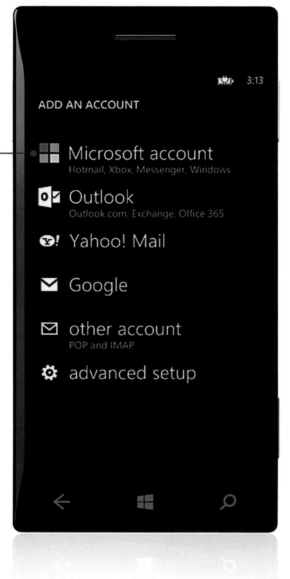

ADD AN ACCOUNT

Microsoft account
Hotmail, Xbox, Messenger, Windows

Outlook
Outlook.com, Exchange, Office 365

Yahoo! Mail

Google

other account
POP and IMAP

advanced setup

3:13

In this chapter, you will learn about Windows Phone 8's ability to send and receive email. Some of the topics covered in this chapter include:

→ Setting up a Microsoft account
→ Linking your phone to your email account
→ Using Outlook Mobile to send and receive mail

Messaging

Messaging is one area in which Windows Phone 8 really excels. Whereas many cellphones limit you to connecting to a single email account, Windows Phone 8 supports simultaneous connectivity to a virtually unlimited number of mailboxes. Furthermore, the phone offers native support for Microsoft Live, Office 365, Exchange Server, Yahoo!, and Gmail. Of course, you also have the option of connecting to just about any mail server using POP3 or IMAP4.

Accessing Email Settings and Configuring Accounts

This chapter guides you through the process of setting up different types of email accounts. All of the accounts types are configured through the phone's Email+Accounts screen, which is accessible by going to the Apps List (swipe left from the Start screen), opening the Settings page, and tapping Email+Accounts.

From here, you can set up a Microsoft account or a variety of email account types, which I cover in the following sections.

Microsoft Accounts

Although the use of a Microsoft account is optional, you can only get the full benefit of using your device if you use a Microsoft account. Microsoft accounts provide access to Hotmail, SkyDrive, Xbox, and Xbox Live, and they are also used for phone backups, phone location services, and even social networking.

Connecting Your Microsoft Account

Regardless of whether you use Microsoft's Outlook.com email service (or Live or Hotmail), you should configure your phone to use a Microsoft account. Microsoft accounts are required for using a number of the phone's features, such as backups and Find My Phone. You can link the phone to your existing Microsoft account by going to the Settings Email+Accounts screen and completing these steps:

1. Tap Add an Account.

2. Tap Microsoft Account.

3. Enter your email address.

4. Enter your password.

5. Tap Sign In.

6. Decide whether you want to back up your phone; tap either Yes or Not Now. At this point, your phone is configured to access your Microsoft account.

Automated Setup

Depending on how you have used your Microsoft account in the past, you might find that Windows Phone 8 automatically sets up other types of accounts on your behalf. For example, when I provisioned my Windows 8 phone with my Microsoft account, the phone automatically set up Twitter and LinkedIn because those accounts were cross-referenced with my Microsoft account.

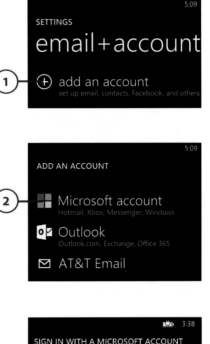

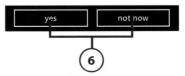

Setting Up a Microsoft Account

If you don't have a Microsoft account, you can easily create one for free. To do so, go to http://login.live.com and click the Sign Up Now link.

Setting Up Exchange Email

As you probably expect, Windows Phone 8 has the capability to connect to Microsoft Exchange Server using ActiveSync. Microsoft provides two different methods for connecting to Exchange Server. The first method is a simplified method that works only with Exchange Server 2007, 2010, and 2013. The second method is a little more advanced and is used for connecting to older Exchange Servers or attaching to Exchange Servers that do not fully support automatic configuration.

What Is Microsoft Exchange?

Microsoft Exchange is Microsoft's email messaging server and is commonly used in corporate environments. If you are attempting to connect your Windows Phone 8 to a corporate email account, there is a good chance that you will need to follow the instructions for Exchange Server connectivity.

Simplified Exchange Server Connectivity

If you have an Exchange Server 2007, 2010, or 2013 that supports automatic configuration for external clients, you can use the simplified connectivity method. To connect to your Exchange mailbox, go to the Email+Accounts screen, tap Add an Account, and complete the following steps:

1. Tap Outlook.

2. Enter your email address.

3. Enter your password.

4. Tap the Sign In button.

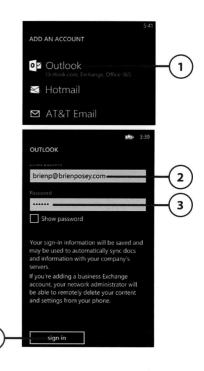

Advanced Exchange Server Connectivity

The connectivity can be used only for connecting to a supported version of Exchange and only if the Exchange Server organization is configured to support automatic configuration. To use Exchange Server connectivity, go to the Email+Accounts screen, tap Add an Account, and follow these steps:

1. Scroll to and tap Advanced Setup.

2. Enter your Exchange email address.

3. Enter your password.

4. Tap Next.

5. Tap Exchange ActiveSync.

6. Fill in the name of your Windows domain.

What's Your Domain?

Information about your domain, as well as some of the other settings listed here, typically comes from your employer or network administrator.

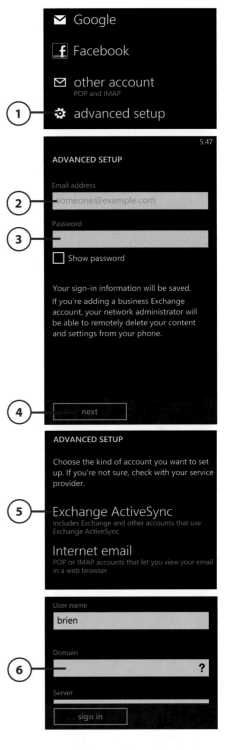

7. Enter the fully qualified domain name (FQDN) of your Client Access Server (or front-end server, for Exchange 2003 and earlier).

8. If your Exchange environment requires SSL encryption for ActiveSync, verify that the Server Requires Encrypted (SSL) Connection check box is selected. Otherwise, deselect it.

9. Set the Download New Content option to As Items Arrive. You can choose a longer interval, if you prefer.

10. Choose how much message history you want to store on the phone (this does not affect your actual Exchange mailbox—only the amount of mail stored on the phone).

11. Choose the types of content you want to sync. Normally, you sync the Email, Contacts, and Calendar items.

12. Tap Sign In.

5:50

EXCHANGE ACTIVESYNC

cas

☑ Server requires encrypted (SSL) connection

Account name

Mysmartphoneanswers

5:50

EXCHANGE ACTIVESYNC

Download new content

as items arrive

Download email from

the last 7 days

Content to sync

☑ Email

☑ Contacts

☑ Calendar

☑ Tasks

sign in

It's Not All Good

You might discover that, even after performing an advanced setup, Windows Phone 8 cannot connect to Exchange Server. If this happens, verify that you have correctly spelled the fully qualified domain name of your Client Access Server and that the server is externally accessible using this name. In some cases, you might have to use the server's IP address instead of its name.

The other thing that tends to go wrong is that Windows Phone 8 might have trouble using SSL encryption. Exchange Server uses a certificate to perform SSL encryption. For Windows Phone 8 to be capable of using SSL encryption, the phone must trust the certificate authority (CA) that issued the certificate to Exchange. This is accomplished by using something called a CA certificate. Windows Phone 8 has built-in CA certificates for the most popular commercial certificate authorities. However, if your company uses a certificate that was generated in-house or by a lesser-known commercial certificate authority, the phone will not automatically trust the certificate authority, and SSL encryption will fail (which causes ActiveSync to fail).

The solution to this problem is to set up another mail account (such as a Yahoo! account or a Gmail account) and configure your phone to access it. Next, ask your network administrator to email the required CA certificate to the account that you have just set up. When you receive the message, open the attachment; the certificate will be installed on your phone. You should now be able to sync with Exchange Server.

One last problem that you might encounter is that mail might not synchronize even if everything is set up correctly. This can happen if you have told Windows Phone 8 to synchronize messages from the last 7 days, but all the messages in your Inbox are more than 7 days old.

Connecting to Yahoo! Mail

Windows Phone 8 includes native support for Yahoo! Mail. To link the phone to your Yahoo! account, go to the Email+Accounts screen and complete these steps:

1. Tap Add an Account.

2. Tap Yahoo! Mail.

3. Enter your Yahoo! email address.

4. Enter your password.

5. Tap Sign In.

Connecting to Google Mail

Windows Phone 8 offers native support for Google Mail (Gmail). To link the phone to your Gmail account, go to the Email+Accounts screen and complete these steps:

1. Tap Add an Account.

2. Tap Google.

3. Enter your Gmail email address.

4. Enter your password.

5. Tap Next.

6. Choose whether you want to synchronize email only or whether you also want to synchronize your calendar and contacts.

7. Tap Sign In.

Setting Up POP3/IMAP4 Messaging

If you need to connect Windows Phone 8 to a mail system other than Microsoft, Exchange Server, Yahoo!, or Gmail, you can do so by using a POP3/IMAP4 account. To establish connectivity to your mail server, go to the Email+Accounts screen and perform the following steps:

1. Tap Add an Account.

2. Scroll to and tap Advanced Setup.

3. Enter your email address.

4. Enter your password.

5. Tap Next.

6. Tap Internet Email.

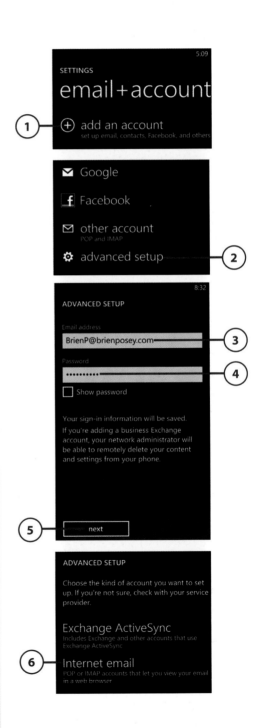

7. Enter your name into the Account Name field.

8. Enter your name (as you want it to be displayed to recipients) into the Your Name field.

9. Enter your server's fully qualified domain name (FQDN) or IP address into the Incoming Email Server field.

What's My Domain?

Specific information about your email account's server domain name, SMTP server, and so on should come from your email provider.

10. Tap the Account Type field and choose either POP3 or IMAP4.

11. Type your username. You can enter your username as a name (BrienP), an email address (BrienP@ BrienPosey.com), or a Universal Naming Convention (BrienPosey\ Brien). Universal Naming Conventions use log-in names in domain\username format.

12. Enter the fully qualified domain name (FQDN) or IP address of your SMTP server.

13. If the outgoing server requires authentication, select the Outgoing Server Requires Authentication check box and the Use the Same User Name and Password For Sending Mail check box.

14. Depending on your mail server's configuration, you might need to enable SSL encryption. If so, tap the Advanced Settings button and then select both the Require SSL for Incoming Mail and the Require SSL for Outgoing Mail check boxes.

15. Tap Sign In.

INTERNET EMAIL ACCOUNT

Account name

Brienposey — **7**

Your name

Brien Posey — **8**

We'll send your messages using this name

Incoming email server — **9**

Account type

IMAP4 — **10**

User name

brienposey\brienp — **11**

Examples: kevinc, kevinc@contoso.com, domain\kevinc

Password

••••••••••

☐ Show password

Outgoing (SMTP) email server — **12**

13 ☑ Outgoing server requires authentication

☑ Use the same user name and password for sending email

14 advanced settings

15 sign in

ADVANCED SETTINGS

The Advanced Settings screen can be used to control how frequently Windows checks for new mail. The default option is to check for new mail every two hours. Checking more frequently can impact battery life and can also result in higher cellular bills if you do not have an unlimited data plan.

The Advanced Settings screen offers an option to control how much mail history is stored on the phone. By default, all mail from the last two weeks is stored on the phone, but you can store more or less mail as your needs dictate. This option affects only the phone's storage, not your actual mailbox.

Removing Mail Accounts

If you no longer need mobile access to a mail account, you can easily remove the account without affecting any of the other mail accounts that might be set up on the phone. To remove a mail account, go to the Email+Accounts screen and complete these steps:

1. Tap and hold the account you want to delete.

2. When the menu appears, tap Delete.

3. You will see a warning message indicating that you are about to delete all the information associated with the account. Tap the Delete key to remove the account.

An Extra Option

When you tap and hold an email account, the menu displays an option to delete the account, but you also see a Sync option. Tapping Sync synchronizes your phone with the mailbox and downloads the most recent messages.

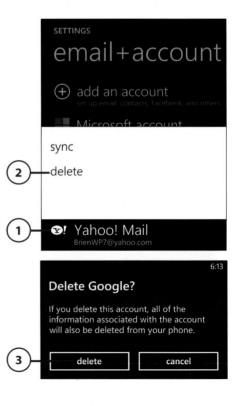

>>>Go Further

TO REMOVE ACCOUNTS, RESET

Because Microsoft accounts are used for more than just email access, Windows Phone 8 does not allow you to remove them in the manner described here. If you want to remove a Microsoft account, you must reset the phone to its factory defaults, as described in Chapter 1.

Microsoft Outlook Mobile

Regardless of whether you get your mail from Outlook.com, Exchange Server, Gmail, or somewhere else, all mail is made accessible through Microsoft Outlook Mobile. The techniques discussed in the following sections, including how to access your email box, open a message, and delete a message, are valid regardless of the type of mailbox you are accessing.

For every mail account that you set up, Windows Phone 8 creates a separate Live Tile on the Start screen. For example, if you set up a Microsoft account and an Exchange Server account, you have a Live Tile for each. The Live Tile displays the name of the mailbox and the number of unread messages waiting for you. In addition, you can find links to each of your mail accounts within the App List.

The Outlook Mobile Interface

When you tap a link to one of your mailboxes, Outlook Mobile opens. The main Outlook Mobile screen contains several different objects:

A. The current time.

B. The name of the mailbox you are currently using. It is important to verify the mailbox that you are connected to because Windows Phone 8 can be connected to multiple mailboxes simultaneously.

C. The current view of your messages. All is selected by default, but you can flick the view option to view unread messages, flagged messages, or urgent messages.

D. Your Mail. Outlook Mobile displays all the messages in the current folder.

E. The New icon. Tap this icon to compose a new message.

F. The Select icon. Tap this icon to access a screen that lets you perform bulk operations on your messages.

G. The Sync icon. Tap this icon to manually check for new mail.

H. The Search icon. Tap this icon to search your mail.

I. The Menu icon. Flick this icon upward to reveal various menu choices.

Identifying Unread Mail

In the image shown here, the messages with red subject lines are new messages that have not been read. Messages displayed in black and white are messages that have already been read.

The Anatomy of a Message

When you open Outlook Mobile, you see the messages in your Inbox. Several pieces of information are listed for each message.

A. **Sender:** The name of the person who sent the message

B. **Time stamp:** When the message arrived

C. **Subject line:** Displayed in red (or whatever theme color your phone uses) if the message is unread; otherwise, shown in gray

D. **Message preview:** The first several words of the message, displayed beneath the subject line

E. **Flag:** (Optional) Indication of whether a message is important, unimportant, flagged for follow-up, or complete, as well as whether the message contains an attachment

F. **Attachment:** Paper clip icon indicating that the message contains an attachment

G. **Urgent:** Exclamation point icon indicating that the message is urgent

H. **Forward icon:** Icon that appears next to messages that have been forwarded.

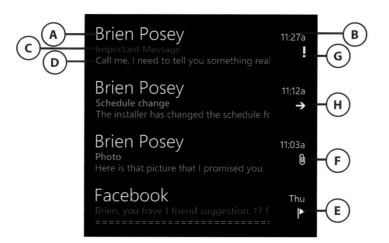

Opening a Message

You can view a message by simply tapping it.

Several items display on the message screen:

A. The sender's name

B. The message subject

C. The message's date and time

D. The address the message was sent to

E. The attachment (if any)

F. The message body

G. The Respond icon

H. The Delete icon

I. The Older icon, for returning to the previous message

J. The Newer icon, for advancing to the next message

K. The Menu icon, for accessing more options

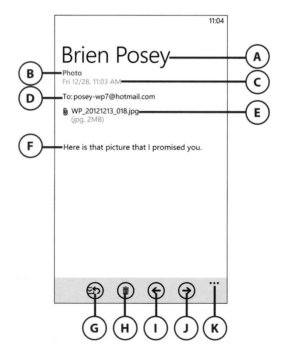

Opening an Attachment

If a message contains an attachment, you can view the attachment by following these steps:

1. Tap the message to open it.

2. Tap the attachment to download it.

3. When the attachment has finished downloading, tap the attachment to open it. Windows Phone 8 automatically opens the application that is associated with the attachment file type (assuming that such an application is installed on the phone).

Unknown File Types

If an email message contains an unknown file type, Windows Phone 8 devices still downloads the attachment, but are unable to open it.

The paperclip icon indicates that the message has not yet been downloaded.

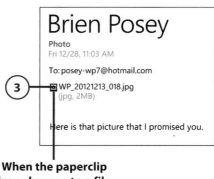

When the paperclip icon changes to a file icon the attachment has been downloaded and is ready for viewing.

Replying to a Message

To reply to a message, follow these steps:

1. Tap the message to open it.

2. Tap the Respond icon.

3. Tap Reply.

Reply All

You can reply to every recipient of an email, not just the sender, by instead tapping the Reply All option, shown here.

---

4. Compose your response.

5. Tap the Send icon.

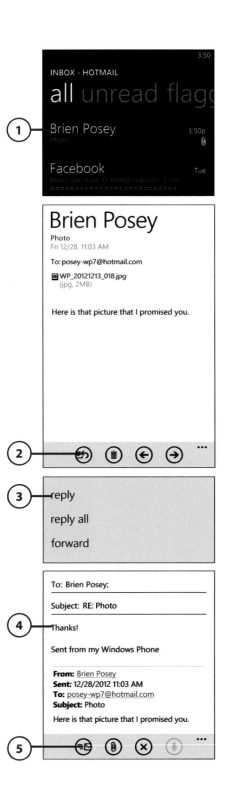

Forwarding a Message

To forward a message to an existing recipient, follow these steps:

1. Tap the message to open it.

2. Tap the Respond icon.

3. Tap Forward.

4. Enter the message recipient's email address.

5. Compose your response, if you have anything more to add.

6. Tap the Send icon.

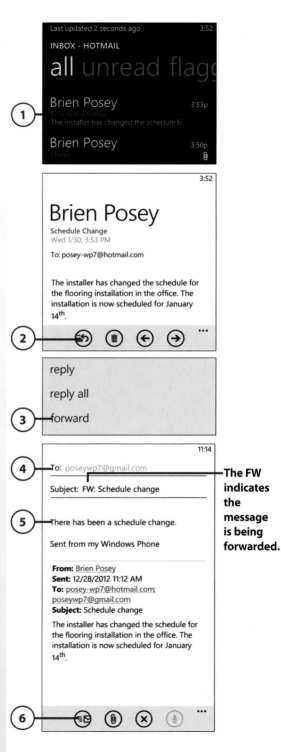

The FW indicates the message is being forwarded.

Viewing New Mail

As mentioned earlier, Outlook displays the subject line of new messages in red, while the subject line is shown in gray for old messages. If you want to temporarily see only the new messages in your mailbox, you can do so by following these steps:

1. Open your mailbox.

2. Flick the view setting from All to Unread. To return the view to normal when you are done, flick the view from Unread to All.

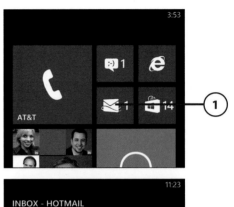

Viewing Urgent Mail

When you receive an urgent message, Windows Phone 8 displays a red exclamation point alongside the message, to indicate that the message is important. However, Outlook Mobile also has an option for viewing only the most important messages. To do so, follow these steps:

1. Open your mailbox.

2. Flick the view setting from All to Urgent. When you are done, you can return the mailbox to its previous state by flicking the view setting from Urgent to All.

Viewing Flagged Messages

Some people flag messages as a way of reminding themselves to look at the messages again later. However, flagged messages can become buried under newer messages over time. The easiest way to access all your flagged messages is to use the Flagged view. To view your flagged messages, complete these steps:

1. Open your mailbox.

2. Flick the view setting from All to Flagged. When you are done, you can return the mailbox to its previous state by flicking the view setting from Urgent to All.

Deleting a Message

To delete a message without opening it, follow these steps:

1. Tap and hold the message you want to delete.

2. When the menu appears, tap Delete.

3. To delete a message that is open, tap the Delete icon.

A Word of Caution

Exercise caution when deleting messages. Neither of the methods just mentioned ask for confirmation before deleting a message.

---

delete

mark as unread

move

set flag

clear flag

Brien Posey   11:03a
Photo
Here is that picture that I promised you.

Facebook   Thu

Brien Posey

Schedule change
Fri 12/28, 11:12 AM   →

To: posey-wp7@hotmail.com; poseywp7@gmail.com

Show all recipients (2)

The installer has changed the schedule for the flooring installation in the office. The installation is now scheduled for January 14th.

Deleting Messages in Bulk

If you need to delete more than one or two messages, consider performing a bulk delete:

1. Go to the Inbox.

2. Tap the Select icon.

3. Select the check boxes corresponding to the messages that you want to delete.

4. Tap the Delete icon.

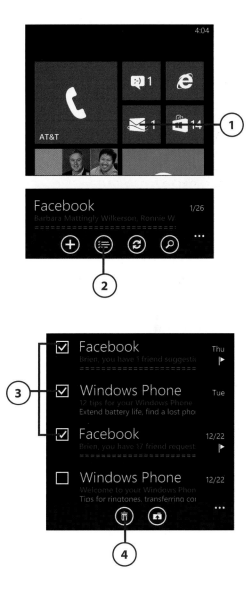

Recovering a Deleted Message

If you accidentally delete a message, you can recover it from the Deleted Items folder. To do so, follow these steps:

1. Open your mailbox.

2. Tap the Menu icon.

3. Tap the Folders option.

4. Tap Show All Folders.

5. Tap Trash.

6. Tap and hold the message that you want to recover.

7. Tap Move.

8. Tap Inbox.

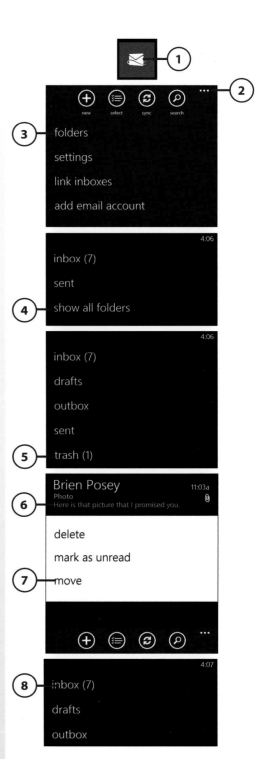

Marking a Message as Read

To mark a message as read, open the folder containing it and follow these steps:

1. Tap and hold the message.

2. Tap Mark as Read.

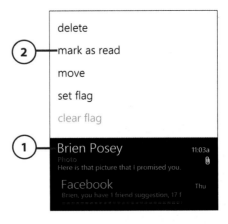

Marking a Message as Unread

To mark a message as unread, open the fold containing it and follow these steps:

1. Tap and hold the message.

2. Tap Mark as Unread.

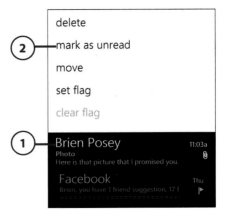

Marking Multiple Messages as Read or Unread

The method discussed in the two previous sections works well for dealing with individual messages, but there is an easier way to mark multiple messages as Read or Unread. To do so, go to the folder containing the messages you want to manage and follow these steps:

1. Tap the Select icon.

2. Select the check boxes corresponding to the messages that you want to flag or unflag.

3. Tap the Menu icon.

4. Tap either Mark as Read or Mark as Unread.

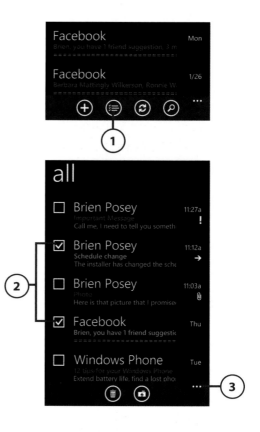

Moving a Message

Windows Phone 8 enables you to move messages into folders for long-term retention. If you need to move a message into a folder, you can accomplish the task by locating the message in a folder and following these steps:

1. Tap and hold the message.

2. Tap Move.

3. Tap the folder where you want to move the message.

all unread flagg

delete

mark as unread

move

complete flag

clear flag

Facebook   Thu
Brien, you have 1 friend suggestion, 17 f

3:34

inbox (6)

drafts

outbox

sent

trash

Junk

Performing a Bulk Move

If you need to move more than one message to another folder, you might be better off performing a bulk move. To do so, go to the folder containing the messages you want to move and follow these steps:

1. Tap the Select icon.

2. Select the check boxes corresponding to the messages that you want to move. All the messages that you select should be destined for the same folder.

3. Tap the Move icon.

4. Tap the folder where you want to move the selected messages.

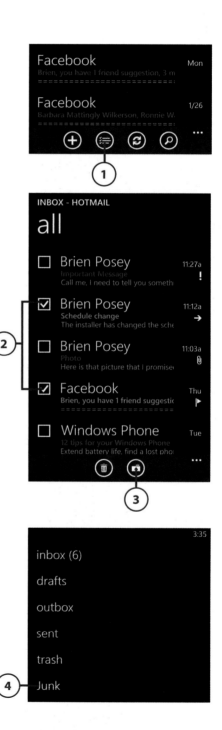

Viewing Folders

Windows Phone 8 displays the Inbox folder by default, but you can view any of your mailbox folders. To do so, open the mailbox you want to access and follow these steps:

1. Tap the Menu icon.

2. Tap Folders.

3. Tap the folder you want to view.

Empty or Missing Folders

Not all folders are displayed on the Folders list by default. If you don't see the folder you are looking for, tap Show All Folders.

When you view a folder, the folder might at first appear empty. In an effort to save space on the phone, Microsoft does not automatically synchronize all folders. For example, it would normally be a waste of space and bandwidth to synchronize the Junk folder. If you need to view the contents of a folder that initially appears to be empty, open the folder and tap Sync This Folder.

Flagging a Message

Windows Phone 8 offers full support for message flags. To flag a message, locate it in your folders and follow these steps:

1. Tap and hold the message.

2. Tap Set Flag.

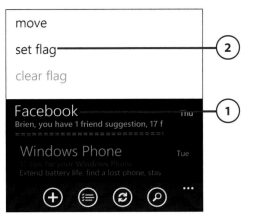

Clearing a Message Flag

To clear the flag from a message, locate the flagged message and follow these steps:

1. Tap and hold the message.

2. Tap Clear Flag.

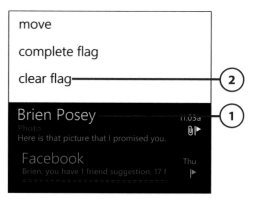

Flagging or Unflagging Multiple Messages

If you need to flag or unflag multiple messages, you can do so by locating the folder containing the messages and following these steps:

1. Tap the Select icon.

2. Select the check boxes corresponding to the messages that you want to flag or unflag.

3. Tap the Menu icon.

4. Tap either Set Flag or Clear Flag.

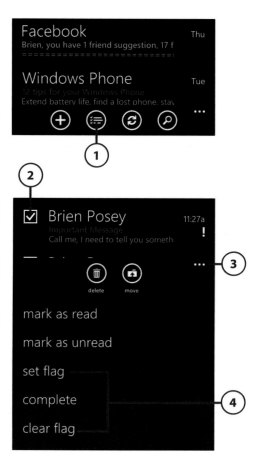

Marking a Message as Complete

If you complete a task related to a flagged message, you might want to flag that message as complete. To do so, locate the flagged message and perform these steps:

1. Tap and hold the message that you want to flag as complete.

2. Tap Complete Flag.

3. When the complete flag is applied, a check mark icon appears next to the message, indicating that the message has been flagged as complete.

delete

mark as read

move

complete flag ──────────── ②

clear flag

Facebook   12/22 ①
Brien, you have 17 friend requests, 1 frie ▶

Windows Phone   12/22
Welcome to your Windows Phone. any
Tips for ringtones, transferring contacts z

Brien Posey   11:03a
Photo   📎
Here is that picture that I promised you.

Facebook   Thu
Brien, you have 1 friend suggestion, 17 f   ✓ ③

Windows Phone   Tue
12 tips for your Windows Phone
Extend battery life, find a lost phone, stav ⋯

⊕   ☰   ⟳   🔍

Marking Multiple Messages as Complete

Just as you can flag a single message as complete, you can mark multiple messages as complete. To do so, locate the folder containing the messages you want to flag as complete and follow these steps:

1. Tap the Select icon.

2. Select the check boxes corresponding to the messages that you want to mark.

3. Tap the Menu icon.

4. Tap Complete.

Accidental Completion
If you accidentally flag a message as complete, you can get rid of the flag by using the Clear Flag option. You can then apply the flag again.

Composing a New Message

One of the most basic messaging tasks is to compose a new message. The message composition screen contains several elements:

A. Time: The current time.

B. To field: You enter the recipient's email address here.

C. Subject line: This is where you type the message's subject.

D. Message body section: Here you actually compose your message.

E. Send icon: Tap this icon to send the message.

F. Attach icon: Tap this icon to add an attachment to the message.

G. Close icon: Tap this icon to cancel the message instead of send it.

H. Speak icon: Use this icon to verbally compose a message.

I. Menu icon: Flick this icon upward to access a menu with access to the CC, Blind CC, and Priority options.

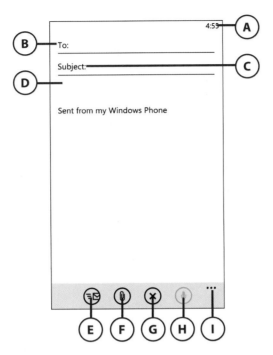

4:55

To:

Subject:

Sent from my Windows Phone

A
B
C
D
E
F
G
H
I

Writing a Message

You can compose a new message by opening the mailbox you want to use and following these steps:

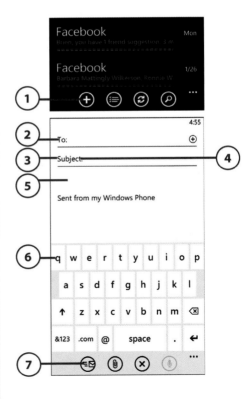

1. Tap the New Message icon.

2. Tap the To field, and then enter the address where you want to send the message.

3. Tap the Subject field.

4. Enter a subject line for the message.

5. Tap the message body.

6. Compose your message.

7. Tap the Send icon.

SENDING MAIL TO YOUR CONTACTS

These above assume that you are going to be manually entering the message recipient's email address. However, Windows Phone 8 gives you the option of sending an email directly to one of your contacts by tapping the Add Contact icon.

Canceling a New Message

Occasionally, you might begin to compose a message and then change your mind about sending it. When this happens, you can cancel the message by performing these steps:

1. Tap the Close icon.

2. If you have not yet entered any information for the new message, the message will be canceled with no further questions. Otherwise, you will see a menu with the following choices:

   Save: The message will not be sent, but it will be saved in your Drafts folder so that you can edit and send it later.

   Delete: The message is deleted without saving a draft copy.

The Back Button

If you tap the Back button while composing a message, Windows Phone 8 displays the menu shown here instead of immediately navigating away from the message (unless the new message is completely empty).

Adding Message Attachments

Windows Phone 8 enables you to send photographs as message attachments. You have the option of sending a photograph either from your Camera Roll (or albums) or directly from the built-in camera.

Sending Pictures from Your Camera Roll or Albums

To send a picture from your Camera Roll or from your albums, open a new message and complete the following steps:

1. Begin composing a new message.

2. Tap the Attachment icon.

3. Tap the Camera Roll icon, or tap the album containing the image that you want to send.

4. Tap the photo you want to send.

5. You return to the message composition screen. Finish composing your message (if necessary).

6. Tap the Send icon.

Multiple Attachments

You can add multiple attachments to an email message, but you must select each attachment separately.

To: poseywp7@gmail.com;

Subject: Picture

05.jpg
remove

5 Here is that picture I was telling you about.

Sent from my Windows Phone

6

Sending a Picture from the Camera

Windows Phone 8 enables you to access the camera from directly within the message composition screen and email a photo immediately after snapping it. To do so, open a new email message and follow these steps:

1. Begin composing a new message.

2. Tap the Attachment icon.

3. Tap the camera icon and snap a picture. Choose if you want to Accept or Retake the photo.

4. You return to the message composition screen, and the new picture is added as an attachment.

5. Tap Send.

To:

Subject:

Sent from my Windows Phone

1

2

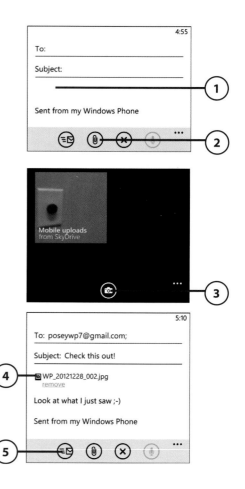

Mobile uploads
from SkyDrive

3

To: poseywp7@gmail.com;

Subject: Check this out!

4 WP_20121228_002.jpg
remove

Look at what I just saw ;-)

Sent from my Windows Phone

5

It's Not All Good

Although the message composition screen contains an attachments icon, the only type of attachment you are allowed to add to messages is a photograph. Windows Phone 8 does allow you to send other types of files as email attachments, but you must do so through the application that created the file. For example, if you want to send someone a Microsoft Word document, you must do so through Microsoft Word Mobile. This option is discussed in more detail in Chapter 6, "Microsoft Office Mobile."

Removing a Message Attachment

When you add an attachment to a message, you have the option to remove the attachment before sending the message. To do so, open a message with an attachment included and follow these steps:

1. Tap the Remove link just beneath the attachment.

2. When Windows asks if you want to remove the attachment, tap Yes.

To: poseywp7@gmail.com;

Subject: Check this out!

🖾 WP_20121228_002.jpg
remove

Look at what I just saw ;-)

Sent from my Windows Phone

4:30

Delete attachment

Are you sure you want to remove 17.jpg from this message?

| yes | no |

Sent from my Windows Phone

Setting Message Priority

When you compose a new message, you have the option to set the message's priority to high, normal, or low. To set the priority for a message, open the message you want to use and follow these steps:

1. From the message composition screen, Tap the Menu icon.

2. Tap Priority.

3. Tap either High, Normal, or Low.

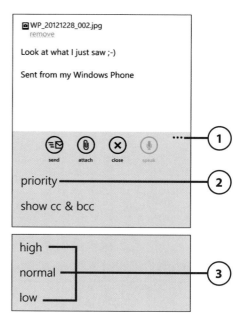

Verifying the Message Priority

When you set a message's priority, Windows does not give you any kind of message telling you that the priority has been set. To verify the message priority, you must look for a flag in the upper-right portion of the message composition screen. Priority flags are displayed for only high- and low-priority messages.

Adding Recipients Through CC and Blind CC

Windows Phone 8 gives you the option to copy or blindly copy other recipients on a message. To do so, create a new message and follow these steps.

1. From the message composition screen, Tap the Menu icon.

2. Tap Show CC & BCC.

3. Enter the email addresses for the recipients that you want to copy or blindly copy on the message.

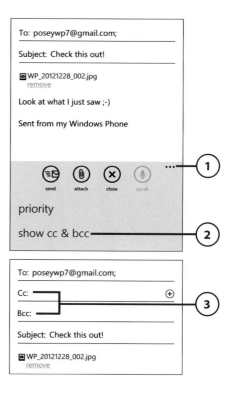

Adding Emoticons and Clip Art

When you compose an email message, Windows Phone 8 gives you an easy and fun way to insert clip art emoticons and clip art images into your message. To do so, open a new message and complete these steps:

1. Tap the emoticon key on the onscreen keyboard.

2. Tap a category key related to the type of image you want to insert.

3. Tap the actual image that you want to insert.

Taking a Shortcut

You might have noticed that one of the category keys looks like a clock. This is a shortcut key. Tapping this key takes you to a screen displaying your most commonly used emoticons or clip art images.

Emoticon Incompatibility

Some of the emoticons only work if the recipient is using a Windows Phone 8 device. Recipients with other types of phones may not receive the emoticons or they might be displayed incorrectly.

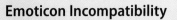

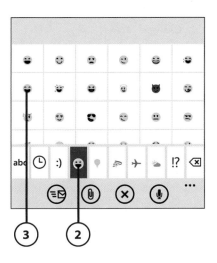

Checking for New Mail

Depending on the type of mailbox you are connected to, new messages might not show up in your Inbox immediately. You can manually check for new messages by completing these steps:

1. Open the mailbox you want to check.

2. Tap the Sync icon.

Configuring Mailbox Settings

Windows Phone 8 provides a number of settings that you can use to control the way that your phone handles email messages. For example, you can use the various settings to do things like linking multiple mailboxes together or enabling conversation view for messages.

Linking Mailboxes

Although Windows Phone 8 supports the use of multiple mailboxes, some people prefer to access all their mail through a single mailbox. This can be accomplished through mailbox linking. When you link mailboxes, all the mail from those mailboxes is displayed as if it existed in a single mailbox. To link mailboxes, open one of the mailboxes you want to link and follow these steps:

1. Tap the Menu icon.

2. Tap Link Inboxes.

3. Tap the name of the mailbox to which you want to link.

4. Tap Rename Linked Inbox.

5. Give your Inbox a name that reflects its purpose.

6. Tap the Done icon.

7. The linked mailbox is displayed on the Start screen under the name you assigned to it. Multiple mailbox icons designate it as a collection of linked mailboxes.

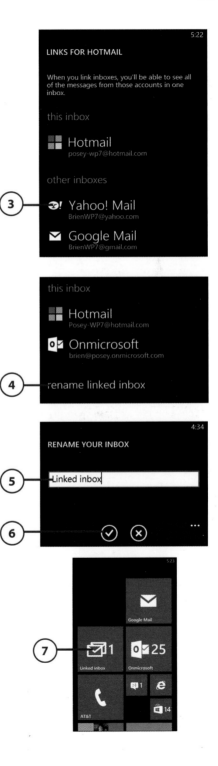

Unlinking Mailboxes

If you later decide that you want to unlink your mailboxes, you can easily do so. To unlink a mailbox, open your linked mailbox and follow these steps:

1. Tap the Menu icon.

2. Tap Linked Inboxes.

3. Tap the name of the mailbox that you want to unlink.

4. Tap the Unlink button.

Conversation View

By default, Windows Phone 8 groups messages into conversation view. Conversation view reduces clutter in your mailbox by grouping messages from each sender into a dedicated conversation container. If you want to disable conversation view, open your inbox and follow these steps:

1. Tap the Menu icon.

2. Tap Settings.

3. Set the Conversation slide bar to Off.

4. Tap the Done icon.

Returning to Conversation View

You can re-enable conversation view by setting the slide bar to On.

Message Signatures

By default, Windows Phone 8 devices add the phrase "Sent from my Windows Phone" to the end of each message that you send. However, you can turn off this signature or customize it. To do so, open your mailbox and follow these steps:

1. Tap the Menu icon.

2. Tap Settings.

3. If you want to customize the signature, tap it and type a new signature.

4. If you want to disable the signature, set the Signature slide bar to Off.

5. Tap the Done icon.

Blind CCing Yourself

Some people like to send a copy of every message that they send to themselves. Windows Phone 8 includes an automatic BCC option. If you want to always BCC yourself, you can do so by opening your mailbox and following these steps:

1. Tap the Menu icon.

2. Tap Settings.

3. Select the Always BCC Myself check box.

4. Tap the Done icon.

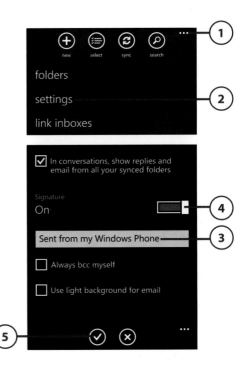

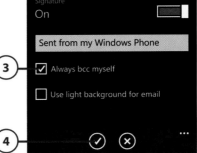

Lightening the Display

You have probably noticed throughout this chapter that the email message composition screens are white with black text, but all the email configuration screens are black with white text. If you prefer to use a white background and black text for all messaging-related functions, you can do so by opening your mailbox and completing these steps:

1. Tap the Menu icon.

2. Tap Settings.

3. Scroll to the bottom of the Settings screen and select the Use Light Background for Email check box.

4. Tap the Done icon.

Changing the Mailbox Sync Settings

Some types of mailboxes download new messages automatically, as they arrive. Other types of mailboxes download mail according to a set schedule. Using the mailbox settings screen, you can customize the download schedule and the retention period for messages stored on your phone. You can access the Mailbox Sync Settings screen by opening your mailbox and completing these steps:

1. Tap the Menu icon.

2. Tap Settings.

3. Tap Sync Settings.

4. Tap Account Name to give the mail account a different name.

5. Tap Download New Content to change the frequency with which new messages are downloaded.

6. Tap Download Email From to control how much email history is stored on your phone.

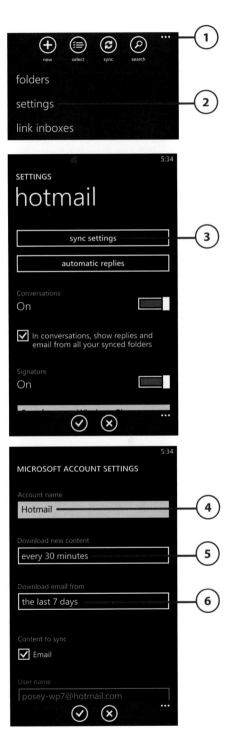

7. Scroll down and tap Content to Sync to choose what you want to sync. Some types of mailboxes allow you to sync only email, but other types of mailboxes permit you to sync calendars and contacts.

8. Tap Username to alter the username that you use to log into the mailbox.

9. Tap Password to change your mailbox password. If you ever change your password, you will need to enter the new password here so that your phone can continue to receive mail.

10. Tap Server to alter the fully qualified domain name (FQDN) or IP address of your mail server. For a properly configured email account, you won't likely ever need to change this setting.

11. Tap Done to save any changes you made here.

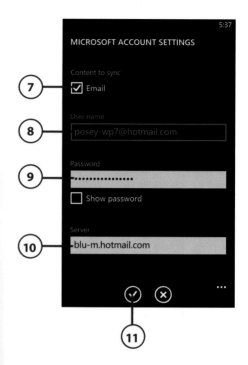

Configuring Automatic Replies

If you are going to be unavailable for a period of time, you might want to configure your phone to answer inbound email with an automated reply telling the person who sent you the message that you are not available. You can configure automatic replies by opening your mailbox and completing these steps:

1. Tap the Menu icon.

2. Tap Settings.

3. Tap Automatic Replies.

4. Move the Automatic Replies slide bar to the On position.

5. Enter your automatic reply message.

6. Tap Done.

Disabling Automatic Replies

When you want to stop using automatic replies, simply go back to the Automatic Replies screen and move the slide bar to the Off position.

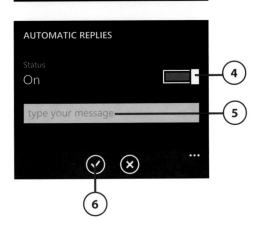

Access a variety of media types directly from the music and video app.

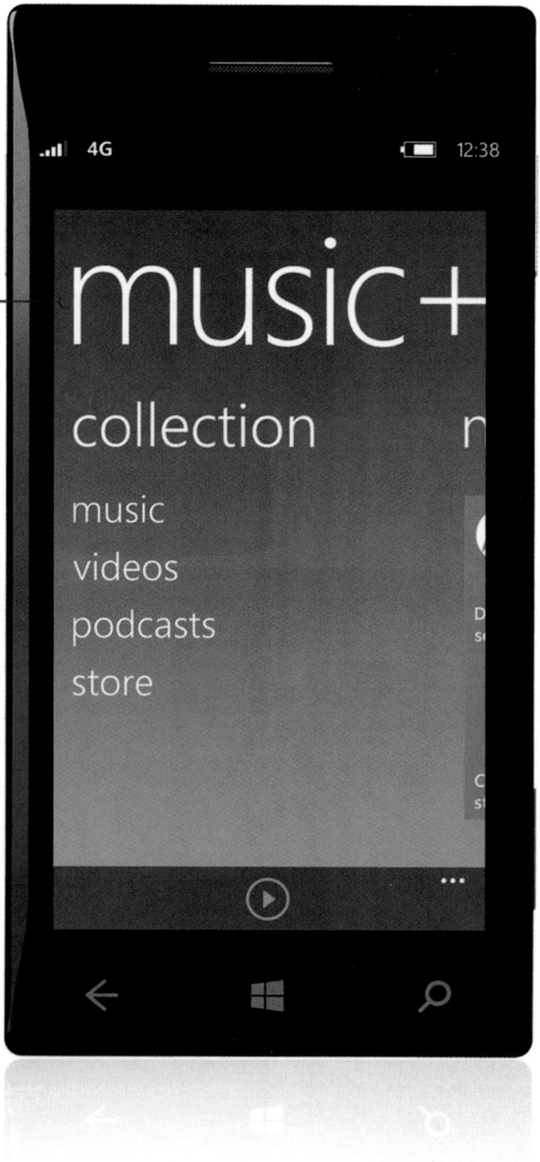
4G
12:38
music+
collection
music
videos
podcasts
store

In this chapter, you learn how to put music and videos on your phone, download podcasts, and much more.

- → Adding photos, video, and audio content on your phone
- → Working with File Explorer
- → Connecting Xbox Music Pass
- → Playing music through your phone
- → Watching videos

The Multimedia Experience

In Chapter 1, "Getting Started with Windows Phone 8," you learned how to install the Windows Phone 8 software to your Windows 8 PC or Microsoft Surface tablet. In this chapter, you learn how to begin using the software to enable your phone to play music and movies.

Working with the Windows Phone Software

Microsoft offers free software for Windows Phone that you can download and install on your Windows 8 PC or tablet. This software, which is available through the Windows Store, makes it easy to copy music, videos, and pictures from your collection to your phone. You can also use the software to check your phone's battery power and to monitor the amount of available storage space on your phone.

The Windows Phone software interface contains several items:

A. The model of phone you are using

B. Your phone number

C. The status of the phone's battery

D. The Add Photos button

E. The Add Video Button

F. The Add Music Button

G. The amount of storage space that has been consumed

H. The amount of free storage space remaining

I. The On Your Phone window, which displays the multimedia content that is currently stored on your phone

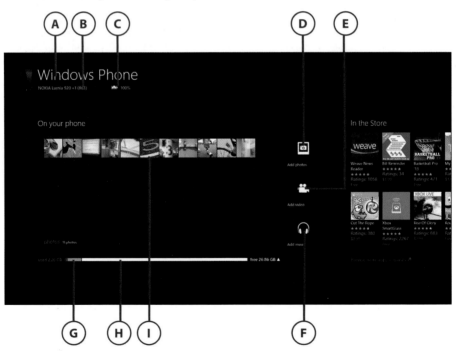

The following sections show you how to add various types of media and content to your phone, including photos and music.

Adding Photos to Your Phone

To add photos to the phone using the Windows Phone software, click the Add Photos button from the On Your Phone window and follow these steps:

1. Click the folder containing the pictures you want to add.

2. Click the pictures that you want to add to the phone. As an alternative, you can click Select All to select all the pictures in the current folder.

3. Click the Add button.

4. The recently added photos appear in the software's On Your Phone window.

Adding Videos to Your Phone

To add videos to the phone using the Windows Phone software, click the Add Video button from the On Your Phone window and follow these steps:

1. Click the folder containing the video you want to add.

2. Click the video that you want to add to the phone. As an alternative, you can click Select All to select all the videos in the current folder.

3. Click the Add button. The recently added videos appear in the software's On Your Phone window.

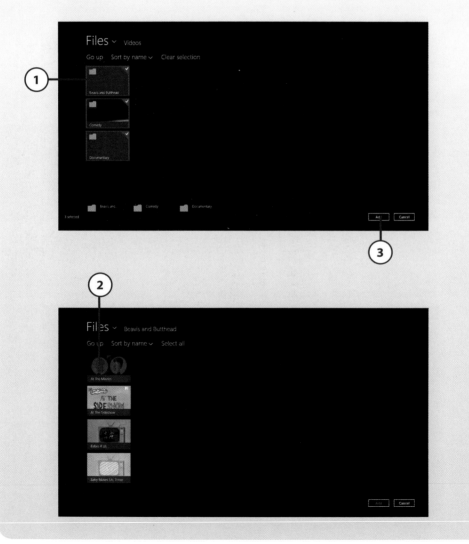

Adding a Song to Your Phone

To add music to the phone using the Windows Phone software, click the Add Music button on the On Your Phone window and follow these steps:

1. Navigate through the folder structure until you locate the song you want to add.

2. Click the song that you want to add to the phone. As an alternative, you can click Select All to select all the songs in the current folder.

3. Click the Add button. The song appears in the software's On Your Phone window.

Adding an Album to Your Phone

To add a music album to the phone using the Windows Phone software, click the Add Music button from the On Your Phone window and follow these steps:

1. Right-click the folder representing the album that you want to add to the phone. When you do, the software indicates that the folder has been selected.

2. Click the Add button. The Album appears in the software's On Your Phone window.

Adding a Musical Artist to Your Phone

To add multiple albums from an artist to the phone using the Windows Phone software, click the Add Music button from the On Your Phone window and follow these steps:

1. Right-click the folder bearing the name of the artist you want to add. When you do, the software indicates that the folder has been selected.

2. Click the Add button. The albums by the selected artist appear in the software's On Your Phone window.

It's Not All Good

The Windows Phone software isn't perfect. As you can see from some of the previous figures, the software often fails to display thumbnail images for music and videos. Furthermore, the software completely ignores your video hierarchy. For example, my video collection is organized into folders by category (comedy, cartoons, and so on). However, the Windows Phone software ignores this folder structure and lumps together all the videos.

Adding Content from Nonstandard Locations

If you have music, video, or photos stored in nonstandard locations on your computer (places outside your Music, Video, or Pictures libraries), it is still possible to add that content to your phone. The process works in nearly the same way as if the music, videos, or pictures are stored in your computer's libraries, but you must complete an extra step. If you want to add content stored in a nonstandard location, select the type of content you want to add from the On Your Phone window and complete these steps:

1. When you reach the Files screen, click Files.

2. Click Add More.

3. Repeatedly click Go Up until you see the Computer container.

4. Click the Computer container.

5. Navigate through the file system to the content you want to add.

6. Select the content that you want to add and then click Add.

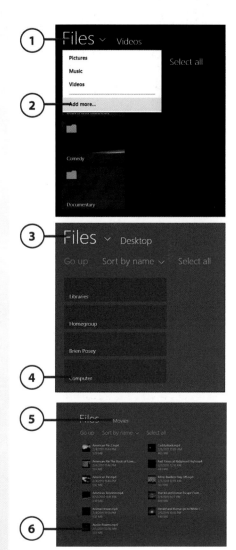

Using the Photo Interface

The Windows Phone software provides some additional options for viewing photos and their attributes. If you click the Photos pane in the On Your Phone window, you can view and select any folders on your phone that contain photos. From there, you need only click the photo to see it full-screen.

When the photo has been displayed as full screen, you can do a few things with it. Right-clicking the photo reveals options to delete the photo or save it to your PC.

The options to delete the photo or save it to your PC are displayed when you right-click on the photo.

Left-clicking the photo displays the photo's attributes, including the date it was taken, its dimensions and size, and its filename.

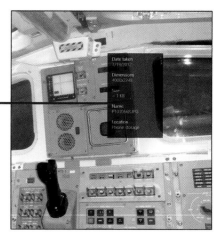

Left-clicking on a photo causes its attributes to be displayed.

It's Not All Good

As you look at the photo's attributes shown here, notice that the Windows Phone software reported the photo's size as less than 1KB. In actuality, however, the photo was 4.11MB in size.

The Windows Phone software is also lacking in its preview capabilities. Although the software enables you to click a photo and view it full-screen, you can't use full-screen mode to flip from one photo to the next. Furthermore, the software does not offer the capability to play music or videos.

Removing Multimedia Content

Occasionally, you might want to remove pictures, videos, or music from your phone to make room for new content. This is easy to accomplish using the Windows Phone software. You can also remove multimedia without the aid of the Windows Phone software. This is discussed later in the chapter.

Removing Music from Your Phone

If you want to remove music from your phone using the Windows Phone software, you can do so by completing these steps:

1. Click the Music pane.

2. Right-click the album, artist, or song that you want to remove from your phone.

3. Click Delete.

4. When asked whether you want to delete the item from your phone, click Delete.

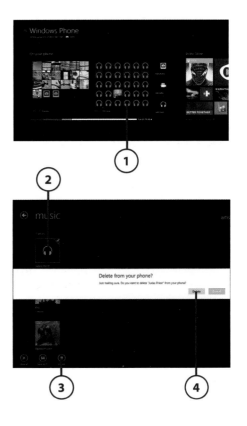

Removing a Video from Your Phone

If you want to remove a video from your phone using the Windows Phone software, you can do so by completing these steps:

1. Click the Videos pane.

2. Right-click the video that you want to remove from your phone.

3. Click Delete.

4. When asked whether you want to delete the item from your phone, click Delete.

Removing Pictures from Your Phone

If you want to remove a picture from your phone using the Windows Phone software, you can do so by completing these steps:

1. Click the Photos pane.

2. Right-click the photo or album that you want to remove from your phone.

3. Click Delete.

4. When asked whether you want to delete the item from your phone, click Delete.

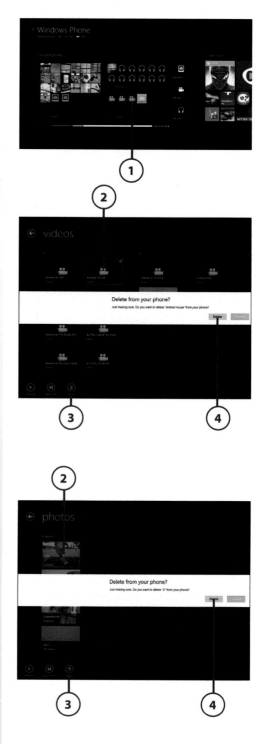

Copying Phone Content to Your PC or Tablet

Although the Windows Phone software is primarily intended as a mechanism for copying content from your PC to your phone, you can also do the reverse. If you have photos, pictures, or videos stored on your phone and you want to copy them to your PC or tablet using the Windows Phone software, you can do so by following these steps:

1. Click either the Music, Videos, or Photos pane, depending on the type of content that you want to copy to your computer or tablet.

2. Right-click the item that you want to copy to your computer or tablet.

3. Click Save to PC.

Working with File Explorer

As previously mentioned, you do not have to use the Windows Phone software to copy music, pictures, and videos to your phone. You can also use File Explorer (known as Windows Explorer in Windows 7 and earlier versions) to drag and drop content directly to your phone. The exact steps that you use vary depending on the operating system you are running on your computer. The procedures in this section are based on Windows 8, although these steps are similar for previous Windows versions.

The following sections show how you can add music to your phone and then remove it, but the procedures are identical for working with videos and pictures. The only difference is which folders you select to copy files from and where you place them on the phone. For example, to add a photo from your PC to your phone, instead of copying to your Windows Phone's Music folder, you copy it to the phone's Pictures folder.

Adding Media to Your Phone

The easiest way to add media to your phone is to simply drag and drop items from your collection. To do so, you must connect your phone to your computer or tablet using a USB cable. However, the Windows Phone software is not required. After you've connected your phone, follow these steps:

1. Open a File Explorer window on your Windows desktop and click Computer in the Navigation pane.

Opening File Explorer

You can open File Explorer in any version of Windows by holding down the Windows key on your keyboard and pressing E.

2. Double-click Windows Phone. (If Windows Phone doesn't appear here, check to make sure it's properly connected to your computer.)

3. Double-click the Phone folder and then the folder for the type of media you want to add (in this case, Music).

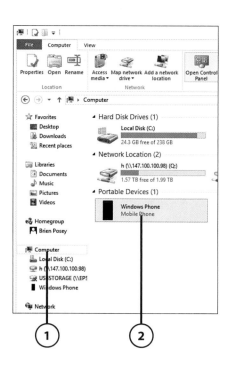

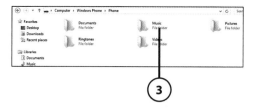

4. Open a second File Explorer window (WinKey+E) and select the media library containing the files you want to copy.

5. Right-click the content you want to copy. This can be individual files or a folder that contains multiple pieces of media.

6. Chose the Copy command from the shortcut menu.

7. Switch back to the other open copy of File Explorer. Right-click inside File Explorer and choose the Paste command from the shortcut menu. The content you copied is then accessible from your Windows Phone.

Missing Media

If you copy the wrong kind of media to a folder—for example, music files to a video folder—Windows Phone 8 will either ignore the file or generate an error when you try to play it.

Removing Media from Your Phone

Just as you can use File Explorer to copy media to your phone, you can use it to remove media from your phone. To do so, follow these steps:

1. Open File Explorer on your Windows desktop and click Computer in the Navigation pane.

2. Double-click Windows Phone.

3. Double-click Phone and then click the folder containing the files you want to remove (Music, in this case).

4. Right-click the file or folder you want to remove.

5. Click the Delete option on the shortcut menu.

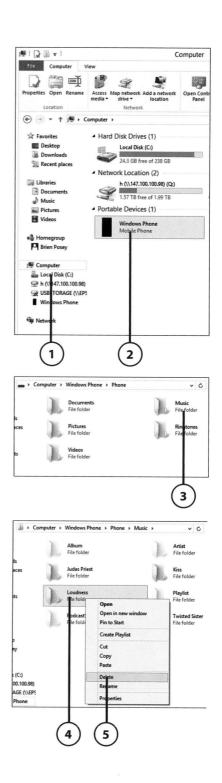

Copying Multimedia Content to Your PC

In the previous sections, you saw how to use File Explorer to copy media from your PC to your phone. However, this process also works in reverse. You can easily use File Explorer to copy phone content to your PC by dragging and dropping music, video, or picture files from the phone and onto a computer's hard drive. To do so, connect your phone to your PC and then follow these steps:

1. Open File Explorer (press WinKey+E) and select Windows Phone in the Navigation pane, under the Computer section.

2. Navigate through the phone's file system and locate the content you want to copy to your computer.

3. Right-click the file (or entire folder) that you want to copy.

4. Select the Copy command from the shortcut menu.

5. Navigate to the folder on your hard drive to which you want to copy the media files.

6. Right-click an empty area within File Explorer.

7. Select the Paste command from the shortcut menu.

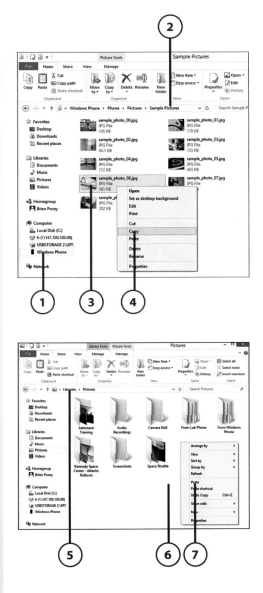

Xbox Music Pass

Microsoft offers a subscription-based music service called Xbox Music Pass (www.xbox.com/en-US/music/music-pass). An Xbox Music Pass subscription enables you to play unlimited music on your Windows Phone 8 device or other compatible devices.

After you have registered for an Xbox Music Pass subscription, you can link your phone to your Xbox Music account and have full access to it from your phone.

Connecting Your Phone to Xbox Music Pass

To connect to Xbox Music Pass, you must configure your phone to use the same Microsoft account as you used when you signed up for it. You can connect your phone to your Xbox Music Pass by opening Music+Videos from your phone's Home screen (or accessing it from the App List) and then following these steps:

1. Tap the Menu icon.

2. Tap Settings.

3. Verify that the Connect with Xbox Music slide bar is set to On.

4. Verify that the Xbox Music Cloud Collection slide bar is set to On.

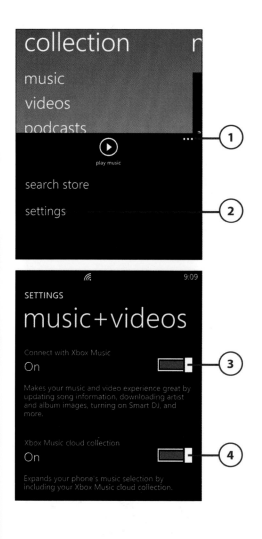

It's Not All Good

For Xbox Music Pass to work, you must configure your phone to use the same Microsoft account that you used when you signed up for Xbox Music Pass.

The phone can be a little misleading because the configuration screen that you used when you enabled Xbox Music Pass support contains a link called Xbox Music Account Settings. However, this link does not seem to do anything to actually authorize the phone to play Xbox music. While writing this book, I struggled for several hours trying to figure out how to authorize my phone. I didn't realize that Windows Phone 8 devices are authorized automatically.

Playing Music from the Xbox Music Pass

After you've connected your phone to your Xbox Music Pass subscription, you have immediate access to everything Xbox Music Pass has to offer. To find some music to play, open your Music+Videos app from your phone's Home screen or app list and complete these steps:

1. Tap the Menu icon.

2. Tap Search Store.

3. Enter the name of the song, artist, or album you want to play.

4. When the search results display, tap the item you want to play.

5. Tap the Play icon next to the item you want to play.

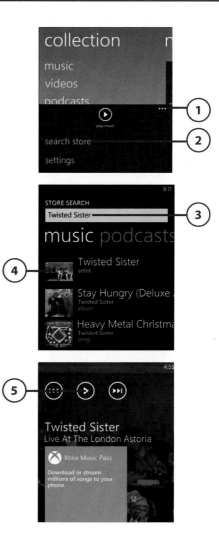

Playing Music Through the Phone

Windows Phone 8 gives you several options for playing music. For example, you can play individual songs, an entire album, all the songs by a particular artist, or even all the songs from a certain genre. You can access and play music through the phone's Music+Videos hub, which you can access from your phone's Start screen or from the App List.

Playing Songs

If you want to play an individual song, you can do so by opening the Music+Videos hub, tapping Music, and following these steps:

1. Flick the Music menu left or right to access the Songs container.

2. Tap the song you want to play.

Using Jump Lists

If you have more than a couple albums stored on your phone, the list of songs can be pretty long. Instead of scrolling through a list of hundreds or even thousands of songs trying to find the song you are looking for, it is usually faster to use jump lists. To use jump lists, open the Songs container as described in the previous section and follow these steps:

1. Tap one of the icons containing a letter of the alphabet.

2. The phone takes you to a screen displaying the alphabet. Tap the letter the song starts with. Windows displays the songs starting with the selected letter.

The Play Screen

After you've selected a song to play, you see the Play screen. The Play screen contains several elements:

A. The name of the artist.

B. The name of the album the song is from.

C. The album art (when available).

D. The timeline, which shows the length of the song and how far into the song you are.

E. The name of the song.

F. The next two songs that will play.

G. The Rewind button. Pressing this button once restarts the song. Pressing it twice plays the next song.

H. The Pause button.

I. The Fast Forward button. Pressing this button skips to the next song.

J. The Rate icon. Tapping this icon so that the heart is colored indicates that you like this song. Tapping the icon again turns the icon into a broken heart, indicating that you do not like the song. A heart with a black center, like the one in the figure, indicates that the song is unrated.

K. The Shuffle icon. This icon causes the phone to play music in a random order.

L. The Repeat icon. The song will play repeatedly.

Playing an Album

Just as you can play an individual song, you can play an entire album. To do so, go to the Music section of the Music+Videos hub and complete these steps:

1. Flick to Albums.

2. Tap the album art to play the album. (To instead see the songs on the album, tap the album name.)

Playing a Music Genre

If you want to hear all the songs on your phone that belong to a certain genre, open the Music section of the Music+Videos hub and complete these steps:

1. Flick to Genres.

2. If you want to play all the songs listed for that genre, tap the Play icon next to the genre's name. If you want to see a list of the songs in that genre and then choose which ones to play, tap the genre name instead.

Playing a Specific Artist

Windows Phone 8 also enables you to play songs from a certain artist, even if those songs span multiple albums. To do so, open the Music section of the Music+Videos hub and follow these steps:

1. Flick the screen to Artists.

2. To play all the songs you have for an artist, tap the Play button next to that artist. To see all the songs you have for that artist, tap the artist's name.

Playing Music in the Background

Windows Phone 8 devices are capable of playing music in the background. In other words, if you start up some music and then press the Start button, switch to another app, or even turn off the phone's display, that music continues to play. You can control music that is playing in the background by using either the Music+Videos hub or the phone's lock screen.

Controlling Background Music Through the Music+Videos Hub

One way to control music that is playing in the background is to simply return to the Music+Videos hub. Upon doing so, you can access the controls for the media player by completing these steps:

1. Flick to the Collection page.

2. Tap the track that is currently playing.

3. The resulting screen includes audio controls that you can use to pause the audio or switch tracks.

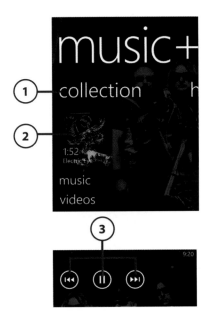

Controlling Background Music from the Lock Screen

Even if you've set aside your phone for a bit and it has returned to the lock screen you, can control music playback without returning to the Music+Videos hub. When music is playing and you activate your phone's display, the lock screen includes audio controls like the ones shown here.

Use these buttons to control audio playback from your phone's lock screen

Missing Audio Controls

The audio controls display on the lock screen for only a few seconds.

Sharing Music

Occasionally, you might play a song that you want to recommend to a friend. If this happens, you can easily send a copy of the song by following these steps:

1. From the song's play screen, tap the menu icon.

2. Tap the Share option.

3. Choose the mechanism you want to use to share the song. You can share the song through e-mail or through Tap+Send. If you choose to use Tap+Send, NFS must be enabled on your phone and on the recipient's phone.

Playing Music Using Smart DJ

Windows Phone 8 devices include a Smart DJ feature that automatically plays a music mix based on the contents of your collection. The device provides one-touch access to the Smart DJ feature. To use it, simply go to the Artist screen and complete these steps:

1. Tap a favorite artist.

2. Tap the Smart DJ icon. The Smart DJ then plays tracks from similar artists.

___

Why Is Smart DJ Grayed Out?

The Smart DJ option is only available if you have enough music available for it to work. Unless you have a sufficient amount of music stored on your phone (or a Music Pass subscription) the option is grayed out.

___

>>>Go Further

SAVE AS PLAYLIST

If you like the Smart DJ mix, you can save it as a playlist that you can then play again. From the Smart DJ mix screen, tap the menu icon and choose Save as Playlist. Your phone asks you to give it a name. The playlist then is saved for you to return to whenever you like.

Accessing Playlists

You can play any playlists you've created by going to the Music+Videos hub, tapping Music, and following these steps:

1. Flick the screen to the Playlists page.

2. Tap the Play icon next to the playlist you want to play. To see the contents of the playlist, tap the list name.

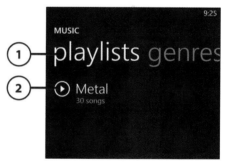

Playing Videos

You can play videos by going to the Music+Videos hub, tapping Videos, and then tapping the video you want to play.

Simply tap the video that you want to play.

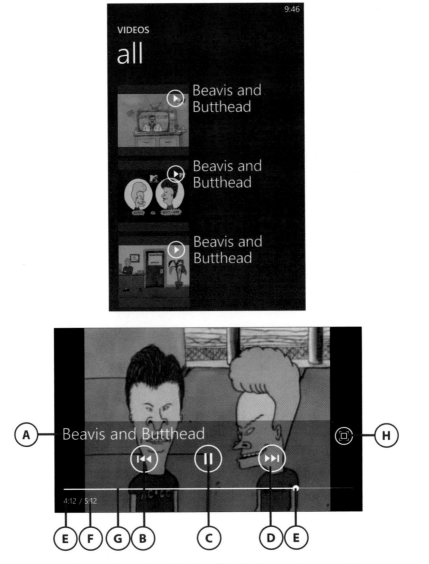

When you play a video , the video itself is displayed alone on the screen. However, if you tap the screen, Windows displays a set of controls, which contains the following:

A. The name of the video

B. Rewind button

C. Pause button

D. Fast Forward button

E. Current video position

F. Length of video

G. Progress bar

H. Full Screen icon

Pause and Play

If you pause a video, the Pause button turns into a Play button that you can press to resume video playback.

When you access the Videos hub shown here, the phone shows you all the available videos stored on it. However, you can sort the videos by category by flicking the screen to choose a different video category. The available categories include these:

- **All:** All the videos on the phone.

- **TV:** Television shows. TV shows can be grouped into subcontainers, with one container for each series (a container for *MythBusters,* a container for *Beavis and Butthead,* and so on).

- **Music:** Music videos.

- **Movies:** Movies

- **Personal:** Videos that you record.

It's Not All Good

As you synchronize your videos to the phone, you might discover that, regardless of the video type, all your videos are lumped into the All container and are not listed in other containers. This happens because Windows Phone looks at information embedded in video file, called metadata, to determine which container to place it into. If your collection consists of DVD rips, home movies, YouTube downloads, or video sources that were not specifically intended to be played on Windows Phone devices, your videos likely are missing the metadata used to sort the videos into containers.

History

The Music+Videos hub's History screen displays the media you have played most recently. You can use the History screen as a quick playlist if you want to replay something that you recently listened to or watched. You can access the History screen by going to the Music+Videos hub and completing the following steps:

1. Flick to the History screen.

2. Tap the item you want to play.

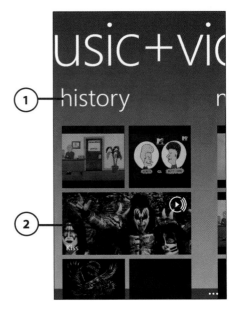

Displaying New Content

The Music+Videos Hub provides quick access to the media that you added to the phone most recently. You can access the phone's most recently added media by going to the Music+Videos hub and following these steps:

1. Flick the screen to access the New page.

2. Tap the item you want to play.

Not-So-New Content

The New screen continues to display the most recently added content, even after you have played that content. Items remain on the New screen until you add media to the phone.

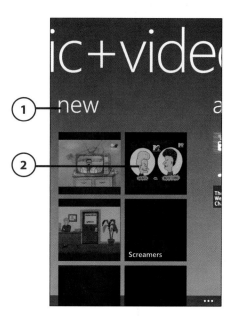

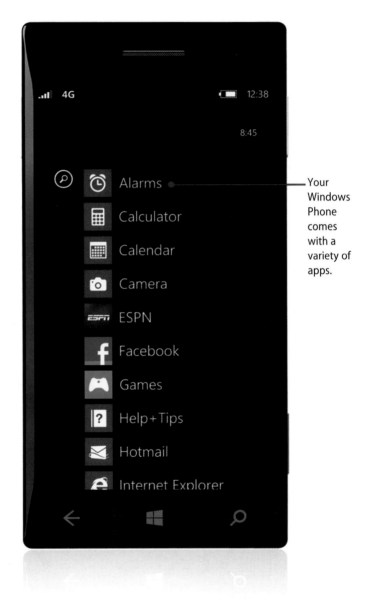

Your Windows Phone comes with a variety of apps.

Windows Phone 8 comes with many built-in applications and gives you the option to download additional apps through the built-in Store. In this chapter, you learn about the most useful standard built-in apps on your phone, as well as how to find and install apps from the Store.

→ Searching for apps
→ Setting alarms
→ Setting up your calendar
→ Using your camera
→ Managing photos
→ Using Internet Explorer
→ Searching the built-in store
→ Setting up Kid's Corner
→ Making payments with Wallet

Windows Phone 8 Apps

Some apps, such as the Office and Mail apps, are larger topics that I cover in other chapters. Also keep in mind that mobile phone manufacturers and cellular service providers typically add their own proprietary apps to their phones. Because these apps aren't technically part of the Windows Phone, I don't cover them in this chapter.

Searching for an App

All apps covered in this chapter are accessed from the Apps screen and listed in alphabetical order. You can access this screen by pressing the Start button and flicking the screen to the left.

As you begin downloading apps from the store, you will likely end up with a relatively large app collection. The list of apps shown on the app screen can thus become quite long. Windows Phone 8 contains a search function that lets you search for apps that are currently installed on your phone. To search for an app, go to the Apps screen and complete these steps:

1. Tap the search icon.

2. Begin typing the name of the app you are looking for.

Limited Search Results

This type of search looks only for apps that are currently installed on the phone. It does not search the Store.

Alarms

Windows Phone 8 has a built-in app that enables the phone to act as an alarm clock. This app can be handy if you travel and either forget to bring an alarm clock or prefer not to bring one.

Setting an Alarm

You can set an alarm on your phone by opening Alarms from the Apps screen and completing these steps:

1. Tap the Add icon.

2. Tap the Time field and set the time for the alarm.

3. Tap the Repeats field and select the check boxes corresponding to the days you want the alarm to sound. Choose Only Once if you don't want the alarm to go off on subsequent days.

4. Tap the Sound field. Choose the alarm sound you want to use. You can preview an alarm sound by tapping its Play icon.

5. Tap the Name field to enter a specific name for your alarm. This way, if you have more than one alarm, you can easily differentiate between them.

6. Tap the Save icon.

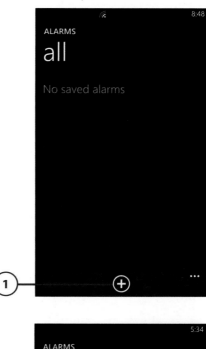

Disabling an Alarm

If you set a recurring alarm and decide that you don't need it now but want to keep it for later use, you can easily disable it. To do so, go to the Apps screen, tap Alarms, and follow these steps:

1. Locate the alarm you want to disable.

2. Set the alarm's slide bar to Off.

Deleting an Alarm

Disabling an alarm simply suspends the alarm so that it is not active—it does not delete the alarm. If you want to delete an alarm, you can do so by going to the App screen, tapping Alarms, and completing these steps:

1. Tap the alarm you want to delete.

2. Tap the Delete icon.

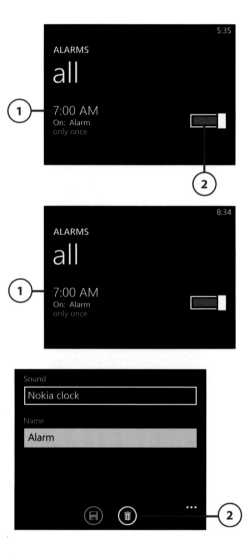

Calculator

A good calculator has become a staple for almost every mobile device, and Windows Phone 8 is no exception. The built-in calculator is useful for simple arithmetic or for scientific calculations.

You can access the phone's calculator by going to the App screen and tapping Calculator.

The Calculator app at first appears to be very basic.

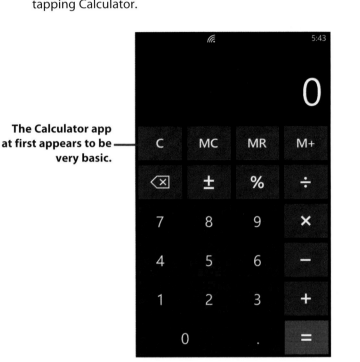

The Calculator app at first appears to be very basic, but Windows Phone 8 does include a scientific calculator. You can access the scientific calculator by opening the Calculator app and then turning the phone sideways. When you do, the Calculator displays in scientific mode.

Turning the phone sidewise causes the calculator to become a scientific calculator.

Calendar

As you probably expect, the Calendar app is designed to help you keep track of your daily activities. In addition, you can use this app to create and manage meetings in much the same way you can through Microsoft Outlook. In fact, the Calendar app can be synchronized with the calendar associated with your E-mail account. If you have multiple E-mail accounts, the Calendar app can even display an aggregate view of all your different calendars.

The calendar is accessible directly from the Start screen. If it's pinned there, you can, of course, access the Calendar app by pressing the Start button and tapping the Calendar tile. The Calendar is also accessible from the Apps list.

If you have the Calendar app on your Start screen at a medium or large size, the Live Tile displays the next appointment on your phone's Start screen.

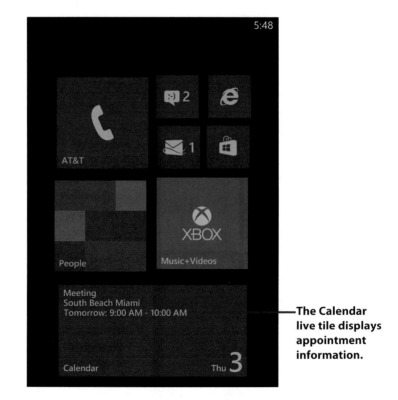

The Calendar live tile displays appointment information.

When you launch the Calendar app, you have access to all parts of your included calendars, including agenda items, to-do lists, the monthly calendar view, and so on.

Calendar Views

The Calendar opens to Day view, which displays all your appointments for today. To see different calendar views, flick left or right on the current view.

From Day view, you can scroll the screen up or down to see previous or future days.

Day view contains several elements:

A. The current time: Shows the current time.

B. The view: Flick the view to switch among Agenda, To-Do, and Day views.

C. Your appointments: Tap an appointment to see it in more detail.

D. Today's date: This icon shows today's date, and you can tap it to quickly return to today if you have scrolled the calendar to another date.

E. The New icon: Tap this icon to create a new appointment.

F. The Month icon: Tap this icon to view the calendar in Month view.

G. The menu icon: Flick this icon upward to access the calendar settings.

If you swipe to the left where Day view is highlighted, you can see Agenda view, which displays your upcoming appointments. What makes Agenda view different from Day view is that all appointments are displayed sequentially on a single screen instead of being displayed in a more traditional calendar format.

Agenda view contains several elements:

A. Shows the current time.

B. Flick the view to switch among Agenda, To-Do, and Day views.

C. Confirmation that this is today's agenda.

D. The time of the next appointment.

E. The name of the appointment.

F. The appointment's scheduled duration.

G. Your availability is color-coded to reflect your appointment status. Availability is discussed later in this chapter.

H. Today icon, which displays the current date. When you tap this icon, it returns you to today on the calendar.

I. The New icon. Tap this icon to create an additional appointment.

J. The Month icon. Tap this icon to access Month view.

K. The Menu icon. Flick this icon upward to access the calendar settings.

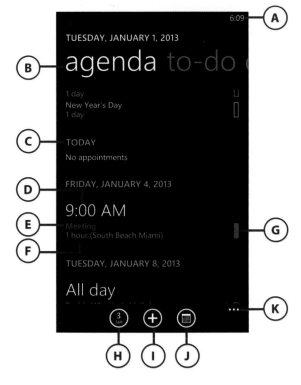

To-Do view enables you to view your task list (your to-do list). To-Do view includes several elements:

A. The current time

B. The currently selected view

C. The task name

D. The task details

E. The priority flag

F. The New button

G. The Select button

H. The menu icon

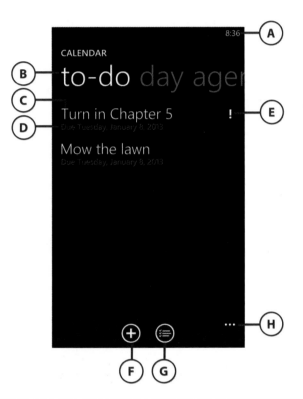

What's the Difference

To-Do view displays your task list. Tasks are different from calendar appointments: Items that appear on your calendar don't usually appear on the task list.

Viewing Another Day's Agenda

1. Although you can scroll to another day through Agenda view, it can sometimes take a lot of scrolling to get to the day you are looking for. As a shortcut you can look at another day's agenda by first going to Month view. To do so, open Calendar's Agenda view and complete these steps: Tap the Month icon.

2. Tap the day you want to view.

Getting Back to Today

You can revert to the present day by tapping the Today icon while in Agenda view.

Accessing a Full Month

Even though, from Day view, the Calendar app defaults to displaying the current day's events, you can view appointment information on a monthly calendar as well. To do so, open the calendar and complete these steps:

1. From either Day view or Agenda view, tap the Month View icon. Windows displays a calendar for the current month.

The Small Print

Even though Month view displays your appointments for the month, the text is generally way too small to read. You can access Day or Agenda views for a specific day by going into Month view and then double-tapping the day you want to look at.

2. To navigate to a different month, tap the name of the month that is displayed above the calendar.

3. Choose the month and year you want to view.

4. Tap the Done icon.

Faster Navigation

You can also swipe up or down just beneath the calendar in Month view to see the next month or the previous month.

Appointments

The Calendar app enables you to create appointments. An appointment is essentially a scheduled event for which you want to be reminded. When you create an appointment using the Calendar app, the appointment can be synchronized to the calendar that is associated with your E-mail mailbox.

Creating an Appointment

You can add an appointment to the calendar from the Day view or Agenda View screen by completing the following steps:

1. Tap the Add Appointment icon.

2. Tap the subject field to enter a name for the appointment.

3. Tap the Location field to indicate where the appointment takes place.

4. Tap Calendar to choose in which of your available calendars you want to log the appointment.

5. Tap the date and time fields located under When to change when the appointment takes place.

6. Tap the How Long field to set the anticipated duration of the appointment.

7. Tap the Save button to log the appointment in the selected calendar. (You can also cancel the appointment by tapping the Cancel button.)

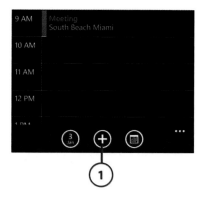

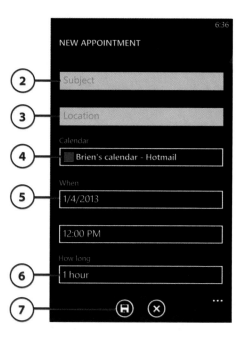

ADDING ADDITIONAL DETAIL

When you create a new appointment, you have the option to supply some additional details that are geared more toward business users. To do so, begin creating a new appointment and then flick up on the screen to scroll up and reveal the More Details button. These extra details are available:

- **Reminder:** Specify when you want your phone to remind you of an upcoming appointment.

- **Occurs:** By default, appointments occur only once, but you have the option to set up a recurring appointment.

- **Status:** Specify how you want your status to display to those with whom you have shared your calendar.

- **Attendees:** Invite someone to a meeting here.

- **Private:** Select this checkbox to block people with whom you have shared your calendar from viewing the appointment details.

- **Notes:** Enter additional required information about the appointment.

It's Not All Good

Limited Recurrence Options

Even though the phone allows you to create recurring appointments, the recurrence options are somewhat limited. For example, even though you can set an appointment to recur on the 10th of every month or on every Saturday, there is no way to set a custom recurrence schedule. For example, you can't create a recurring appointment for the second Tuesday of each month.

Understanding Appointment Status

When you create a new appointment, one of the options that you can set (after tapping the More Details button) is the appointment's status. When you set an appointment's status, you are actually configuring your free/busy information for the block of time the appointment occupies.

When you create an appointment, Windows automatically sets the status for the corresponding block of time to Busy. That way, if someone looks at your shared calendar or tries to schedule a meeting with you, that person will see that you are busy at that time. Although Busy is usually an appropriate status, you have four status options:

Free: Even though an appointment is on your calendar, it isn't important, and you can be available at that time, if necessary.

Tentative: The appointment has not yet been confirmed.

Busy: The appointment is a firm commitment, and you are unavailable during that time slot.

Out of the Office: This option is most appropriate when you are on vacation or you are traveling for business.

The Status indicates how the block of time will be marked on your calendar.

Occurs

once

Status

free

tentative

busy

out of office

Creating a Meeting

Windows Phone 8's Calendar app contains native functionality for creating meetings, in which you pick people from your contacts to invite. If you want to schedule a meeting, open a new appointment in Calendar, enter the baseline information covered in the section, "Creating an Appointment," and follow these steps:

1. Tap the More Details button.

2. Tap the Add Someone button.

   The Calendar differentiates between required and optional attendees for a meeting. For required attendees, tap the Add Someone button, located in the Required section.

3. Tap the name of the person you want to invite as a required attendee. If you have additional required attendees, tap the Add Someone icon again and choose the attendees.

4. If you want to invite any optional attendees, tap the Add Someone icon found in the Optional section, and select them from your contacts the same way you did for the required attendees.

Meeting Options

Although the app doesn't offer all the options of the full-blown version of Outlook, such as automatically searching attendees' calendars for a meeting time that works for everyone, the phone has the basics covered.

5. Tap the Done icon.

6. Tap the Save icon.

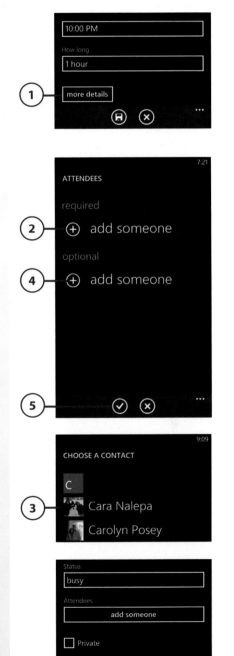

Responding to a Meeting Invitation

When someone sends you a meeting invitation, that invitation shows up in your inbox just like any other meeting invitation. When a meeting invitation is viewed through the phone, it looks like any other e-mail message. You can respond to the invitation by completing these steps:

1. With the e-mail meeting invitation open, tap the Respond button.

2. Tap Accept, Tentatively Accept, or Decline for the invitation.

3. Optionally, enter any text to go with your response.

4. Tap Send.

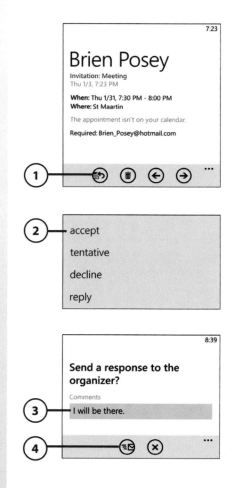

PROPOSE NEW TIME

Occasionally, someone might send you an invitation for a meeting that is scheduled for an inconvenient time. When this happens, you have the option to propose a different time. To do so, instead of tapping Accept or Decline, tap the Menu icon and then tap Propose New Time. From here, you can then suggest a new day, time, or duration for the meeting and send the response as normal.

Enabling, Organizing, and Disabling Calendars

When you link your phone to multiple email accounts and their associated calendars (or if you have more than one calendar for an account), the Calendar app aggregates them all into a unified calendar view. However, you can color-code your calendars or choose which of your included calendars appear. To do so, open the Calendar and follow these steps:

1. Go to Day view or Agenda view.

2. Tap the Menu icon.

3. Tap Settings.

4. Use the slide bar to disable any calendar whose contents you do not want to display.

5. To change the color coding for a calendar, tap its color indicator.

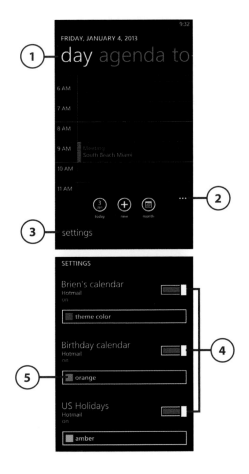

6. Tap the color you want to associate with the selected calendar.

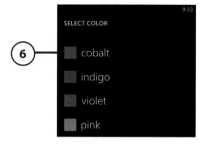

The To-Do List

If you choose to synchronize the Task List from your Exchange Server mailbox
(this can include Microsoft Hotmail, Live, and Outlook.com email accounts),
the items from the Task List display in the calendar's To-Do view. Of course,
you are free to use To-Do view whether or not you are synchronizing tasks
with an Exchange mailbox.

Creating a New Task

You can create a new task by opening
the calendar and following these steps:

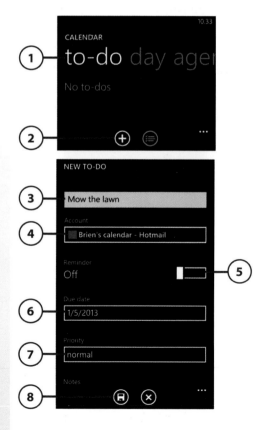

1. Switch to To-Do view.

2. Tap the New icon.

3. Tap Subject to enter a name for
the task.

4. Tap Account to change the
email account associated with
the task. Remember that only an
Exchange-based account works
with To Do items.

5. Flick right on Reminder if you
want to set up an alert for when
the task is due.

6. Tap Due Date to select when the
task needs to be completed.

7. Tap Priority to assign the task a
priority of High, Low, or Normal.

8. Tap Save to save the task.

Notes

If you scroll down the screen, you can also access a Notes field to add notes about the to-do task that you want to keep in mind.

Editing a Task

If you need to modify a task, you can do so by opening the Calendar and following these steps:

1. Switch to To-Do view.

2. Tap the task you want to edit.

3. Tap the Edit button.

4. Make your modifications.

5. Tap the Save button.

>>>Go Further

POSTPONING A TASK

If you need to postpone a task, you can easily do so by modifying the task as described here. However, Windows Phone 8 also provides a shortcut that you can use if you want to postpone a task until tomorrow. To move a task to tomorrow, open the Calendar, go to To-Do view, tap and hold the task you want to postpone, and select Postpone a Day. You can use this same procedure to delete a task or move up its due date to the current calendar day.

Completing a Task

When you have finished a task, Windows expects you to mark the task as completed. This ensures that the task does not continue to appear among future tasks. You can tell Windows that you have completed a task by opening the calendar and following these steps:

1. Switch to To-Do view.

2. Tap the task you have completed.

3. Tap Complete.

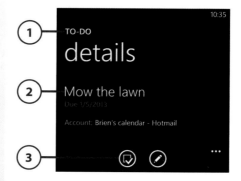

COMPLETING MULTIPLE TASKS

Occasionally, you complete several tasks at once. In this type of situation, it is easier to perform a bulk completion than flag each individual task as complete. If you have completed several tasks, you can designate them as complete by navigating to To-Do view, tapping the Select button to pick the to-do items you want to mark as complete, and then tapping the Complete button.

Viewing and Reactivating Completed Tasks

Sometimes you need to look back or reactivate a completed task. You can see your completed tasks by opening the Calendar, going to To-Do view, and following these steps:

1. Flick the menu icon upward.

2. Tap Show Completed.

3. Tap and hold the task you want to reactivate (or use the Select icon to select multiple completed tasks).

4. Tap the Activate icon.

Viewing Tasks by Priority

As previously mentioned, Windows Phone 8 enables you to prioritize your tasks. You also can sort the list of upcoming tasks by priority. To do so, open the Calendar, go to To-Do view, and follow these steps:

1. Tap the Menu icon.

2. Tap Sort by Priority.

Sorting by Due Date

If you sort tasks by priority, you can always put them back in order by due date by repeating this procedure and using the Sort by Due Date option (instead of using Sort by Priority).

Displaying Tasks on Your Calendar

Although Windows Phone 8 has a dedicated screen for displaying tasks, it is possible to display tasks on your calendar as well. To do so, open your calendar and complete these steps:

1. Tap the Menu icon.

2. Tap Settings.

3. Swipe up on the Settings screen until you see the Preferences section.

4. Select the Show To-Dos on the Calendar check box.

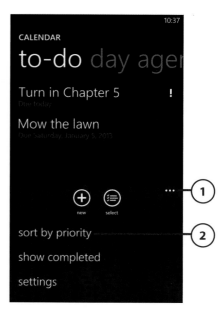

Camera

Every Windows Phone 8 device is equipped with both a front-facing and a rear-facing camera that can take pictures and record video. You can store the pictures and video that you record with the built-in camera on the device, play them back through the phone, and share them with others.

To take a still photo using a Windows Phone 8 device, you need to launch the Camera app by pressing the Camera button on the side of the device or activating it from the App list (or Start screen).

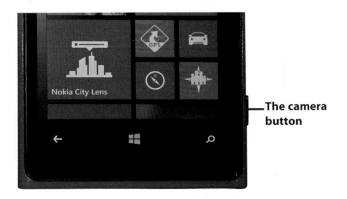

The camera button

At that point, you aim the device at the subject you want to capture and then press the Camera button halfway down to focus the camera. When you're ready to take the picture, push the button all the way down.

Geotagging

Windows Phone 8 devices contain a geotagging feature that appends your GPS location to your photos. When you use the camera for the first time, you see a prompt asking you if you want to allow location data to be used.

Windows Phone 7 devices contained zoom icons, which are noticeably absent from Windows Phone 8. Instead of using icons to adjust the camera zoom, Windows Phone 8 uses gestures. Simply use two fingers to make a pinching or unpinching motion on the screen to control the camera's zoom.

Adjusting Photo Settings

Different camera settings are useful to adjust before snapping a picture. These settings affect things like the picture's brightness and aspect ratio. You can adjust the photo settings by activating the Camera app and following these steps:

1. Tap the menu icon.

2. Tap Photo Settings.

3. Adjust the available photo settings to suit your needs.

Photo Settings

The actual settings that are available vary widely from one device to another. Each manufacturer integrates settings specific to their camera. Some commonly available settings include these:

Scenes: Setting for the type of photo you are taking. Available scenes might include close-up, night, night portrait, sports, or backlight.

ISO: The 35mm ISO equivalent.

Exposure Value: Manual exposure control.

White Balance: Control over the photo's white balance.

Aspect Ratio: Choice between wide photos (16:9) and standard photos (4:3).

Focus Assist Light: Control over the behavior of the light used to focus the camera.

Adjusting the Camera's Configuration Settings

In addition to the manufacturer specific camera settings discussed in the previous section, You have some global configuration options for the camera. You can access these configuration options by going to the phone's Settings screen and following these steps:

1. Flick the screen to the left to access the Application Settings page.

2. Tap Photos+Camera.

3. Enable the Tap on Screen to Take Pictures and videos check box if you want to be able to snap a picture without pressing the shutter button.

4. Enable the Press and Hold Camera Button to Wake Up the Phone check box if you want to be able to access the camera functions without first activating the Lock screen.

5. Enable the Prevent Accidental Camera Launch When Phone Is Locked check box to prevent the Camera app from launching with an inadvertent press of the Camera button.

6. Enable the Include Location Info in Pictures I Take check box to enable geotagging for your photos (that is, storing information in the photo's metadata about where the picture was taken).

>>>Go Further

AUTO UPLOAD AND RESET CAMERA

Also on this screen are options for Auto Upload and Reset Camera. Auto Upload includes options for uploading files to your SkyDrive or to a third-party service you might have installed (these are listed under the Apps option). If you enable either of these settings, every photo you take automatically uploads to the service or your SkyDrive. It's a good way to back up your photos as soon as you take them, but it can be annoying if you take a lot of unimportant pictures that you don't plan to keep. The Reset Camera option restores the camera to its factory default settings.

Controlling the Camera's Flash

Windows Phone 8 cameras are equipped with a flash that you can set to Enabled, Disabled, or Auto by activating the Camera app and following this step:

1. Tap the Flash icon to change its state among On, Off, and Auto. Auto allows the camera's own light sense to determine whether a flash is needed.

Flash States

Note that the flash is used only for the rear-facing camera. The front-facing camera is not equipped with a flash.

Changing the Camera's Behavior with Lenses

Windows Phone 8's camera is extensible through the use of software add-ins called lenses. Lenses change the camera's behavior according to the lens design. Some lenses are purely artistic. For example, a lens might make the camera take black-and-white photos, or it might produce a psychedelic effect. Other lenses actually provide functionality such as turning the camera into a barcode reader. You can access the phone's lenses by activating the Camera app and completing these steps:

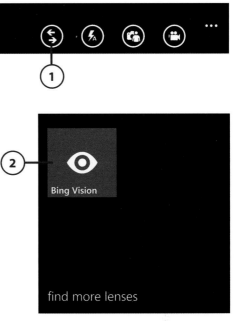

1. Tap the Lenses icon.

2. Tap the lens you want to use.

Acquiring Additional Lenses
You can download additional lenses by instead tapping Find More Lenses option.

Using the Front Camera

Windows Phone 8 devices include a front-facing camera that can take self-portraits or handle videoconferencing. By default, Windows Phone 8 devices use the rear-facing camera, but you can easily switch to the front-facing camera by launching the camera and following these steps:

1. Tap the Front icon.

Using the Front Camera

The Front icon toggles between the front camera and the rear camera. Most of the features that are available for the rear camera are also available for the front camera, but with one notable exception: The front camera has no flash.

Activating Video Mode

Although the phone's camera is configured by default to take still pictures, you can also use it to record video. You can switch the camera to video mode by activating the Camera app and following these steps:

1. Tap the Video icon.

Switching Back

The video icon toggles between video mode and still photography mode.

2. Aim the camera and tap the screen (or press the phone's Camera button) to begin recording. A counter appears on the screen to let you know how long you have been recording.

3. Tap the screen (or press the Camera button) a second time to stop recording.

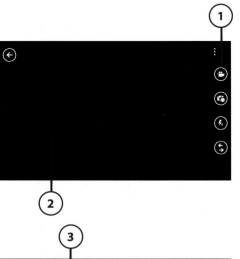

A counter appears when the phone is in video mode.

Adjusting Video Settings

Just as you can configure various settings for the still camera, you can adjust various video settings, such as the video resolution and the focus mode. Again, the actual settings that are available are device specific and vary among phone models. To access the video settings, activate the Camera app and follow these steps:

1. Tap the menu icon.

2. Tap the Video Settings.

①

lenses   flash   front   video

photo settings...

video settings...   ②

video settings

White Balance

Auto (default)

Continuous Focus

On (default)

Video Mode

Standard Quality (720p) (default)

save   reset

>>>Go Further

The available video settings differ among devices, but some settings are commonly available:

White Balance: Enables you to adjust the video's white balance

Continuous Focus: Helps you keep the video in focus while recording

Video Mode: Enables you to switch between video resolutions (720p, 1080p, and so on)

Before you record a video, it is worth checking to make sure that your phone is set to use the optimal video resolution. Some phones default to using relatively low resolution (720p), even though the camera supports full high-definition video at 1080p (1920×1080). Of course, lower video resolutions consume less storage space, so consider that if your phone is short on storage.

Using the Video Light

If you need extra light for your video, you will be happy to know that the camera's flash doubles as a video light. To enable the video light, activate the Camera app and follow these steps:

1. Ensure that the device is in video mode by tapping the Video icon, if necessary.

2. Tap the Lamp icon to toggle the camera light on and off.

Malfunctioning Video Light

If the video light doesn't come on, it doesn't necessarily mean that you're doing something wrong. Some phones are designed to override the video light setting if sufficient lighting is available.

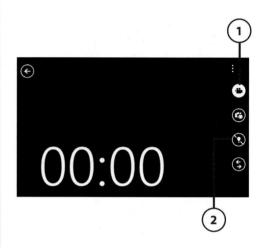

Photo

The Photo app is used for viewing and managing the photos that are stored on your camera. You can use the Photo app to arrange photos into albums, edit, and even share photos.

Photo 177

Viewing Your Pictures

You can view the pictures you have taken by activating the Photos app and following these steps:

1. Tap either Camera Roll or Albums.

2. Tap the picture you want to view.

3. You can view other pictures by flicking the screen left and right.

SORTING BY DATE

As you can see here, Windows Phone 8 also gives you the option to view your pictures based on the date they were taken or the album they are stored in (you can create your own custom albums), or to view photos from People that are in your contacts list. The People option is particularly interesting: After you choose a contact, you can see albums they've made publicly available, such as albums in their Facebook account, if you are a Facebook friend of that person.

Adding a Picture to Your Favorites

Windows Phone 8 enables you to flag your favorite photos so that you can view them all together in the Favorites folder. To add a picture to your favorites, open the Photos app and follow these steps:

1. Locate and select the picture you want to add to your favorites.

2. Tap the menu icon.

3. Tap Add to Favorites.

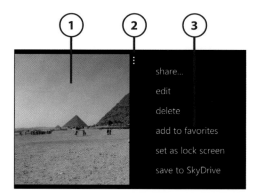

Viewing Your Favorite Pictures

You can view your favorite pictures at any time by opening the Photos app and following these steps:

1. Flick the screen to access Favorites view.

2. Tap the picture you want to view.

Deleting a Favorite

If you accidentally add a photo to your favorites, you can remove it by selecting the picture as described here, tapping the menu button, and tapping Remove from Favorites on the menu that appears.

Photo   **179**

Deleting a Picture

Not every picture that you snap is something you want to keep forever. You can delete a picture by opening the Photos app and completing these steps:

1. Locate the picture you want to delete.

2. Tap the Menu icon.

3. Tap Delete.

4. When Windows asks if you want to delete the picture, tap Delete.

Uploading a Picture to SkyDrive

Microsoft accounts include free access to Microsoft's online storage service, SkyDrive. SkyDrive is a 25GB pool of cloud storage that you can use to store files and documents and access them from virtually any web-enabled device. Windows Phone 8 has the capability to upload pictures from the phone directly to SkyDrive (assuming that the phone has been provisioned with a Microsoft account, as discussed in Chapter 3). To upload photos to SkyDrive, open the Photos app and follow these steps:

1. Locate the picture you want to upload to SkyDrive.

2. Tap the Menu icon.

3. Tap Save to SkyDrive.

Automatic Uploads

You can automatically update any photo you take to your SkyDrive using the option discussed earlier in the section, "Adjusting the Camera's Configuration Settings."

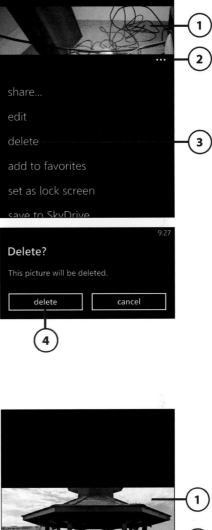

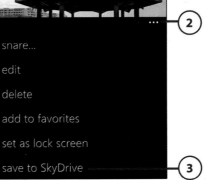

Sharing Your Pictures

After you snap a photo, you can immediately share the picture with your friends by sending the picture through email or through a text message or by using the Tap to Share feature. To do so, open the Photos app and follow these steps:

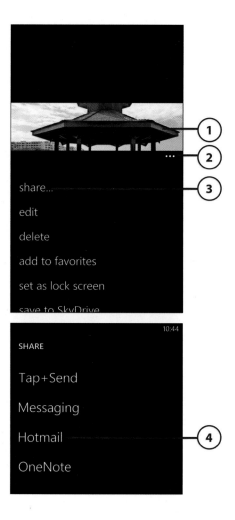

1. Locate the picture you want to share.

2. Flick the menu icon upward.

3. Tap Share.

4. Tap the mechanism you want to use to send the picture. You can use email, text messaging, or Tap+Send, or you can add the picture to OneNote.

Editing a Photo

Windows Phone 8 includes some lightweight photo-editing capabilities. You can access the photo editor by opening the Photos app, tapping the photo you want to edit, and tapping Edit from the Menu options.

The Edit screen includes three primary editing tools: Rotate, Crop, and Fix. The following sections discuss each of these tools.

Photo   **181**

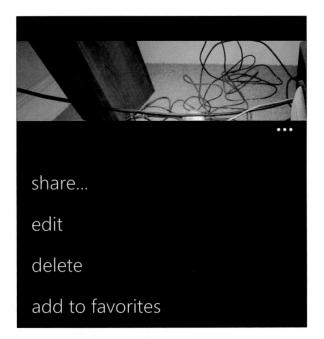

Rotating a Photo

To rotate a photo from within the Photos app, tap the photo you want to edit and then complete these steps:

1. Tap the Rotate icon.

2. Tap the Save icon

Cropping a Photo

To crop a photo from within the Photos app, tap the photo you want to edit and then complete these steps:

1. Tap the Crop icon.

2. To make the crop box adhere to a specific aspect ratio, tap the Aspect Ratio icon.

3. Select the desired aspect ratio.

4. Drag the orange arrows to select the picture's new boundaries.

5. Tap the Done icon.

6. Tap the Save icon.

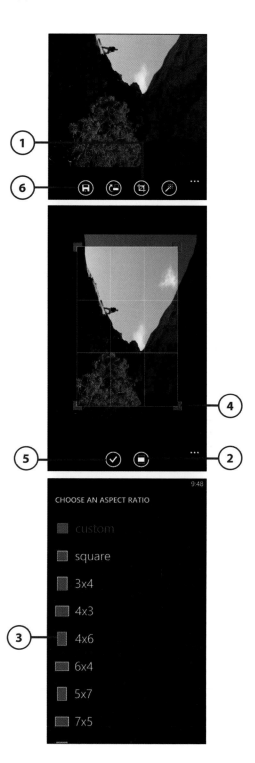

Photo   **183**

Fixing a Photo

Windows Phone 8 can fix a photo by automatically adjusting its brightness, contrast, white balance, and so on. To fix a photo in this way, open the Photos app, tap the photo you want to fix, and then complete these steps:

1. Tap the Fix icon.

2. Tap the Save icon.

Fixing the Fix

Sometimes the automated fix doesn't give you the results that you want. In these cases, you can revert the picture to its previous state by tapping the Undo Fix icon (which replaces the Fix icon after the fix is applied).

Using a Photo on the Lock Screen

Windows Phone 8 enables you to add a favorite photo to the phone's Lock screen. To do so, open the Photos app, tap the photo you want to use, and complete these steps:

1. Tap the menu icon.

2. Tap Set As Lock Screen.

3. Drag the crop the rectangle into position. Only the portion of the photo inside the rectangle is displayed on the lock screen.

4. Tap the Crop icon.

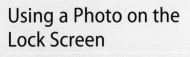

Your Picture Is Okay

You don't have to worry about the cropping process altering your photo. The cropping process applies only to the lock screen; your original photo is left unaltered.

Playing a Video

In the previous chapter, you learned how to play videos through the Music+Videos hub. Oddly enough, videos that are recorded through the phone are not included in the Music+Videos hub. To play a video that you have recorded, open the Photos app and complete these steps:

1. Tap Camera Roll.

2. Tap the video you want to play.

3. Tap the Play icon. The video playback screen contains various elements, including the usual icons for rewind, fast forward, play/pause, and video progress bar.

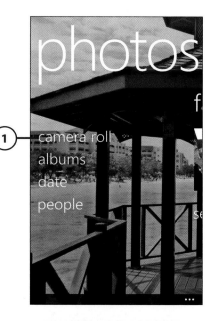

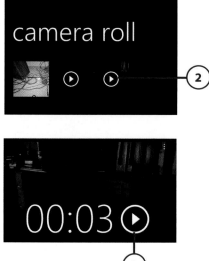

Internet Explorer

Perhaps none of Windows Phone 8's features has been more improved over the previous version than Internet Explorer. Some of the previous mobile editions of Internet Explorer were difficult to use, and many times web pages did not display properly. Windows Phone 8 includes a version of Internet Explorer 10 that is similar to the desktop version and that renders most web pages in exactly the same way a desktop computer would.

When you open Internet Explorer for the first time, Windows asks whether you want to use the recommended settings or whether you prefer to use custom settings. If you choose to use the recommended settings, your browsing history is sent to Microsoft to help improve Bing search results. Windows SmartScreen also then is enabled, to guard against unsafe websites and to inform certain websites that you don't want to be tracked.

11:44

Use recommended Internet Explorer settings?

This will send browsing history to Microsoft to help improve Bing services, use SmartScreen Filter to help protect against unsafe websites, and inform websites that you don't want to be tracked.

Learn more

We won't use this info to identify or contact you, and you can turn these features off at any time.

Privacy Statement

| recommended | custom |

You can use custom settings or the recommended settings.

Using Custom Settings

To use Internet Explorer's custom settings, follow these steps:

1. Click the Custom button.

2. Choose whether you want to send your browsing history to Microsoft, to help improve Bing search results.

3. Choose whether you want to use SmartScreen to protect against unsafe websites.

4. Choose whether you want to send a Do Not Track request to the websites you visit.

5. Tap Done.

Privacy Statement

recommended   custom   —①

11:44

CUSTOM SETTINGS

② — ☑ Send browsing history to Microsoft to help improve Bing services

③ — ☑ Use SmartScreen Filter to help protect against unsafe websites

④ — ☑ Send a Do Not Track request to websites you visit

Learn more

Privacy Statement

⑤ — done   cancel

>>>Go Further

CHANGING SETTINGS LATER

If you later decide to change these elements, you can do so by going to the phone's Settings screen, and then flicking the screen to the left to access the Applications page. Next, choose the Internet Explorer option. When the Internet Explorer screen opens, tap the Advanced Settings button to access the browser settings.

Browsing the Web

Browsing the web on a Windows Phone 8
device is just as simple as doing so from
a computer. To visit a web page, open
Internet Explorer and follow these steps:

1. Enter the URL for the website you
   want to visit.

Refresh icon — Address bar — Menu icon

Zooming a Page

Because Windows Phone 8 devices have a much smaller screen than a
typical computer, reading the text on a web page can be difficult. One way
to improve a page's readability is to turn the phone sideways. The browser
rotates to display the page in landscape format.

**Web pages are often easier to read if you turn the phone sideways
and view the page in landscape mode.**

Sometimes even viewing a page in landscape mode isn't enough to make the
page readable. In such cases, you can zoom in on the page using the unpinch
gesture. After doing so, you can flick the screen in any direction to view the
rest of the page or pinch in on the screen to zoom back out again.

Adding a Page to Your Favorites

Just as desktop versions of Internet Explorer enable you to maintain a list of favorite web pages, so does Internet Explorer on your Windows Phone. You can add a web page to your list of favorites by opening Internet Explorer and following these steps:

1. Enter the URL for the web page you want to add to your favorites list.

2. Tap the Menu icon.

3. Tap Add to Favorites.

4. When prompted, verify the name of the page and its URL, and make any necessary corrections.

5. Tap the Done icon.

Accessing Your Favorites List

You can access your favorite web pages at any time by opening Internet Explorer and following these steps:

1. Tap the Menu icon.

2. Tap Favorites.

3. Tap the page you want to visit.

Removing a Page from Your Favorites

If you no longer need a page included in your favorites list, you can easily remove it from the list by opening Internet Explorer and following these steps:

1. Flick the menu icon upward.

2. Tap Favorites.

3. Tap and hold the item you want to remove.

4. Tap Delete.

Editing Your Favorites

When you tap and hold an item on your Favorites list, the menu also displays an option to edit the item. You can use the Edit option to change the name of the page or the URL.

It's Not All Good

Deleting Vendor's Favorite Sites

Some phone manufacturers clutter your favorites list with a bunch of vendor websites. You can see a couple examples of these types of sites in the previous figure. You might want to take some time to get rid of the vendor's favorite sites before you populate the Favorites list with your own favorite sites.

Accessing Your Browsing History

Just as desktop versions of Internet Explorer keep track of the sites you visit, so does Internet Explorer on your Windows Phone. You can use your browsing history list as a handy mechanism for revisiting recently visited websites. You can access the browsing history by opening Internet Explorer and completing these steps:

1. Flick the menu icon upward.

2. Tap Recent.

3. To return to a previously visited site, find it in the list and tap it.

Clearing Your Browsing History

As a matter of privacy, you might want to periodically clear your browsing history. To do so, tap the Delete icon that you see here at the bottom of the Recent screen.

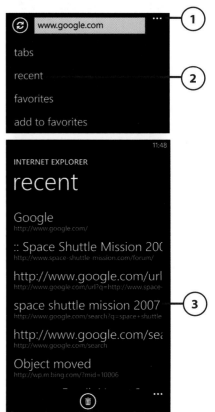

Tabbed Browsing

Most modern browsers for desktop computers offer a tabbed browsing feature that lets you open multiple web pages and go back and forth between them. The mobile version of Internet Explorer 10 includes this functionality as well.

Opening a New Tab

To open a new browser tab, open Internet Explorer and complete these steps:

1. Tap the Menu icon.

2. Tap Tabs.

3. Tap the New icon to open a new tab.

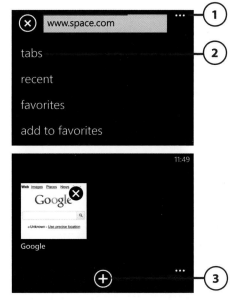

Switching to a Different Tab

You can access any of your open tabs by completing these steps:

1. Tap the Menu icon.

2. Tap Tabs.

3. Tap the tab you want to view.

Multitasking

Tabbed browser sessions remain open even after you press the Start button to move on to something else. This enables you to quickly return to them later.

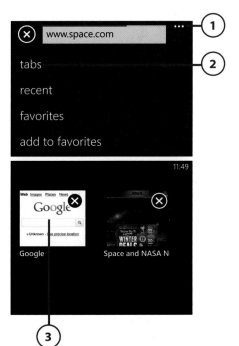

Closing a Tab

If you no longer need a tab, you can close it by completing the following steps:

1. Tap the Menu icon.

2. Tap Tabs.

3. Tap the Delete icon on the tab you want to close.

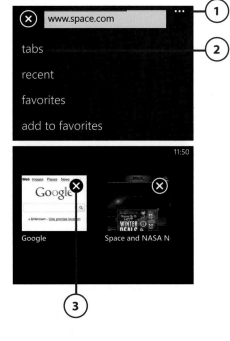

Sharing a Web Page

You can share a web page with a friend by emailing or texting the name of the page and the URL. To send a web page to someone, follow these steps:

1. Navigate to the web page you want to share.

2. Tap the Menu icon.

3. Tap Share Page.

4. Choose the Messaging option to send the web page by text, or pick the email account that you want to use to send the page. You can also share a page using Xbox or Tap+Send. Where you go from here depends on how you choose to share the web page.

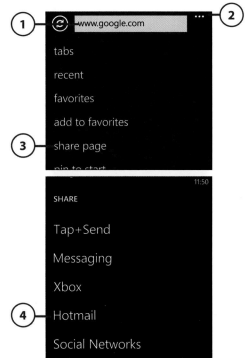

>>>Go Further

SHARING OPTIONS

Using Tap + SendWindows Phone 8 gives you a variety of options for sharing content. Tap + Send is a feature that you can use to share content with another Windows Phone 8 user by tapping your phones together. Xbox sharing makes use of Microsoft Smartglass to send the website that you are viewing to the Xbox 360's built-in web browser.

Adding a Page to the Start Screen

If you use a particular web page often, you might want to pin a shortcut to your Start screen instead of merely adding it to your favorites. To do so, open Internet Explorer and follow these steps:

1. Navigate to the page you want to add to the Start menu.

2. Flick the menu icon upward.

3. Tap Pin to Start.

___

Pin to Start Option Unavailable
You cannot use the Pin to Start option until the web page has finished loading. Until then, the option is grayed out.

___

(1)

(2)

www.google.com   •••

tabs

recent

favorites

add to favorites

share page

pin to start (3)

Internet Explorer Settings

You can manage several settings for Internet Explorer, including settings related to cookies, suggested sites, and website preferences. You can access the Internet Explorer settings by going to the Applications page on the Settings screen and tapping Internet Explorer.

The Settings page provides the following options:

A. Website Preference: By default, the phone displays the mobile version of a website, if a mobile version exists, but you can choose to always display the desktop version instead.

B. Use Address Bar Button For: You can choose the function that is available from the address bar. By default, Stop and Refresh are available on the address bar, but you can include a link to your favorites or to the browser tabs instead.

C. Delete History: Clicking the Delete History button clears your browser cache and clears your browsing history.

D. Advanced Settings: The advanced settings are listed next.

You can access these advanced settings by clicking the Advanced Settings button:

A. **Allow Access to My Location:** Allows web pages (such as Bing) to use GPS data

B. **Get Suggestions from Bing as I Type:** Displays popular URLs as you enter the URL for the page you want to visit

C. **Send Browsing History to Microsoft to Help Improve Bing Services:** Need author to add Text here

D. **Use SmartScreen Filter to Help Protect Against Unsafe Websites:** Need author to add Text here

E. **Send a Do Not Track Request to Websites You Visit:** Need author to add Text here

F. **Cookies from Website and Apps:** Controls whether all cookies and apps are accepted or blocked, or whether cookies and web apps are handled on a case-by-case basis

G. **Open Links from Other Apps In:** Enables you to control whether links are open on the current tab or on a new tab

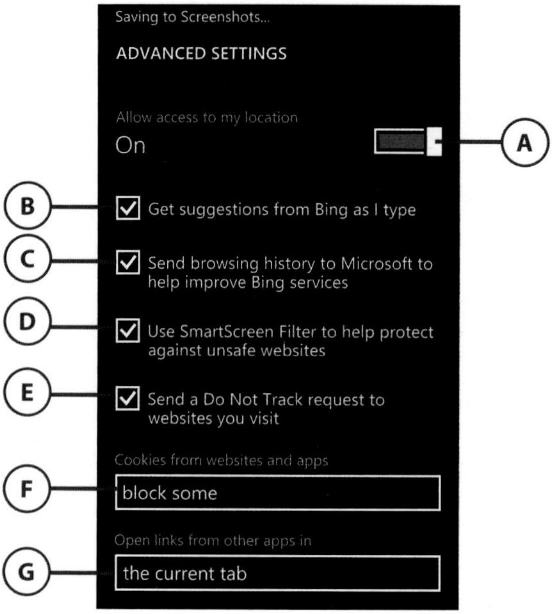

Manage Storage

You also have a Manage Storage option, which is not shown here. Some websites store data on your phone. These sites are listed on the Manage Storage screen, and from there you can choose to clear this data.

Finding an Item on a Web Page

Sometimes locating exactly the information you are looking for is difficult on a lengthy web page. In this situation, you can use the Find on Web Page feature to locate the information you are most interested in on the current page. To use this feature, follow these steps:

1. Navigate to the web page you are interested in.

2. Tap the Menu icon.

3. Scroll down and then tap Find on Page.

4. Enter your search query.

5. You can use the right and left arrow icons to locate the previous and next instances of the item you searched for.

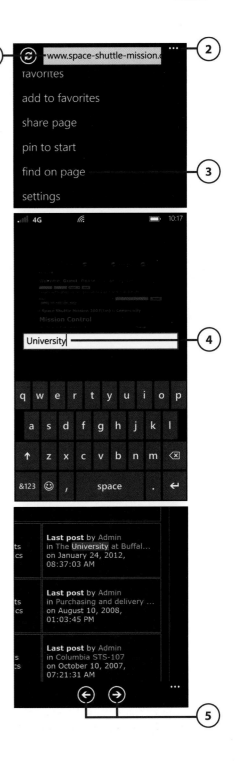

Store

The Store app on your Windows Phone represents an online portal where you can download apps, games, music, and podcasts for your phone. Many of the apps (and a few of the songs) are free, but plenty require paying a fee.

You can access the Store by tapping its tile on the Start screen or from the App List. When the Store opens, you see a screen that lists the types of items you can find in the Store.

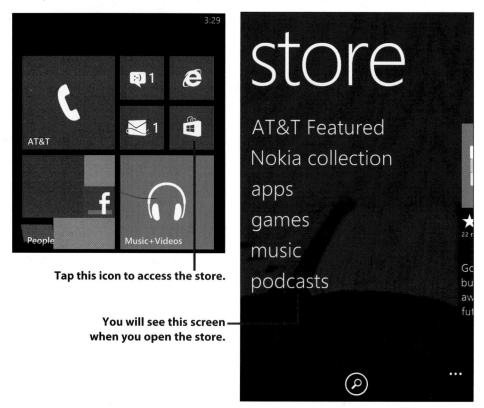

Tap this icon to access the store.

You will see this screen when you open the store.

Although the Store defaults to the Category screen shown here, you can flick to the right or the left to scroll through four more screens:

Featured: This screen doesn't really have a name. It displays whatever games, apps, or music are being promoted.

Apps: You browse the available apps here.

Games: The Games screen is like the Apps screen, but it focuses solely on games.

Music: You use the Music screen to browse and download music.

If an update is available for any of your apps, a number appears on the Store's tile on the Start screen. This number indicates the number of available updates.

The number 14 indicates that there are 14 updates available.

Downloading App Updates

If updates are available, you can access them through the Categories screen. The bottom of this screen provides a link to any available updates for apps you have already downloaded. To apply updates, return to this screen and follow these steps:

1. Tap the update notification.

2. Tap the app that you want to update, or tap the Update All button.

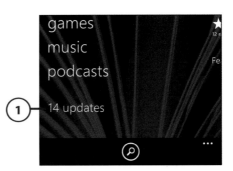

Finding New Applications

Windows Phone 8 makes it easy to search for new apps. To do so, open the store and follow these steps:

1. Tap Apps.

2. Flick to the Categories screen.

3. Tap the type of app you are interested in (Games, Entertainment, Photo, Lifestyle, and so on).

4. Browse the list of applications until you find the one you are interested in. When you find one, tap it.

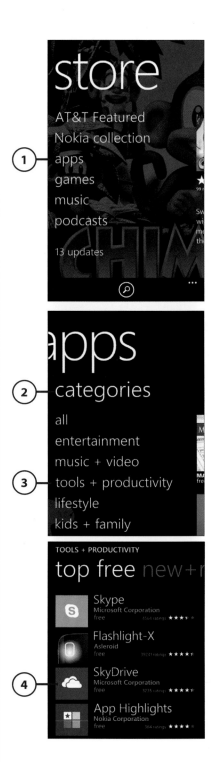

Searching for an App

If you are looking for a specific app, it is easier to search for the app than to browse for the app. You can search for an app by opening the Store and following these steps:

1. Tap the Search button.

2. Enter your search criteria.

3. Browse the search results for an application that meets your needs. When you locate one, tap it.

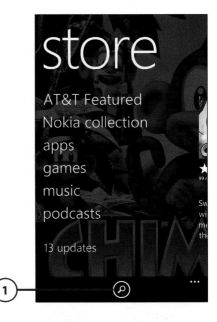

Viewing an Application

When you tap the icon for an app you're interested in, Windows displays a screen with more detailed information about the app:

A. The name of the app: You can see the name of the application and the name of the publisher.

B. The app's icon: This icon appears in the App List if you choose to install the app.

C. Price: Some apps are free; some are not.

D. The App rating: This is a star rating based on feedback from other users.

E. A description of the app: The description typically outlines the app's features and capabilities.

F. Show Details: Most app descriptions include a Show Details button that reveals more detailed information about the app.

G. The Try button: Tap the Try button to install a free trial version of the app.

H. The Buy button: Tap the Buy button to purchase the app.

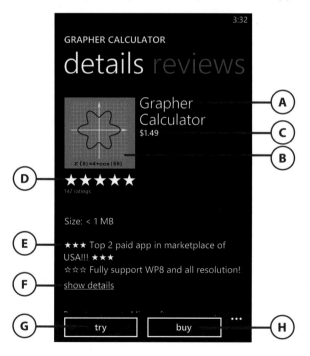

Viewing More Information

You can flick the screen to the right or left to view user reviews for the app, screenshots, and a list of related apps.

Installing an Application

When you find an application you want to install, you can install it by completing these steps.

1. Tap the app's icon to reveal its details screen.

2. Tap Try. d(You can also choose to purchase the app or, if it's free, download it in full.)

Extra Steps

Some apps display a screen asking if you want to allow the app to access device functions such as location information. If such a screen displays, tap Allow. Additionally, you might have to accept the app's terms of use.

3. The app installs automatically and can be either accessed from the App List or pinned to the Start screen.

INSTALLING AN APP THROUGH THE WINDOWS PHONE SOFTWARE

>>>Go Further

Just as you can download and install apps directly through the phone, you can do so through the Windows Phone software by connecting your phone to your computer, launching the Windows Phone software (see, "Working with the Windows Phone Software," in Chapter 4), and scrolling to the In the Store section of the app. From here, you have full access to the Store from your PC, which gives you a bit more screen real estate from which to find, purchase, and download apps for your Windows Phone.

When you choose to install an app using Windows Phone Software, you must choose whether you want the app to download to your phone using messaging or whether you want instructions emailed to you so that you can download the app later.

Deploying an app using messaging can cause you to rack up a hefty phone bill unless you have a plan that supports unlimited SMS text messaging. Because apps are not downloaded to your PC and then copied to your phone (they are downloaded straight to your phone from the Internet), either deployment method supported by the Windows Phone software causes your phone to download the apps directly, which can incur data usage fees.

Removing an App

If you want to remove an app that you have installed, you can do so by going to the app list and following these steps:

1. Tap and hold the app you want to remove.

2. Tap Uninstall.

3. Tap Yes.

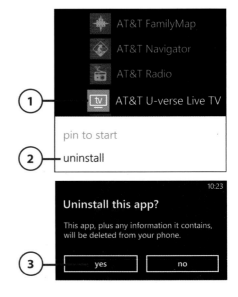

Xbox Music Downloads

Although the Store focuses heavily on apps, you can also use it to purchase and download music through an area known as Xbox Music. You can access music downloads by opening the Store and tapping Music from the Categories screen. This takes you to the Xbox Music screen shown here.

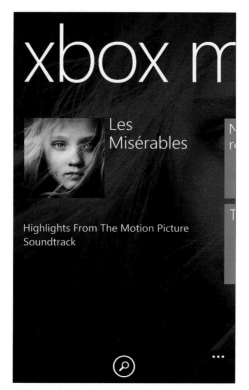

The Store contains several screens that you can flick between:

Featured: You can find a direct link to the album of the moment.

Quick Access: This screen doesn't really have a name. It contains a collection of shortcuts that give you fast access to new releases, top albums, and top artists.

Spotlight: This screen gives you quick access to new albums from a variety of genres.

Genres: Browse specific genres here.

Unless you have very diverse musical tastes, you will probably be happier browsing Xbox Music by music genre. That way, you can filter the browsing results based on your musical tastes.

It's Not All Good

Not All Genres Shown by Default

Although Windows Phone 8 gives you many different music genres to choose from, not all genres are represented by default. For example, heavy metal, bluegrass, and opera are all missing from the list. However, as you add items from your music collection, genres that are not otherwise supported might be added to the list. In the previous figure, for instance, Hard Rock appears on the list because I have some selections in my music collection, not because Hard Rock is one of the phone's default genres.

When you choose a music genre, you go to a page that enables you to browse the available music by several categories:

- New Releases
- Top Albums
- Top Artists
- Top Songs
- Top Playlists

There are a number of different screens displayed within each genre.

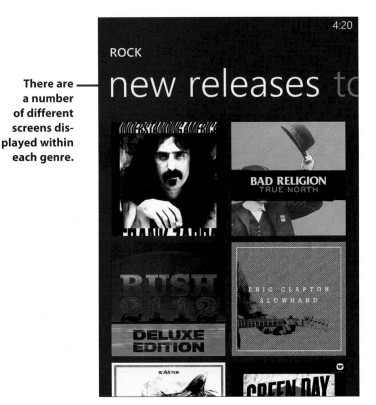

If you want to purchase a specific song or album from Xbox Music, it is easier to search for what you are looking for than to browse through an entire musical genre. To search for an artist, song, album, or playlist, tap the Search icon and enter your search criteria, as shown here.

Iron Maiden
iron maiden Apps+Games
iron maiden no Apps+Games
Iron Maiden Music
A Matter Of Life And Death Music

The search results contain a mix of albums, artists, songs, playlists, and even podcasts. Note that this particular search searches only the Store, not your personal music collection. Chapter 4 discusses searching your music collection.

Podcasts

The Store enables you to download a variety of podcasts. You can browse the available podcasts by opening the Store, navigating to the Categories screen, and completing the following steps:

1. Tap Podcasts.

2. Locate and tap the podcast that you want to subscribe to. You can search for a specific podcast, use one of the featured podcasts, or sort through available podcasts by flicking across the categories at the top of the screen.

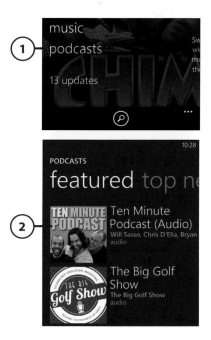

3. Tap Subscribe if you want to receive not only the current episodes, but future episodes as well. (You can also download just a single episode by tapping it in the listing shown here.)

4. Choose the number of episodes you want to keep on your phone.

5. Choose the play order (either oldest first or newest first).

6. Tap Confirm to subscribe to the show and begin downloading episodes.

Kid's Corner

One of the most innovative features of Windows Phone 8 is Kid's Corner. Although I don't have any kids of my own (nor are there any future plans for rug rats in the Posey house), I have plenty of friends with kids. Almost all those kids like to play with their parents' smartphones.

The problem is that kids can get into trouble with unrestricted access to a smartphone. For example, they might reset the phone to its factory defaults (erasing all the data), send an email or a text to everyone on the address book, order every app in the App Store, or press enough random buttons to make a call to Zimbabwe.

This is where Kid's Corner comes in. Kid's Corner lets you lock down your phone so that your kids have access to only the apps and features you want them to have. Of course, Kid's Corner doesn't take all the risk out of letting a kid play with your phone. My sister's toddler once flushed her iPhone. Good riddance!

Setting Up Kid's Corner

You can set up Kid's Corner by going to the Settings screen and completing these steps:

1. Tap Kid's Corner.

2. Tap Next.

3. Tap the type of category that contains the apps or media you want available to Kid's Corner. For this example, I use Games, but the process works the same way for Music, Videos, and Apps.

4. Select the check boxes for the items you want your children to have access to.

5. Tap Done. Repeat this process for each category of app or media you want to include.

6. Tap Next.

7. Tap Set Password.

8. Enter a password.

9. Confirm your password.

10. Tap Done.

11. Tap Finish.

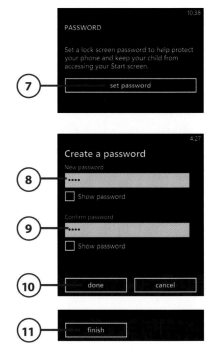

Launching Kid's Corner

You must manually engage Kid's Corner whenever your child wants to use your phone. To do so, go to the Settings screen and follow these steps:

1. Tap Kid's Corner.

2. Tap Launch Kid's Corner. When you do, the phone displays a dedicated lock screen to show you that Kid's Corner is enabled.

3. Flick the Kid's Corner lock screen upward to display the custom Kid's Corner start screen.

When activated, Kid's Corner displays a special lock screen.

MAKING LIFE EASIER

If you use Kid's Corner often, pin it to your Start screen to make launching it easier. If your phone is already at the lock screen, you can go directly to Kid's Corner by swiping left on the lock screen. When you are logged into Kid's Corner, you can return to your own Start screen by pressing the phone's power button to turn off the display and then turning it back on again.

It's Not All Good

Lock Screen Times Out Quickly

The Kid's Corner lock screen times out quickly. When the lock screen times out, your phone's display turns off and you must relaunch Kid's Corner if you still want to use it. My phone timed out in less time than it took me to type this sentence. The screen dimmed after a mere 5 seconds, and the display shut off after 10 seconds. As a parent, you might want to go to the Kid's Corner Start screen before you hand the phone to your child.

Modifying Kid's Corner Permissions

Over time, you will probably want to modify the Kid's Corner permissions. After all, your kid will probably want access to the latest game or social networking app or you might decide to disallow something you previously allowed. To change the permissions, go to the Settings screen and complete the following steps:

1. Tap Kid's Corner.

2. Tap Games, Music, Videos, or Apps (depending on the type of permission you want to change).

3. Select the check box for any new item that you want to give your child permission to access. Likewise, you can deselect the check box for any item for which you want to revoke permission.

4. Tap Done.

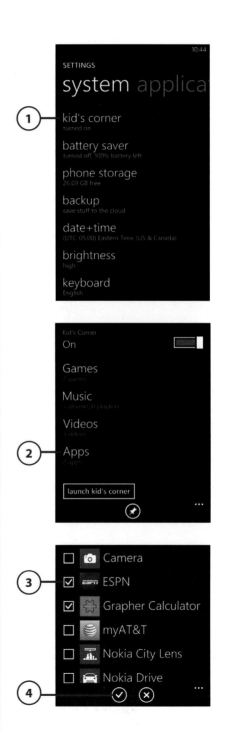

Wallet

Windows Phone 8 devices include a built-in app known as Wallet that enables you to keep track of credit cards, debit cards, gift cards, and even coupons. You can even designate credit cards for use in specific types of electronic purchases.

It's Not All Good

Account Numbers Might Be Stored by Default

The Wallet app is one of those features that simply doesn't appeal to everyone. After all, not everybody likes the idea of having credit card numbers stored in a phone.

If you decide that the Wallet app is not for you, it is critically important to at least open Wallet and see if any forms of payment are set up by default. When I opened Wallet for the first time, I was surprised to see that my AT&T account and my debit card were both entered by default. Apparently, my phone had downloaded my debit card information from my Microsoft account.

If you plan to use the Wallet app, it is essential that you assign a strong password to your phone. Otherwise, if your phone is ever lost or stolen, your payment information could be compromised. The Wallet app also offers the capability to set a PIN that is independent of the device's password. I strongly recommend enabling the Wallet PIN. Instructions for doing so are provided later in this section.

Before you can use Wallet, you must go through a simple initial setup process. To do so, go to the App list, tap Wallet, and, on the ensuing Welcome screen, confirm that you want to use the app by tapping Get Started.

Adding a Payment Method

The whole point of Wallet is that it enables you to enter various forms of payment, including credit cards, debit cards, Microsoft gift cards, and PayPal. You also have an Other option that you can use to enter gift or membership card information from supported merchants. You can add a credit card as a payment type by opening Wallet and completing these steps:

1. Go to the All screen and tap the Add icon.

2. Choose the form of payment you want to add. You can add a credit or debit card, a Microsoft gift card, or PayPal. You can use the Other option if you have a gift card from a provider that offers a Windows Phone app.

Different Steps

The instructions for entering card information can vary significantly, depending on the type of payment that you are entering. These steps are based on adding a credit or debit card.

3. Choose whether you want to authorize the payment method to be used for app or music purchases.

4. Tap Next.

5. Enter the first six digits of your card number (unless instructed to do otherwise).

6. Tap Next. If an app exists that recognizes your card number, the card is added. You're done! Otherwise, you have to tap the Add Your Card Manually link that appears.

MANUALLY ENTERING A CARD NUMBER

If no app recognizes your card number, you must enter your card manually. When you click the Add Your Card Manually link, you're taken to a screen that includes several labels for adding a card name, the cardholder's billing information, extra personalization information (such as a nickname or any notes about the card), extra account details (such as how long you've been a member), and more. The crucial information is all under the Billing Details option, which you have to tap repeatedly to enter content such as your card's expiration date, your billing address, and your phone number.

It's a good idea to go ahead and populate the Issuer Details portion of the payment information section, even though that information is not actually required. That way, if your card is ever lost or stolen, then the contact information for the bank is stored in your phone. Doing so could be handy even if you do not want to use your phone to make electronic payments.

Editing a Payment Method

You might occasionally need to edit your payment information. For example, if you move, you might need to update the billing address for a card. Likewise, if a card expires, you need to enter a new expiration date. You can edit payment information by opening Wallet and performing the following steps:

1. Tap the payment method you want to edit.

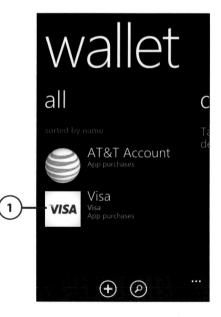

2. Tap the Edit icon.

3. Make any necessary changes to the payment method.

4. Tap the Save icon.

Removing a Payment Method

You can easily remove a payment method from your phone by opening Wallet and completing these steps:

1. Tap and hold the payment method you want to delete.

2. Tap Delete.

It's Not All Good

Deleting Account Info Not Always Easy

Some payment forms are easier to delete than others. If your cellular account is listed as a default payment method, you might not be able to get rid of it. Likewise, if your credit or debit card information was downloaded from your Microsoft account, the only way to get rid of that information is to log into your Microsoft account and remove the billing information. Only then can you delete the card data from your phone.

Pinning Payment Information

You can pin payment information to your phone's Start screen by opening Wallet and completing these steps:

1. Tap and hold a payment method.

2. Tap Pin to Start.

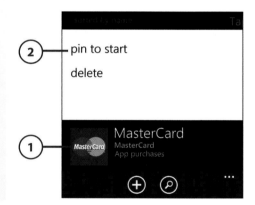

The Wallet PIN

Given the sensitive nature of the information stored in the Wallet app, it is a good idea to activate the Wallet PIN. The Wallet PIN lets you assign a PIN to the Wallet app. This PIN is independent of the PIN or password you use to sign into your phone.

Security Warning

For the sake of security, it is a good idea to set your Wallet PIN to something different than the device password. That way, even if someone gains access to your device by figuring out your password, that person doesn't have access to Wallet.

Setting a Wallet PIN

To add a Wallet PIN, open Wallet and
complete these steps:

1. Tap the Menu icon.

2. Tap Settings+PIN.

3. Set the PIN slide bar to On.

4. Enter your PIN.

5. Confirm your PIN.

6. Tap Done.

7. Tap the Use Wallet PIN to Protect
   Music, App, and In-App Purchases
   check box.

Changing Your Wallet PIN

You can change your Wallet PIN at any time by opening Wallet and completing these steps:

1. Tap the Menu icon.

2. Tap Settings+PIN.

3. Tap Change PIN.

4. Enter your old PIN.

5. Enter your new PIN.

6. Confirm your new PIN.

7. Tap Done.

Removing Your Wallet PIN

If you want to stop using a Wallet PIN (which I do not recommend doing), you can get rid of the PIN by opening Wallet and completing these steps:

1. Flick the menu icon upward.

2. Tap Settings+PIN.

3. Set the Wallet PIN slide bar to the Off position.

Deals

The Wallet app's Deals feature gives you a way to store coupon information in the Wallet app. You can locate and download electronic coupons, or you can manually enter coupon information. This section shows you how to do both.

Finding Deals

The Finding Deals function enables you to browse for coupons of local interest. You can find deals by opening Wallet and completing these steps:

1. Go to the Deals screen.

2. Tap Add.

3. Tap Find Deals.

4. Browse the list of deals. If you see a deal that interests you, tap it to view more information.

5. Tap Save for Later.

ADDING A CUSTOM DEAL

In addition to finding deals based on your location, you can add a custom deal to your wallet. Instead of tapping Find Deals, as shown here, tap Add Deal Info. Your phone asks you to fill out the following fields:

Deal Details: These details include the deal website, the coupon code, the expiration date, and the start date.

Merchant Details: The merchant details include the merchant's address and phone number.

Issuer Details: These details include the name of the issuer and the issuer's website.

Personalize: This section includes a customer name and a Notes field.

Removing a Deal

Deals tend to expire, and you might need to occasionally remove expired deals or deals that you are no longer interested in. To do so, open Wallet and complete these steps:

1. Go to the Deals screen.

2. Tap and hold the deal you want to remove.

3. Tap Delete. When prompted for confirmation, tap Delete again.

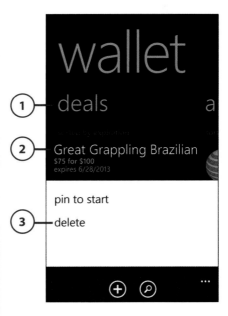

Pinning a Deal

If you want to pin a deal to your Start screen, you can do so by opening Wallet and completing these steps:

1. Tap and hold the deal you want to pin.

2. Tap Pin to Start.

Searching for a Deal

If you use the Deals feature heavily, you might accumulate so many deals in your wallet that finding what you are looking for becomes difficult. In these types of situations, it is helpful to be able to search your Wallet for specific deals. To do so, open Wallet and complete these steps:

1. Go to the Deals screen.

2. Tap Search.

3. Enter your search criteria.

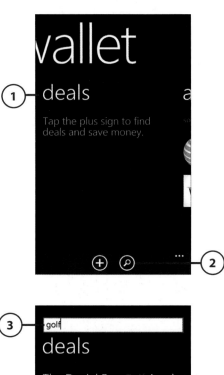

It's Not All Good

No Online Deals Search

Although you can search for deals in your Wallet, Windows Phone 8 does not offer a feature to search for deals online. For now, the only way to locate online deals is to browse.

Sharing a Deal

Sometimes when browsing for deals, you might find a deal that would interest a friend. You can share the deal with your friend, even if that person isn't using a Windows Phone 8 device. To do so, open Wallet and complete these steps:

1. Locate a Deal you want to share. Tap it.

2. Tap Share.

3. Tap the mechanism you want to use to share the deal. The actual available mechanisms vary, depending on how your phone is configured, but some of the options include Tap+Send, Messaging, Email, Xbox, and Social Networks.

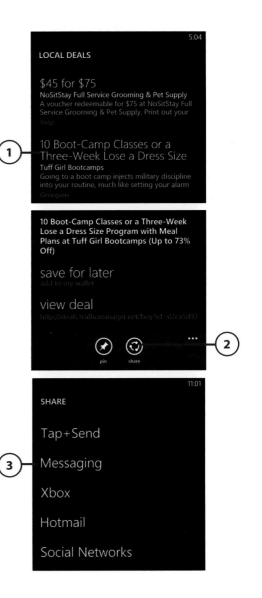

Marking a Deal as Used

The Wallet app's Deals screen can keep track of which deals you have and have not used. To mark a deal as used, open the Wallet app's Deals screen and complete these steps:

1. Tap the deal you have used.

2. Tap the Menu icon.

3. Tap Mark as Used. The Deals screen now places a Used indicator beneath the deal.

   If you accidentally mark a deal as used, you can remove the Used indicator by marking the deal as unused. Repeat the steps listed here. In place of the Mark As Used menu option, you'll see a Mark As Unused option. Tap that instead.

GETTING REMINDERS

If you're concerned that you might forget to use a deal before it expires, you can also set up a reminder for it that works precisely the same as setting up an appointment on your Calendar. (See the "Calendar" section, earlier in this chapter.) To do so, select the deal from the Wallet app's Deals screen, bring up the menu, and tap Add Reminder. Your phone brings up the New Appointment screen, enabling you to set up the reminder and store it in one of your available calendars.

It's worth pointing out that although the reminder configuration screen contains a More Details button, it's there only because, at this point, your phone just thinks you're setting up a standard appointment. Most of the details here aren't really suitable for coupon reminders because they include things like event recurrence, the capability to invite someone to a meeting, or the capability to change your calendar status. Some of these details might be helpful in very specific situations, but you probably won't use them in most cases.

Access Office documents stored on your SkyDrive.

Create, edit, and modify Office documents through your phone!

In this chapter, you learn about Windows Phone 8 mobile versions of Microsoft Word, Excel, PowerPoint, and OneNote. Some of the topics discussed in this chapter include:

→ Accessing Microsoft Office
→ Creating spreadsheets and charts with Excel
→ Working with Word documents
→ Creating PowerPoint slides and presentations
→ Using OneNote to create notes and lists

Microsoft Office Mobile

From the very beginning, Microsoft has included mobile versions of the Microsoft Office applications on its mobile operating systems. This tradition continues in Windows Phone 8. Windows Phone 8 offers mobile versions of Microsoft Word, Excel, PowerPoint, and OneNote. The phone is also designed to interact with SharePoint 2010 workspaces.

In some previous editions of Windows Mobile, the Microsoft Office apps were usually just enough to get by on. For example, it was possible to receive a Microsoft Word document by email, open it, make a few changes, and send it back. However, many important features were missing. For instance, if a document contained comments, those comments could not be displayed.

The other issue that plagued previous editions of Microsoft Office Mobile was that the applications could be difficult to use on a device with a small screen. Many Windows Mobile 6.1 devices, for example, required the use of a stylus. Imagine trying to compose a Word document by using a stylus to tap tiny characters on an onscreen keyboard.

Although none of the Microsoft Office Mobile apps in Windows Phone 8 is as full featured as its Office 2013 counterpart, Microsoft has added a great deal of functionality and designed each app's interface so that you can effectively use it from a Windows Phone 8 touchscreen.

Accessing Microsoft Office

You can get to the Microsoft Office hub by tapping its tile either from the App List or from the Start screen. If the tile isn't already on the Start screen, you can add it from the App List by tapping and holding its icon and tapping Pin to Start, as shown here.

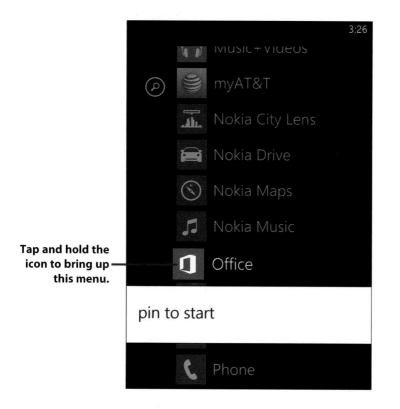

Tap and hold the icon to bring up this menu.

Preexisting Tile

Some Windows Phone 8 devices already include an Office tile on the Start screen. The Start screen configuration differs among manufacturers.

When you initially open Microsoft Office, the Places screen displays. This screen gives you access to Office documents saved in various locations. Places is one of two screens that is accessible by flicking left and right; the other is Recent, which grants access to all your most recently accessed Office documents.

The Recent Screen

The Recent screen displays a list of the most recently opened Word, Excel, and PowerPoint documents. You can tap on a document to open it, but other options are available if you tap and hold a document:

- **Pin to Start:** A shortcut to the document appears on the Start screen.

- **Share:** You can share the document through email or by using the Tap+Send feature.

- **Save To:** You can save the document to a different location.

- **Delete:** The document is erased.

- **Remove from Recent:** The document is removed from the list of recently opened documents.

The Places Screen

Windows Phone 8 devices enable you to save Microsoft Office documents in a variety of locations. In fact, the Office hub contains a Places page that you can use to access documents stored in various locations. These locations are available:

- **Phone:** If you tap the Phone option, Windows takes you to the Documents page, which shows a list of the Office documents stored on your phone. You can tap on a document to open it.

- **Email:** When you tap Email, Windows Phone 8 displays a list of Office documents that have been recently opened as email attachments. When you open an email attachment, that attachment remains open in the background. As such, tapping email gives you a list of any Office documents that were opened as email attachments, since the last time the phone was rebooted. You can tap on a document to view it.

- **SkyDrive:** If you tap the SkyDrive option on the Locations page, Windows displays the contents of your SkyDrive. By default, this includes a Documents folder and a Shared folder.

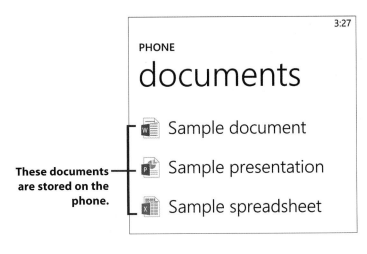

These documents are stored on the phone.

This document is a recently opened email attachment.

These documents are stored on SkyDrive.

- **Office 365:** Windows Phone 8 is also designed so that you can access documents stored within Office 365 SharePoint. This is primarily something that you would only do if you were using your phone in a corporate environment in which Microsoft Office documents were stored in a SharePoint document library.

If you have not yet connected your phone to Office 365, the Office 365 option is listed as Office 365. Tapping the Office 365 option displays a screen stating that your phone must be set up to connect to Office 365. Tapping the corresponding Set Up button takes you to the Email+Accounts screen. Chapter 3 discusses the process of connecting Windows Phone 8 to Office 365.

When Windows Phone 8 has been connected to Office 365, the words "Office 365" are replaced by "Team Site."

After the Windows Phone 8 device connects to Office 365, the Office 365 option on the Places screen disappears and is replaced by the words Team Site. Tapping Team Site takes you to your SharePoint team site. You can open a document within the team site by simply tapping the folder that contains the document and then tapping the document.

Adding a SharePoint Folder

Although Windows Phone 8 automatically populates the team site with your Office 365 SharePoint folders, you might occasionally want to add SharePoint folders that are not a part of your Office 365 account. To do so, go to the Places screen and complete these steps:

1. Tap the New icon.

2. Enter the URL for the SharePoint site you want to open.

Searching for a Document

A quick glance at the Places screen confirms the fact that you can store Office documents in a variety of locations. As such, it can sometimes be tough to remember where a particular document is stored. Fortunately, you can search for an Office document. To do so, open the Places screen and complete these steps:

1. Tap the Search icon.

2. Enter your search criteria.

Search Scope

By default, a search looks for documents in all possible locations. However, you can limit the search scope by flicking the Search screen to the left or right. For example, if you want to search only for documents stored on your phone, you can flick the Search screen to the Phone page and then perform your search.

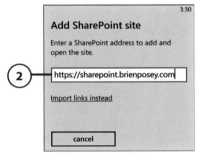

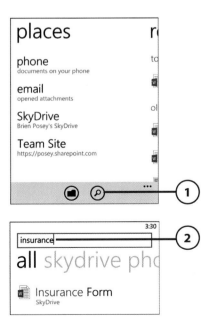

Places Options

As you've seen in the previous sections, the Places screen is designed to give you quick access to Microsoft Office documents stored in various locations. Although you can tap a document to open it, other options are available if you tap and hold a document:

- **Pin to Start:** A shortcut to the document appears on the Start screen.

- **Share:** You can share the document through email or by using the Tap+Send feature.

- **Save To:** You can specify a different location for saving the document.

- **Delete:** The document is erased.

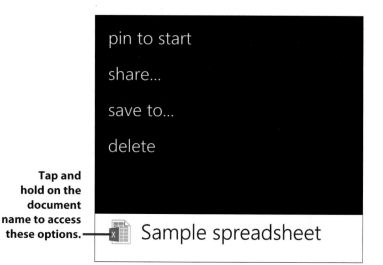

Tap and hold on the document name to access these options.

Office Mobile Settings

You can set a few different configuration options for Office Mobile. To access these configuration settings, navigate to the phone's Settings screen and follow these steps:

1. Flick the Settings screen to the right to access the Applications page.

2. Tap Office.

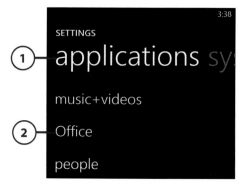

3. Tap User Name to enter your name. This name appears next to any comments that you make within an Office document. If you create a new Office document from your phone, the User Name is used as the document author.

4. Tap Open SharePoint Links in the Office Hub if you want to make any SharePoint links you have access to available through the Office hub.

5. Tap Reset Office to erase all saved Office settings, local files, and online files. Office reverts to its default factory settings. Resetting Office also removes connections to SharePoint and anything Office related that you might have pinned to your Start screen.

SETTINGS

Office

User name

User

Enter your user name to identify yourself in comments, notes, and document tracking.

☑ Open SharePoint links in the Office hub

reset Office

Excel

Although it's not quite as full featured as the desktop version, the mobile version of Excel enables you to create and view spreadsheets with ease. Excel Mobile can even open desktop Excel spreadsheets, although it ignores any unsupported features that are used in the spreadsheet.

Creating a New Spreadsheet

You can create a new Excel spreadsheet by opening the Office hub and following these steps:

1. Flick the screen to access the Recent page.

2. Tap the New icon.

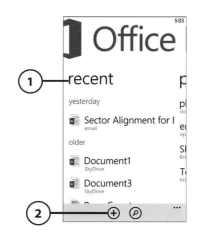

Office

recent

yesterday

Sector Alignment for I
email

older

Document1
SkyDrive

Document3
SkyDrive

3. Tap Excel.

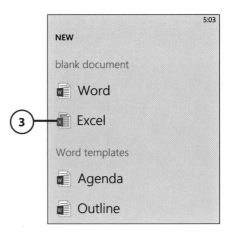

Document Templates

The procedure outlined here assumes that you want to create a blank Excel spreadsheet. However, when you tap the New icon, Windows provides templates you can use to create preformatted spreadsheets. For example, Microsoft provides templates for tracking expenses or vehicle mileage and even an event scheduler. You can create a spreadsheet based on a template simply by tapping the template.

Working with the Excel Interface

When working with Excel, you likely will use two main components: the onscreen keyboard and the Excel icon bar. Unfortunately, you cannot display these items on the screen at the same time; you must switch between them as needed.

The process of entering data into Excel takes some getting used to. The first time you need to enter data into a cell, you have to tap the cell and then tap the text bar at the top of the screen. This reveals the keyboard so that you can begin entering data. However, if the keyboard is already onscreen, you simply tap a cell and begin entering data.

If the onscreen keyboard is currently displayed, you need to access the Excel icon bar and then press the phone's Back button. This hides the keyboard and reveals the icon bar.

Press the phone's Back button to hide the onscreen keyboard.

Adding a Comment to a Cell

Comments are a popular feature in Excel that enable you to enter notes for a spreadsheet cell without altering the spreadsheet itself. You can add a comment to a spreadsheet by following these steps:

1. Tap the cell on which you want to comment.

2. Tap the Menu icon.

3. Tap Comment.

4. Enter your comment.

5. Tap another cell to complete the process.

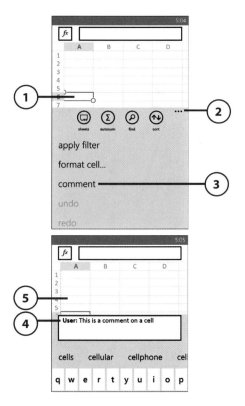

THE COMMENT AUTHOR

In the comment in this example, notice the label User attached to it. The first time you attempt to add a comment to an Office document, you are prompted to enter your name. The name you enter is displayed along with any comments you make. Be careful to enter an appropriate name—the name you enter is semipermanent.

If you do need to change this name at some point, you can either type over the name in any comments you make or use the Microsoft Office Settings page to modify the name so that new name is used in all future comments.

Changing the Comment Author

If you need to change the comment author, you can do so by going to the phone's Settings screen and performing the following procedure:

1. Flick the screen to the right to access the Application settings page.

2. Tap Office.

3. Enter a new name into the User Name field.

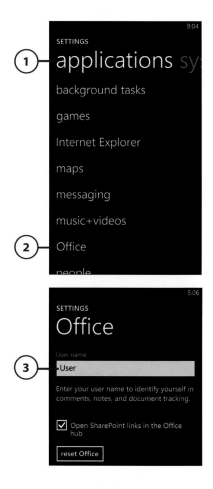

Viewing and Navigating Comments

Even if someone added a comment to an Excel spreadsheet by using a desktop version of Excel, you can read those comments in Excel Mobile. To do so, follow these steps:

1. Look for a cell with a small colored triangle in the upper-right corner, and then tap it to view the comment.

2. If the spreadsheet has multiple comments, you can use the Previous and Next icons to view them.

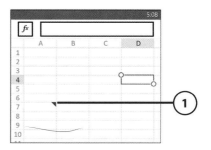

Searching a Spreadsheet

The easiest way to locate text within a large spreadsheet is to use the Search function. To do so, follow these steps:

1. Tap the Find icon.

2. Enter the text you want to search for.

3. Excel locates the nearest cell containing the specified text.

4. You can use the Next icon to find additional occurrences of the text.

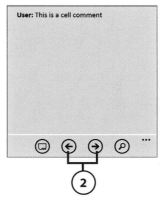

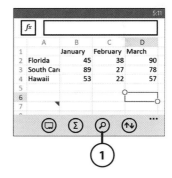

Selecting Multiple Cells

It may occasionally be necessary to select multiple cells within a spreadsheet. For example, if you want to apply formatting to a large area, it is easier to select the full range of cells that you want to format and then apply the formatting to all of them at once.

You can select multiple cells by tapping a cell within the range of cells you want to select and then dragging using the small circle indicators to tap and drag your finger until all desired cells are selected.

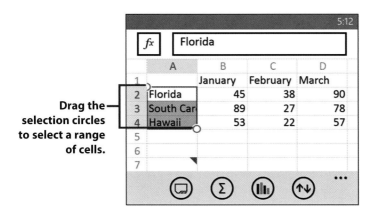

Drag the selection circles to select a range of cells.

Avoid the Keyboard
You can't select multiple cells if the keyboard is displayed onscreen. You must first hide the keyboard by pressing the phone's Back button.

SELECTED CELLS

You can perform various actions after you select a range of cells. Any time that you select a range of cells, Excel displays the Outline, Sort, Filter, and Auto Sum icons at the bottom of the screen. However, tapping the Menu icon makes several other options available.

>>>Go Further

Viewing Cell Text

Occasionally, a cell contains too much data to be able to read the cell's full contents within the confines of the current column. In this situation, you can get Excel to show you the cell's full contents. Follow these steps:

1. Tap and hold the cell you want to view.

2. Tap View Cell Text.

Freezing a Pane

Freezing a pane enables you to keep a range of cells onscreen while you scroll the rest of the cells. For example, you might want to keep the spreadsheet's header rows onscreen while you view data farther down the spreadsheet. You can freeze a portion of the spreadsheet by following these steps:

1. Tap and hold a cell in the column that you want to freeze.

2. Tap Freeze Pane.

3. The thicker line on the Excel grid indicates which column is frozen.

Unfreezing Cells

When you decide to unfreeze the cells, you can do so by tapping and holding a cell above the freeze line and then tapping the Unfreeze Pane option.

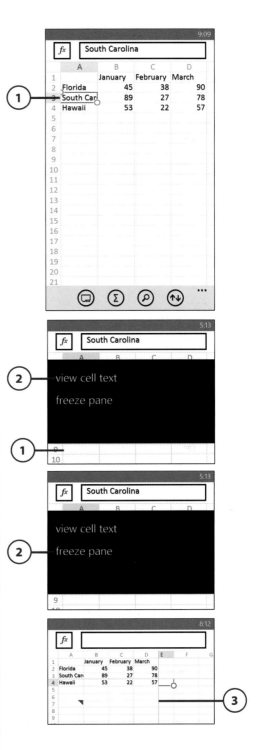

Applying Formatting Options

Excel Mobile enables you to apply text effects to cells within your spreadsheet. To modify the text style, follow these steps:

1. Select the cells to which you want to apply a text effect.

2. Tap the Menu icon.

3. Tap Format.

4. To apply standard formatting such as Bold, Italic, or Underline, tap the applicable button.

5. To format a number as a calendar date or time, tap the Date button.

6. To format a number as a form of currency, tap the Currency button.

7. To format a number as a percentage, tap the Percent button.

8. Tap a color in the Font Color group to change the color of the cell's text.

9. To change the background color of a cell, tap a color in the Fill Color group.

Formatting Ranges

When formatting, you can select a range of cells to which you want to apply these formatting options.

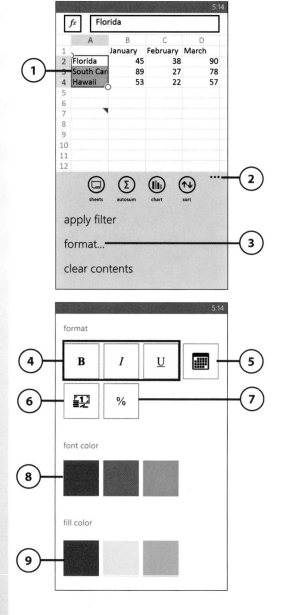

Sorting a Column

Excel Mobile makes it easy to sort a column of data either alphabetically or numerically. To sort a column, follow these steps:

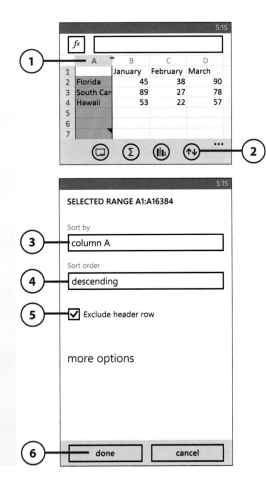

1. Tap the header for the column you want to sort.

2. Tap the Sort icon.

3. Verify that the Sort By field lists the appropriate column.

4. Tap the Sort Order field and choose either Ascending or Descending.

5. Tap the Exclude Header Row check box if your selection includes a header row that you don't want to include in the sort.

6. Tap Done.

MULTI LEVEL SORTING

>>>Go Further

Just as you can sort a single column of data, Excel Mobile enables you to sort multiple columns. To do so, select more than one column before tapping the Sort button. Then, on the Sort screen, tap the More Options button, which enables you to include up to two more columns in your sorting criteria.

Filtering

Excel Mobile contains a powerful filtering mechanism that you can use to hide all the spreadsheet data except for the specific data you are interested in. You can filter spreadsheet data by completing these steps:

1. Tap a cell on the top row of the spreadsheet.

2. Tap the Menu icon.

3. Tap Apply Filter.

4. Tap the icon in the top cell of the column you want to filter.

5. Tap the desired filter options. The filter data should be the data that you want to view, while hiding everything else.

6. Tap Done.

7. All data is hidden except for the filter or filters you have selected.

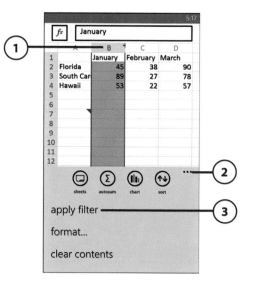

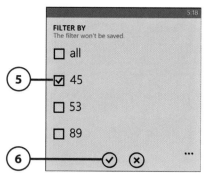

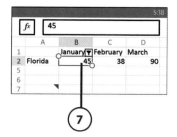

Undo and Redo

When you are working on a spreadsheet on a mobile device using a touchscreen, it is easy to make a mistake. Thankfully, Excel Mobile contains an Undo function and a Redo function. You can access Undo and Redo by following these steps:

1. Tap the Menu icon.

2. Tap either Undo or Redo.

Why Can't I Undo

Keep in mind that Undo and Redo might be grayed out if your last action can't be undone (such as when you apply a filter). Furthermore, Undo and Redo appear only on Excel's main menu. If you are accessing a specific Excel function and look at the menu icon, you won't see them there.

Charting

In spite of its simple interface, Excel Mobile enables you to add charts to a spreadsheet. To do so, follow these steps:

1. Select a range of cells containing the data you want to chart.

2. Tap the Chart icon.

3. Tap the type of chart you want to insert.

Returning to Your Spreadsheet

To get back to your spreadsheet after creating or viewing a chart, tap the Sheets icon.

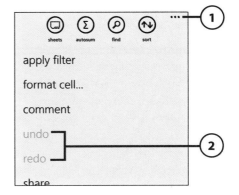

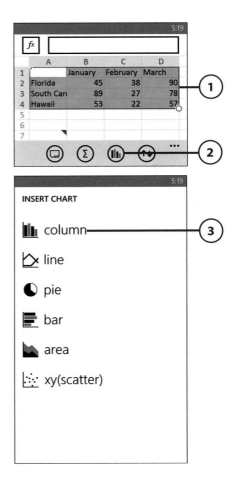

Accessing Charts and Sheets

In desktop versions of Microsoft Excel, a single workbook can contain multiple sheets, which are accessible through tabs at the bottom of the screen. Excel Mobile also supports the use of multiple sheets, but the tabs do not exist. If you want to access alternate sheets (or charts, which are saved as separate sheets), follow these steps:

1. Tap the Sheets icon.

2. Tap the name of the sheet or chart you want to view.

Saving a Spreadsheet

You can save your spreadsheet at any time by completing these steps:

1. Tap an empty cell within the spreadsheet.

2. Tap the Menu icon.

3. Scroll to and then tap either Save or Save As.

4. If prompted, enter a filename.

5. Tap the Save To field and choose the destination where you want to save the file.

6. Tap Save.

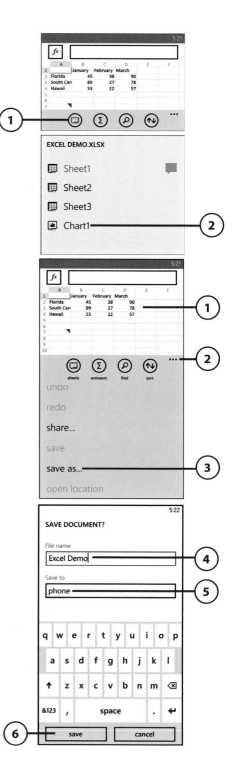

Sharing a Spreadsheet

Windows Phone 8 enables you to share
spreadsheets either by emailing them
or by using Tap+Send. You can share a
spreadsheet by completing these steps:

1. Tap a blank cell.

2. Tap the Menu icon.

3. Scroll to and tap Share.

4. Choose the mechanism you want
   to use to share the spreadsheet.
   You can use email or Tap+Send.

Fitting and Hiding Text

Sometimes a cell is not wide enough to display all the text within it. When
this happens, you can do two things to make the text visible. One option
is to perform an AutoFit. An AutoFit expands the width of the column to
accommodate the text. Another option is to wrap the text so that it fits
within the current column width. Finally, you can simply hide the text from
view on the spreadsheet.

Using AutoFit

To use the AutoFit feature, follow these steps:

1. Tap and hold the cell at the top of the column you want to adjust.

2. Tap AutoFit.

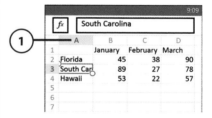

Using Wrap Text

To use the Wrap Text feature, follow these steps:

1. Tap and hold the cell at the top of the column you want to adjust.

2. Tap Wrap Text.

Hiding Columns

The Windows Phone 8 screen has a limited amount of space, and sometimes working with a spreadsheet is easier if you hide columns that you don't currently need. To do so, follow these steps:

1. Tap and hold the column you want to hide.

2. Choose the Hide option from the menu when it appears.

Revealing Hidden Columns

You can reveal a hidden column at any time by tapping and holding the top row of the spreadsheet and then choosing the Unhide option from the resulting menu.

Entering Formulas

Excel Mobile supports the same formulas as the desktop version of Excel. To enter a formula into an Excel spreadsheet, complete these steps:

1. Tap on the cell where you would like to enter the formula.

2. Enter the formula.

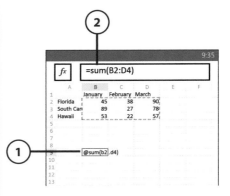

SELECTED CELLS

Formulas are beyond the scope of this book, but if you would like to learn about the various formulas that you can use with Excel, there are some very good references online. Microsoft provides a page with commonly used formulas at: http://office.microsoft.com/en-us/excel-help/examples-of-commonly-used-formulas-HP005200127.aspx. You can also tap on Excel Mobile's Formula icon (the FX icon) to see a list of supported formulas and to get help with formula syntax.

AutoSum

Even though Excel Mobile supports the same formulas as Excel, you might occasionally want to quickly perform a calculation against a range of cells without having to write a formula. This is where the AutoSum feature comes into play. AutoSum provides statistical information about the data in the selected cells, such as the total, the average, and the high and low values. To use this feature, complete the following steps:

1. Select the range of cells you want to include in the results.

2. Tap the AutoSum icon.

3. Tap one of the available Auto-Sum functions. Notice that each one includes the result alongside the functions you can select.

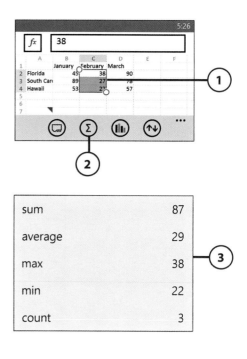

Word

Of all the apps included with Windows Phone 8, perhaps none is more useful than Microsoft Word Mobile. This app enables you to create, view, and edit Microsoft Word documents on the go.

Creating a New Word Document

The technique for creating a new Word document is similar to that of creating an Excel document. To create a Word document, open the Office hub and follow these steps:

1. Flick the screen to access the Recent page.

2. Tap the New icon.

3. Tap Word.

Microsoft Word Templates

Windows Phone 8 includes a series of built-in templates that are available on the New document screen. You can use these templates to create an agenda, outline, or report. Simply tap the template instead of tapping Word.

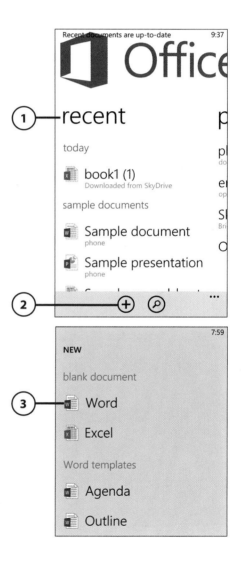

The Microsoft Word Interface

As you can see here, Word Mobile resembles a watered-down version of Notepad. It consists of a blank screen, a keyboard, and a few icons. Fortunately, all is not what it seems—there is much more to Word Mobile than meets the eye. This section explains in detail which features are available through Word Mobile. For right now, here are the elements that are present on the screen when you create a new document:

A. The current time

B. The document body

C. The onscreen keyboard

D. The Outline icon

E. The Comment icon

F. The Find icon

G. The Format icon

H. The Menu icon

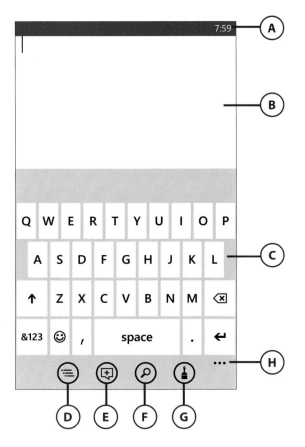

Copy and Paste

Windows Phone 8 devices fully support the use of Copy and Paste within Microsoft Word and other apps. To use Copy and Paste within a Word document, follow these steps:

1. Tap a word that you want to include within the text you want to copy.

2. When the word is selected, drag the circles beneath the word to select any additional words that you want to include.

3. Tap the Copy icon.

4. Tap the location within the document where you want to paste the newly copied contents.

5. Tap the Clipboard icon.

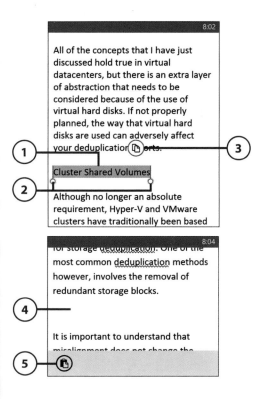

Applying Text Effects

As you enter text into a Word document you have the option to format that text using various styles. For instance, you can make text bold or you can highlight the text. To do so, follow these steps:

1. Move the cursor to the appropriate location within the document, or select the text to which you want to apply the effect.

2. Tap the Format icon.

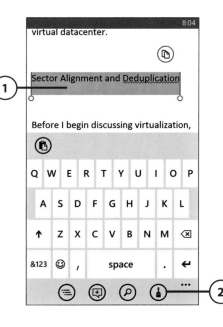

3. To apply standard formatting, such as Bold, Italic, or Underline, tap the applicable button.

4. To apply strikethrough formatting to the selected text, tap the Strikethrough button.

5. To increase or reduce font size, tap the Increase or Decrease button.

6. Tap a color in the Highlight group to add highlighting to the selected text.

7. Tap a color in the Font Color group to change the color of the cell's text.

Locating Text Within a Document

When viewing or editing longer word documents, it can sometimes be helpful to search for keywords or phrases within the document. If you need to locate specific words or phrases, follow these steps:

1. Tap the Find icon.

2. Enter your search text.

3. Word marks the first occurrence of the search text. You can find additional occurrences by clicking the Next icon.

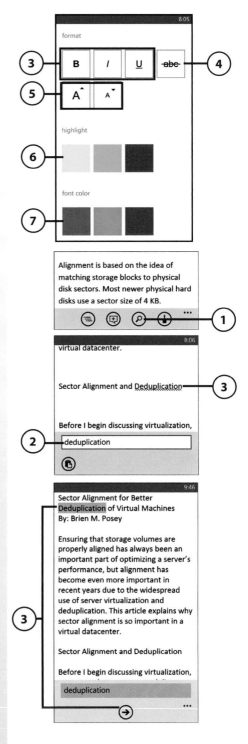

Adding a Comment

If you want to add a comment to a document, you can do so by following these steps:

1. Select the location for the comment within the document.

2. Tap the Comment icon.

3. Type your comment.

4. Tap the document to complete the process.

Viewing and Navigating Comments

If you receive a Word document that contains comments, you can view those comments by following these steps:

1. Locate the text for which a comment has been made. The commented text is flagged with a Comment icon. Tap the commented text.

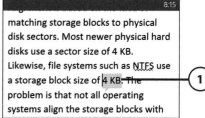

2. The comment displays at the bottom of the screen.

3. Tap the Next icon to view the next comment.

4. If necessary, tap the Previous icon to view the previous comment.

Grayed Out Icons
If the Previous and Next icons are grayed out, the document has no additional comments.

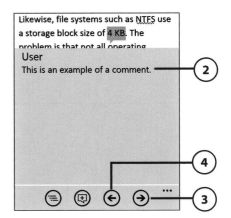

Deleting a Comment

If you want to remove a comment from a Word document, you can do so by completing these steps:

1. Tap a Comment icon to view the comment.

2. Flick the menu icon upward.

3. Tap Delete Comment.

Be Careful Deleting Comments
Use caution when deleting comments: Word Mobile does not ask for confirmation before removing a comment.

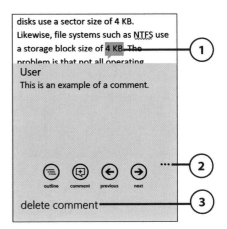

Sharing the Document

After you create or edit a document, you might want to email it to yourself or to others. Word Mobile lets you share documents through email or by using the Tap+Send feature. To share a document, follow these steps:

1. Tap the Menu icon.

2. Tap Share. If your document needs to be saved, you are prompted to do so now.

3. Select the mechanism you want to use to share the document. You can share the document using email or Tap+Send.

Saving the Document

You can save a Word document at any time by following these steps:

1. Tap the Menu icon.

2. Tap Save or Save As.

3. If you have not previously saved the document (or if you chose the Save As option), you are prompted to enter a filename.

4. Tap the Save To field and choose a destination.

5. Tap Save. The next time you access the Office Hub, the document appears within the Documents list on the Recent screen.

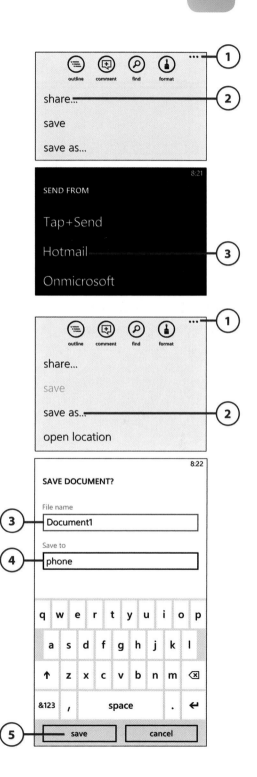

It's Not All Good

Missing Features

Although Word Mobile is suitable for light editing, it lacks a couple crucial features that are required for composing any document of significant length. For starters, Word is missing the Undo/Redo option.

The other crucial feature that is missing from Word Mobile is a spelling check. However, Word does take some steps to prevent misspellings within your documents. An AutoCorrect feature automatically corrects suspected typos, and as in desktop versions of Office, Word Mobile underlines misspelled words in red. However, the AutoCorrect feature has a bad habit of correcting things that aren't actually wrong (in essence, introducing mistakes into your document), and there is no option to spell-check the entire document.

Correcting Spelling Errors

Word Mobile underlines misspelled words in red. If your document contains a misspelling, you can simply retype the misspelled word, or you can fix the error by following these steps:

1. Tap the misspelled word.

2. Choose a replacement word from the list of suggestions.

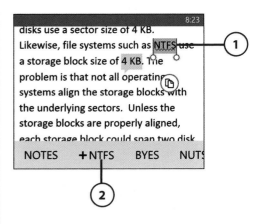

Adding Words to the Dictionary

Sometimes Word flags a word as being misspelled, even though the word is spelled correctly. When this happens, you can add the word to the dictionary by tapping the suggestion that has the + in front of it. In the previous screen capture, for example, the word NTFS is listed as being misspelled. To add NTFS to the dictionary, tap +NTFS.

PowerPoint

Windows Phone 8 lets you watch PowerPoint presentations right on your phone. You can even open PowerPoint documents, make changes, and send the presentation to others.

It's Not All Good

PowerPoint Presentations

For some reason, Windows Phone 8 lacks the capability to create new PowerPoint presentations. The phone has no trouble creating new Word, Excel, and OneNote documents, but this essential feature was omitted from PowerPoint. The only way to create a new presentation from within the phone is to open the "sample presentation," save it under a new name, and then erase the existing slides and create your own.

Opening a PowerPoint Document

To open a PowerPoint document, go to the Office hub and follow these steps:

1. Flick the screen to access the Recent page.

2. Tap the PowerPoint document you want to open.

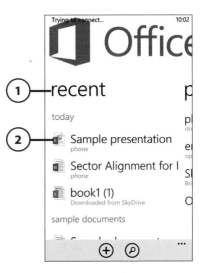

Emailed Documents

Although the previous example deals with opening a document that is already on your phone, you can also open PowerPoint documents as email attachments. If you have a PowerPoint document stored elsewhere, but the document is not displayed on the Recent list, you can locate and open the document using the Find feature.

Viewing PowerPoint Slides

When you open a PowerPoint document, several items display on the screen:

A. The current slide

B. The current slide number

C. The slide notes

D. The Slides icon

E. The Edit icon

F. The Menu icon

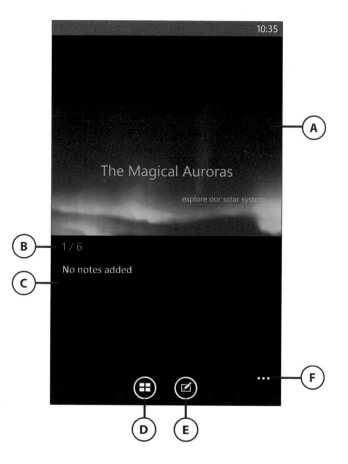

>>>Go Further

THE HIDDEN ICON BAR

To save space on the device's screen, PowerPoint tends to hide the icon bar. If this happens, you can reveal the icon bar by orienting the phone so that the top of the slide is facing up and then tapping the empty margin.

You can view the previous slide or the next slide simply by flicking the currently displayed slide left or right. Flicking to the left displays the previous slide, and flicking to the right displays the next slide.

Viewing a Specific Slide

If you want to view or edit a specific slide, you don't have to go through every slide in the presentation to access it. You can go directly to the desired slide. To do so, follow these steps:

1. Tap the Slides icon.

2. Tap the icon for the slide you want to view.

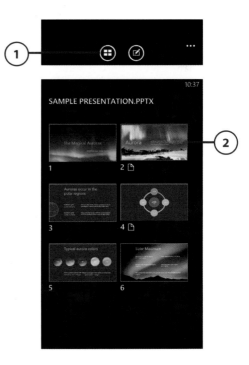

Adding Notes to a Slide

PowerPoint Mobile supports adding speaker notes to your slides. To add a note to a slide, follow these steps:

1. Go to the slide you want to add the note to.

2. Orient the phone in portrait mode. When you do, the slide's notes appear beneath the slide.

3. Tap the notes section.

4. Compose your notes.

5. Tap the Done icon. From now on when you view that slide, the note appears beneath it.

Modifying Notes

If you want to view the slide notes on a dedicated screen or you want to edit the notes, simply tap the notes. This displays the notes within an editor. When you are finished viewing or modifying the notes, tap the Done icon.

Editing a Slide

PowerPoint Mobile offers limited options for editing slides. Before you can begin the editing process, you must put PowerPoint Mobile in edit mode. To do so, follow these steps:

1. Navigate to the slide you want to edit.

2. Tap the Edit icon.

3. When PowerPoint is in Edit mode, the top text box is selected by default. You can choose another text box by tapping it. To edit a text box, double-tap it.

4. Make any necessary changes to the text.

5. Tap the Done icon.

6. To exit Edit mode, tap the Slide Show icon.

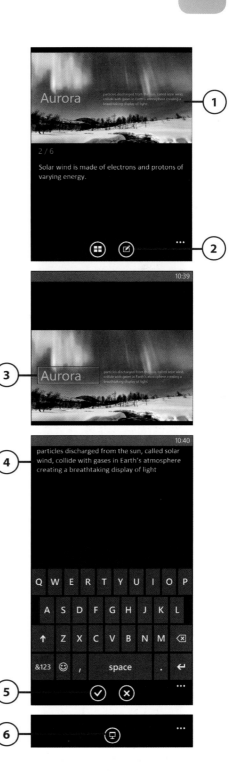

It's Not All Good

Editing Text Styles

PowerPoint Mobile has no capacity for editing text styles or adding other visual elements (such as images) to a slide deck. When you edit a text box, your edits are done on a plain black-and-white screen in plain text. However, any changes you make will adopt the style of the selected text box.

Moving a Slide

PowerPoint Mobile enables you to move a slide to another location within the document. To do so, complete these steps.

1. While in Edit mode, tap the Menu icon.

2. Tap Move Slide.

3. Choose the location within the document where you want the slide moved.

4. Tap Done.

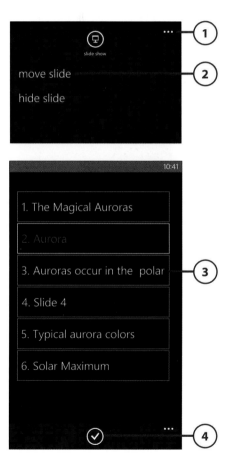

Hiding a Slide

PowerPoint Mobile also gives you the option to hide a slide while in Slide Show mode. To do so, follow these steps:

1. While in Edit mode, flick the menu icon upward.

2. Tap Hide Slide.

Unhiding a Slide

You can unhide a hidden slide at any time by accessing the slide in Edit mode, flicking the menu icon upward, and choosing the Unhide Slide option.

Saving the PowerPoint Presentation

To save your PowerPoint presentation, complete the following steps:

1. Make sure PowerPoint is not in Edit mode, and tap the Menu icon.

2. Tap either Save or Save As.

3. If you choose the Save As option, you are prompted to provide a filename.

4. Specify a destination for the saved presentation.

5. Tap Save.

Accessing Your PowerPoint Presentation

The next time you access the Office hub, your PowerPoint presentation is available from the Documents list on the Recent screen.

Sharing Your PowerPoint Presentation

PowerPoint Mobile gives you the option to share your PowerPoint presentation either through email or by using the Tap+Send feature. To share your PowerPoint presentation through email, follow these steps:

1. Make sure PowerPoint is not in Edit mode, and tap the Menu icon.

2. Tap Share. If you have not yet saved the PowerPoint presentation, you are prompted to save your changes.

3. Choose the mechanism you want to use to share your PowerPoint presentation. You can share the document using email or Tap+Send.

OneNote

Microsoft OneNote is an application that is designed to enable you to keep track of multiple notes in a single place. A single OneNote document can contain a combination of text, images, and audio notes. Some common uses for OneNote documents include shopping lists, meeting notes, invention ideas (with diagrams), and to-do lists. To access OneNote, locate it on the Start screen or Apps list and tap its tile.

Adding OneNote to the Start Screen

You can add OneNote to the Start screen by tapping and holding the OneNote icon in the App List and then tapping Pin to Start.

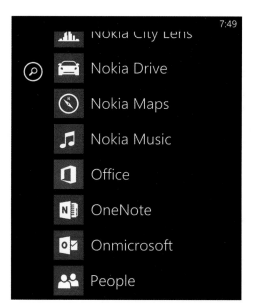

When you open OneNote, you go to the Quick Notes screen. This screen contains several elements:

A. The time.

B. OneNote documents.

C. The New icon. Tap this icon to create a new OneNote document.

D. Search, which enables you to search for existing OneNote documents.

E. The Menu icon. Tap this icon to access the submenu.

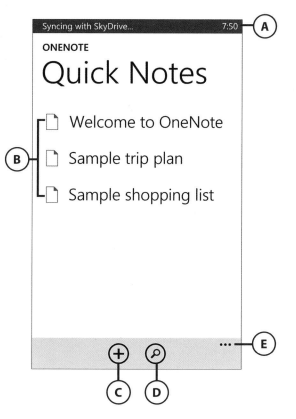

As you create OneNote notes for your notebooks, you can open a specific note by opening the notebook and section in which you created it and then tapping the note. For example, as shown here, Document 1 is a note I recently created in the Unfiled Notes section of one of my notebooks that I can open by tapping it. You can also open a Recent screen to see a list of the notes you've opened most recently.

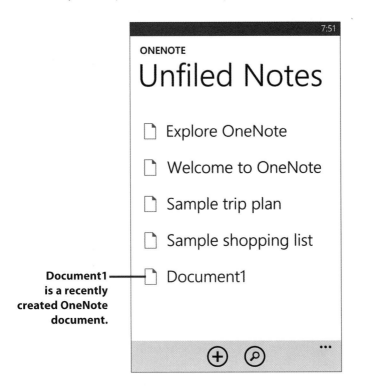

Document1 is a recently created OneNote document.

Opening a Note

OneNote documents are referred to as Notes. Notes are stored in sections, and sections are grouped together into a notebook. In essence, a note is a page in a much larger notebook. Opening a OneNote document involves opening a Notebook, tapping on a section, and then opening a note.

To open a note, open OneNote and complete the following steps:

1. Tap on the notebook containing the note that you want to open.

2. Tap on the section containing your note.

3. Tap on the note that you want to open.

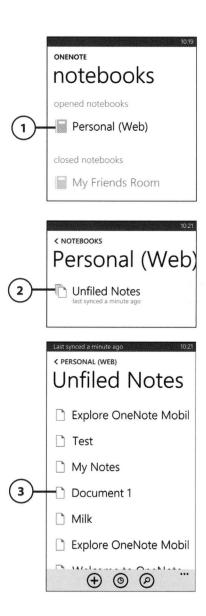

Searching for Notes

Although you can open most OneNote documents by tapping them on the Recent screen or by opening the Notebook they're located in, if you're not sure where a specific note is located, you can also search for it by following these steps:

1. Open OneNote and tap the Search button.

2. Enter your search query.

3. From the list of results that appears, tap the document you want to open.

Deleting a Note

As you begin to accumulate notes on your phone, you might eventually decide to free up some space by getting rid of some older notes. To delete a note, complete these steps:

1. Navigate to the section of a notebook that contains notes you want to delete.

2. Tap and hold the note you want to delete.

3. Tap Delete.

4. You see a message indicating that the document will be permanently deleted. Tap Yes to delete the document.

Limited Delete Options

You can delete notes from any section of any notebook, but you cannot delete sections or notebooks using your phone's version of OneNote. You can Close a notebook, but that does not remove its data from where it's stored (usually a SkyDrive folder).

Closing Notebooks

You can close a notebook by completing these steps:

1. Tap and hold the notebook that you want to close.

2. Tap Close Notebook.

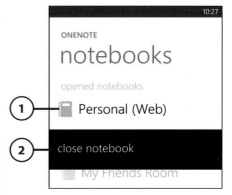

Pinning a Document to the Start Screen

As is the case with other types of documents, you can pin OneNote notes to the Start screen. To do so, follow these steps:

1. Navigate to the notebook section that contains the page you want to pin.

2. Tap and hold the document you want to pin to the Start screen.

3. Tap Pin to Start.

Creating a Note

You can create a new OneNote document by opening OneNote and completing these steps:

1. Navigate to a section in one of your notebooks.

2. Tap the New icon to create the note.

3. When the new note appears, tap Enter Title and type in a name for the note.

4. Tap the note body and enter the information you want it to include. You can return to the previous screen by tapping the Back button on your phone.

You Don't Have to Save Your Work

No Save option exists for OneNote documents. Changes that you make to OneNote documents are saved automatically.

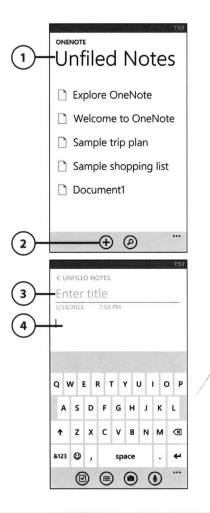

EDITING EXISTING NOTES

When you create a note, you immediately go into OneNote's edit mode, which includes icons for adding lists, images, and even audio (as you'll see in the following sections). If you open an existing note, however, you see the same New, Recent, and Search icons you see at the notebook and section views. To edit an existing note, you need to tap the note itself to open it and then also tap inside the body of the note to begin making changes to it. You can return to the previous view at any time by tapping your phone's Back button.

Creating a List

You can easily create a numbered or bulleted list in OneNote by following these steps:

1. Open or create a note and then tap inside the note's body.

2. To start a numbered list, tap the Menu icon.

3. Tap Numbered List.

4. The number 1 automatically is added to the document. Type your first list item next to 1.

5. Press Enter and type the next list item. When you get to the end of your list, press Enter twice to end the numbering.

6. To create a bulleted list, tap the List icon.

7. Type your first item next to the bullet that Windows adds to the screen, and press Enter.

8. Add any additional list items, pressing Enter after each. When you're done, press Enter twice.

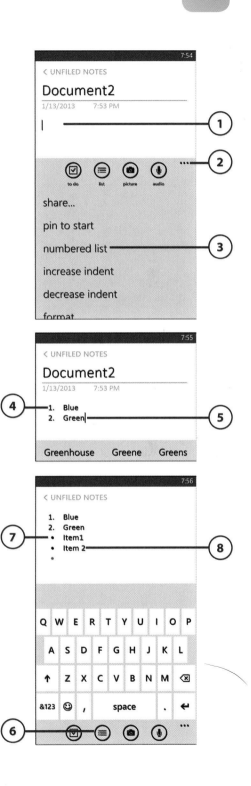

Using Indentation

You can have even finer control over the list indentation by tapping the Menu icon and choosing the Increase Indent or Decrease Indent options. Using this option, you can create lists within lists. You can also use them to place paragraph text or other types of content further across the page.

Adding Pictures to a Note

You can add pictures to your OneNote document by following these steps:

1. Open or create a note and then tap inside the note's body.

2. Tap the Picture icon.

3. Navigate to and then tap the picture you want to add to the document.

4. Tap the Done icon.

Adding Pictures

Note that you can add a picture only if it is stored on your phone (or you can add a picture from the phone's camera). You cannot add images from the Internet without first using the Windows Phone software to add the image to your collection.

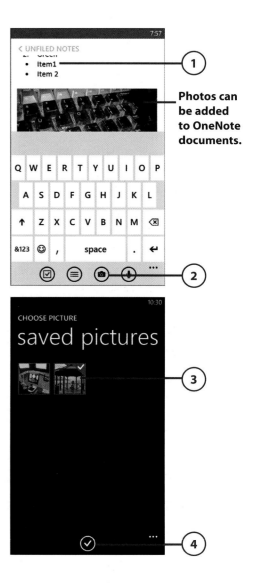

Photos can be added to OneNote documents.

Adding Audio

OneNote lets you add audio notes to your documents. To add an audio note to your OneNote document, follow these steps:

1. Open or create a note and then tap inside the note's body.

2. Tap the Audio icon and record your note (recording begins automatically).

3. Tap Stop when you're done recording.

Recordings are displayed using this icon.

Playing an Audio Note

You can play an audio note at any time simply by tapping it.

It's Not All Good

Prerecorded Audio

Even though the desktop version of OneNote enables you to add prerecorded audio files to your documents, the mobile version does not support doing so. You can add only audio that you record on the spot.

Adding a To-Do List

Just as you can add bulleted and numbered lists to a OneNote note, you can add a to-do list. To do so, follow these steps:

1. Open or create a note and then tap inside the note's body.

2. Tap the To Do icon.

3. OneNote automatically creates a check box. Enter a to-do item next to the check box, and press Enter.

4. Either enter another to-do item or press Enter again to end the list.

Using the Check List

After you create a check list, using it is simple. Tapping a check box causes it to become checked. You can remove the check mark by tapping the box again.

It's Not All Good

No Importing To-Do

If you read Chapter 3, you know that Outlook Mobile supports the creation of to-do lists. However, OneNote does not allow you to use the To-Do icon to import an Outlook To-Do list.

Formatting Text

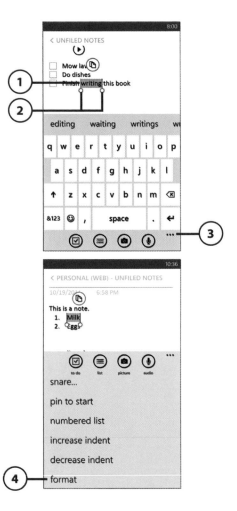

OneNote enables you to apply various visual elements to the text that you type. You can format text that you have already typed by following these steps:

1. Double-tap a word within the block of text that you want to format. This selects the word you tapped.

2. Tap and drag the circle icons beneath the selected text to select any additional required text.

3. Tap the Menu icon.

4. Tap Format.

5. To apply standard formatting such as Bold, Italic, Underline, or Strikethrough, tap the applicable button.

6. To apply highlighting to the selected text, tap the color in the Highlight section of the screen (yellow is the only color available in OneNote). When you return to the document, tap an empty area of the screen to reveal the new formatting.

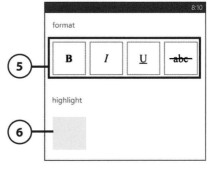

Formatting Existing Text

Although the technique shown is intended for formatting existing text, you can also format brand-new text as you type it. To do so, simply pick a formatting style and then start typing.

Sharing a Note

You can share a OneNote note via email or Tap+Send by following these steps:

1. Tap the Menu icon.

2. Tap Share.

3. Choose the mechanism that you want to use to share the document. You can use Email or Tap+Send.

Play games and
access Xbox Live
right from your
phone!

Browse your gaming
Achievements.

Give your Xbox
Live avatar fresh,
swanky looks that
are all their own.

In this chapter, you learn how to download and play games on the Windows Phone 8. Some of the topics covered in this chapter include:

→ Using the Games hub
→ Joining Xbox Live
→ Interacting with friends
→ Setting beacons
→ Finding and playing games
→ Using Xbox SmartGlass

Gaming

One of the features that makes Windows Phone 8 stand out from competing devices such as the iPhone is that Windows Phone 8 has extensive support for Xbox Live. You can't use your phone to play Xbox 360 games, but you can access your Xbox Live profile through the phone and download a variety of games from the Store.

The Games Hub

The Games hub is an area of your phone that is dedicated to gaming. When you install a game from the Windows Phone Store, the game is made available through the Games hub, rather than through the phone's Apps list. The Games hub also provides access to Xbox Live. You can use the Games hub to modify your Xbox Live profile, keep track of friends, and even compare game stats.

You can access the Games Hub directly through the Start screen by tapping the Games icon. If the Games icon gets removed from the Start screen, you can still access it from the App List and pin it back to the Start screen, if you want, by tapping and holding its icon and then selecting Pin to Start.

Tap the Games tile to access the Games hub.

You can also access the Games hub from the App list.

Where Are My Games?

Unlike other types of apps, games are not listed individually on the App List screen. Although you can also pin them to the Start screen, by default, games are listed only on the Games Collection screen in the Games hub.

Games Hub

The Games hub consists of two screens. You can switch between these two screens by flicking the phone's display left or right.

The Games hub consists of multiple screens.

If you haven't already joined Xbox Live, the Games hub initially consists of two screens, Collection and Xbox. After you connect your phone to an Xbox Live account, you have access to a couple additional screens:

- **Collection:** This is where you go to play a game. Any game you've downloaded from the Store appears here.

- **Xbox:** The Xbox screen lets you configure connectivity to Xbox Live. When you're connected, you can see baseline information about your Xbox Live account, as well as access options that let you go a bit deeper (such as see your achievements list). A secondary Xbox screen provides links to Xbox SmartGlass, the Games Store, and a Find Friends option.

- **Notifications:** Any notifications or messages appear here, such as if it's your turn to play a game or you've received a message from a friend.

- **Spotlight:** Here you can see games and other promotional materials that Microsoft is promoting on the network.

If it's not connected already, the first thing to do when you go into the Games hub for the first time is connect your Xbox Live account. This happens automatically if your Xbox Live account is already associated with the same username and password as your Windows Phone. If you don't have an Xbox Live account already, however, creating one is easy.

Joining Xbox Live

You have several options for joining Xbox Live. You can create an Xbox Live account directly through your phone, or you can do it from your Xbox 360 console or from an Internet-enabled PC. You can set up an Xbox Live account from your phone by going to the Games hub and following these steps:

1. From the Xbox screen, tap either Join Xbox or Sign In.

Xbox Live Accounts
Your phone must be connected to a Microsoft account before you can join Xbox Live.

2. When prompted, specify your country or region.

3. Enter your date of birth.

4. Tap Accept.

Temporary Tags
You will surely want to use a more personalized Gamertag than the one Live assigns to you. Unfortunately, you can't change it using your phone. You learn more about this later in this chapter, in the section "Modifying Your Xbox Live Bio."

5. After you create your Xbox account, make note of your Gamertag. Your friends need your Gamertag to find you online on Xbox Live.

6. Tap Done. You return to Xbox Live and are automatically signed in using your new Xbox Live account.

1:31

SET UP ACCOUNT

Congratulations! Your setup is complete. Here's your gamertag:

(5) — **Player583901175**

You can change your gamertag by tapping on it in the Games hub and editing your bio.

Change Xbox Privacy Settings

(6) — [done]

>>Go Further

XBOX LIVE ACCOUNTS

Microsoft offers two types of Xbox Live accounts. The free basic Xbox Live account enables you to preview games through free demos and to download new games or game add-ons. As with all Xbox Live accounts, a free account enables you to play games purchased through the Store.

If you want more than just the basics, you can upgrade to the Xbox Live Gold package. The price of the Gold package varies, depending on how many months you pay for. Xbox Live Gold offers the same benefits as a free account, but you also can play games online with friends, watch live sports from ESPN, and get personalized music from Xbox Music Pass.

You need an Xbox 360 game console to get the full benefit from an Xbox Live Gold membership.

Installing Xbox Extras

To get the maximum benefit from the Games hub, install the Xbox Extras app. This app gives you access to your Xbox Avatar, a little animated version of you that's associated with your Live account. You can install Xbox Extras by opening the Games hub and completing these steps:

1. Go to the Xbox screen.

2. Tap the Avatar tile, which looks like a little T-shirt icon.

Already Installed

If you've already installed Xbox Extras, tapping this icon takes you to the Avatar screen, where you can customize the look of your miniature you.

3. Tap Install.

Customizing Your Avatar

Xbox 360 has numerous options for creating and customizing your avatar. Many of these options are also available on Windows Phone 8. To customize your avatar, open the Gaming hub and follow these steps:

1. Go to the Xbox screen.

2. Tap the Avatar tile.

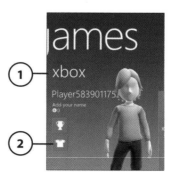

3. The avatar customization screen is similar to what is available on the Xbox 360 console. You can see a Change My Style option and a Change My Features option, as well as a link to the Store. Tap Change My Style.

4. On the Style screen, tap the icon that corresponds the clothing or accessories you want to customize.

5. Tap an item that you want to apply to your avatar.

6. You see a close-up of how your avatar looks with the selected item. Tap Apply if you want to keep it (tap Discard if you don't); you then return to the Style screen. Press the phone's Back button to go back to the Avatar screen.

Changing Features

The process for changing features, which lets you customize physical features such as hairstyle, face, and body, works identically to the process for changing your avatar's style.

7. When you're done making changes to your avatar, tap Save.

>>>Go Further

GOING SHOPPING

If you want to see more avatar customizations, tap the Store icon on the Avatar screen. This icon takes you to a specialized corner of the Store that's just for adding new outfits and features to your avatar. Just as in the regular Store, these items usually cost a bit of money to purchase and download.

Modifying Your Xbox Live Bio

Windows Phone 8 gives you the capability to modify your Xbox Live bio directly through the phone. To do so, open the Games hub's Xbox screen and complete these steps:

1. Tap your Gamertag.

2. On the Profile screen, tap Bio.

3. The Bio screen shows the name, motto, location, and bio associated with your Xbox live account. Tap the Edit icon to change any of these details.

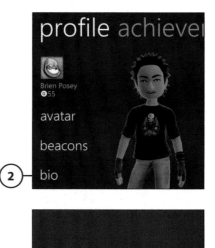

4. Tap Name to change the name (not Gamertag) associated with your account.

5. Tap Motto to change the motto associated with your account. There's a 21-character limit for this, so don't get too wordy.

6. Tap Location to include the area where you live in your account profile.

7. Tap Bio to enter any information about yourself that you want other Xbox Live users to know.

8. Tap Save.

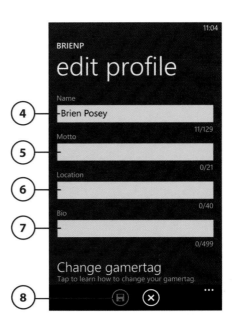

It's Not All Good

Options at the bottom of the Edit Profile screen enable you to change the name of your Gamertag or to change the Gamertag associated with your Microsoft account. You need to know two points about these options. First, tapping Change Gamertag does not actually change your Gamertag; it merely opens a web page with instructions for changing your Gamertag using an Xbox 360 game console. Windows Phone 8 does not have the capability to change Gamertags, so if you don't have access to an Xbox 360, you're out of luck. There's is a way to change your tag using Games for Windows Live on a PC, but it's even more convoluted than doing it on the console. To learn how to do that, go to support.xbox.com and search for "How to change your Xbox Live Gamertag."

The other point to know is that changing the Gamertag associated with your Microsoft account is not an option to be used lightly. If you associate your Gamertag with a different Microsoft account, you have to reset the phone to its factory defaults so that you can begin using the alternate account ID (and your Gamertag). This means erasing all the configuration settings and data (music, videos, pictures, games, and so on) that is stored in your phone.

Achievements

Xbox Live has a rewards system called achievements, which are little rewards you get for accomplishing specific tasks in games. You can view your achievements by opening the Games hub and following these steps:

1. Flick the screen to access the Xbox page.

2. Tap the Achievements icon.

3. The Achievements screen lists the games you've played and how many achievement points you've earned from those games. If you want to access achievement information about a specific game, tap the name of the game.

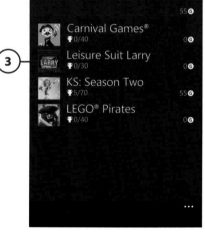

Configuring Games Hub Settings

The Games hub contains a selection of settings that you can use to control the way Windows Phone 8 interacts with Xbox Live. You can access these settings by opening the Games hub and completing these steps:

1. Tap the Menu icon.

2. Tap Settings.

3. To prevent your phone from synchronizing things like game scores and achievements with Xbox Live, drag the Connect with Xbox slider to the off position.

4. If you don't want to receive multiplayer game requests on your phone, drag the Sync Game Request slider to the off position.

5. To stop Windows Phone 8 from alerting you to notifications that come from Xbox Live, drag Show Game Notifications to the off position.

Adjusting Your Privacy Settings

When you initially create your Xbox Live profile, various privacy settings keep it from being displayed to anyone. You can access privacy settings from the Settings page on the Games hub by tapping the Privacy Settings link at the bottom of the screen.

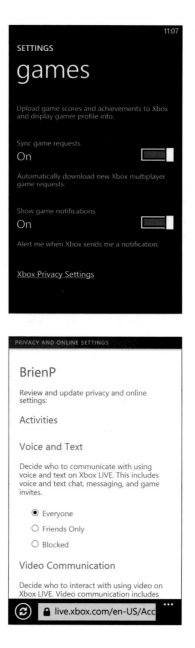

Each available privacy setting has three options: Everyone, Friends Only, and Blocked (some settings use Allowed or Blocked instead). The individual settings that you can control include these:

- **Voice and Text:** The Voice and Text setting controls who can communicate with you using voice or text on Xbox Live. This setting applies to voice and text chat, as well as messaging and game invites. This setting is blocked by default, which could prevent you from receiving messages and game invites.

- **Video Communications:** The Video Communications setting determines who is allowed to interact with you using video on Xbox Live. This includes both Video Kinect and in-game video chats.

- **Profile Sharing:** The Profile Sharing option controls who can see your profile. A profile contains more than just your name, motto, location, and bio. It also includes your gaming history, your achievements, and, in some cases, even a picture.

- **Game History:** The Game History determines who is allowed to see your gaming history and your achievements.

- **Online Status:** The Online Status setting controls who can see your online status. Your online status reflects the last time you were online, your current or previous online activity, what you are playing right now, and your availability to play with others.

- **Video and Music Status:** Use this setting to determine who can see the titles of the videos or music being played. If you have blocked Online Status, then Video and Music Status is also blocked.

- **Friends List:** You can use the Friends List setting to control who can see your friends list. When you give others access to your friends list, your friends' profiles also are visible.

- **Voice Data Collection:** This setting controls whether you want to allow Microsoft to collect samples of voice commands spoken within Kinect games, for the sake of improving speech recognition.

- **Kinect Sharing:** The Kinect Sharing setting controls whether content that was created using Kinect can be shared outside Xbox Live.

- **Social Network Sharing:** You can use the Social Network Sharing setting to control whether Xbox Live content can be shared on other social networks.

- **Exercise Info:** The Exercise Info setting lets you control whether you want to share your exercise history (such as exercise duration and calories burned). Data such as your weight or date of birth is not shared.

- **Programming:** The Programming setting controls the types of promotions and offers that appear within Xbox Live. You can opt for standard programming or "family-friendly" programming.

- **Profile Viewing:** The Profile Viewing setting is a bit counterintuitive. Instead of controlling whether others can see your profile, it controls whether you can see your friends' profiles (some profiles might contain objectionable content).

- **Member Content:** This setting controls whether you can see member-created content within games. Member content includes images, text, and custom game content. The setting does not impact your capability to download indie games.

- **Music, Music Videos, and Windows Phone Games:** This setting controls whether you want to allow access to explicit music, music videos, or Windows Phone games. The setting applies only to new content, not to content that you have already downloaded.

The privacy settings are configured through a web interface instead of through a native Windows Phone 8 feature. As such, it might take up to four hours for changes to your privacy settings to take effect. When you're finished making changes to this page, tap the Save button.

Friends

Xbox Live is designed to be a social gaming environment in which you can compete against your friends. As such, the Xbox 360 gaming console enables you to compile a list of your friends. You can then easily connect with them simply by picking a name from your Friends list. Your Friends list is also accessible from Windows Phone 8. To access your Friends list, open the Games hub, go to the secondary Xbox screen, and tap the Friends tile.

Friends who are —— online
currently online   Nobody here

Friends who are —— offline 1
currently offline

                          tazpoz
                          Last played KS: Season Two

The Friends screen organizes your list of friends based on who is currently online. Friends who are not online are listed in the Offline section, along with the date when they were most recently online. If you have any new friend requests, you'll see those listed here, too.

To view a friend's profile, just tap that person's Gamertag in the list.

Your friend's profile appears across several screens, which you can access by flicking the display to the left or to the right. The pages that make up your friend's profile include these:

- **Profile:** The Profile screen lets you send your friend a message (Xbox Live Gold only), remove the friend, or view the friend's bio.

- **Recent Games:** This screen displays the games your friend has played recently.

- **Compare:** You can use this screen to compare your gaming achievements with those of your friend. Tap a game to see a more detailed comparison between you and your friend for that specific game's achievements.

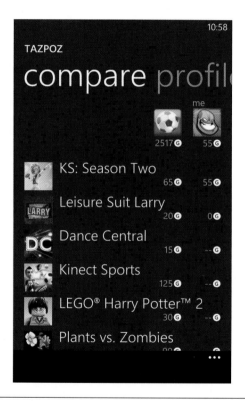

Missing Achievements

The Xbox Live privacy settings have a big impact on what achievements are actually displayed. If you are having difficulty getting the achievements comparison to work correctly, be sure to read the section on privacy settings later in this chapter.

Adding a Friend

The easiest way to add someone to your Friends list is to do so through an Xbox 360 console. However, suppose that, while attending a party, you meet someone and discover that he's into Xbox gaming. In such a situation, you can add the person to your Xbox Live Friends list right from your phone. To do so, open the Games hub and follow these steps:

1. From the secondary Xbox screen, tap the Friends tile.

2. Tap the Add icon.

3. Enter the Gamertag you want to search for.

4. When the search results return, look at the profile to verify that you have added the correct Gamertag. Tap Add Friend. The new Gamertag is added to your Friends list, pending that person's approval of your request.

Getting Approval

Xbox Live is set up so that no one can add you as a friend without your approval. When you add someone to your Friends list, the name is added pending approval. The next time the person you added signs into Xbox Live, he receives a friend request and can approve or deny your request.

It's Not All Good

Windows Phone 8 can give some misleading error messages. While writing this chapter, I tried to add a friend, but without knowing that he had changed his Gamertag. Instead of telling me that the Gamertag doesn't exist, Windows Phone 8 told me it was having trouble connecting to Xbox service and asked me to try again later.

Removing a Friend

You can remove another gamer from your Friends list by opening the Games hub and following these steps:

1. From the secondary Xbox screen, tap the Friends tile.

2. Tap the friend that you want to remove.

3. Tap Remove Friend.

4. When Windows asks if you are sure you want to remove the friend, tap yes.

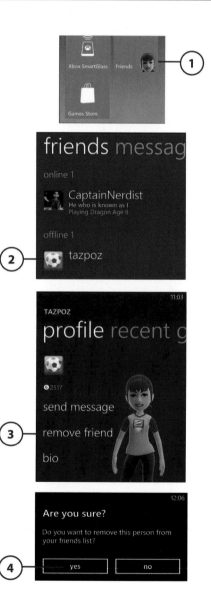

Sending Messages to Friends

Xbox Live contains a messaging system that lets gamers send messages to each other. If you have an Xbox Live Gold subscription, you can send a message to a friend by going into the Games Hub and completing these steps:

1. From the secondary Xbox screen, tap the Friends tile.

2. Tap the friend to whom you want to send a message.

3. Tap Send Message to compose and fire off your message.

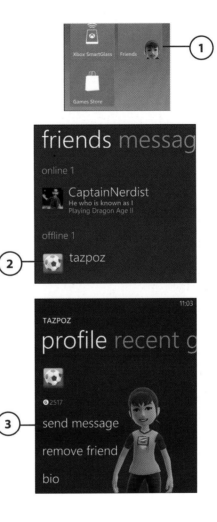

It's Not All Good

Messaging works only if you have an Xbox Live Gold subscription. Otherwise, you receive a prompt to upgrade your membership.

Beacons

Beacons are an Xbox mechanism that is used for telling your friends what game you are playing or what game you want to play. For example, you might send your friends a beacon letting them know that you want to play a certain game. This beacon essentially tells your friends that no matter what you might be doing at the moment, it is okay for them to interrupt you and ask you to play the game that you specified within the beacon.

Setting a Beacon

You can set up a beacon by going to your Profile screen and completing the following steps:

1. Tap Beacons.

2. Tap Set New Beacon.

3. Tap the game for which you want to set a beacon.

4. Tap Set.

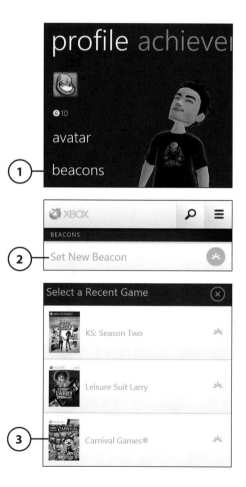

Removing a Beacon

If you want to remove a beacon for a game, you can do so by going to your Profile screen and completing these steps:

1. Tap Beacons.

2. Tap the game for which you want to remove a beacon.

3. Tap Remove Beacon.

4. Tap Remove.

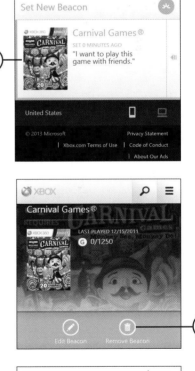

Finding Games

The Store contains free and paid games that you can download to your phone. Microsoft provides several methods for finding and installing games.

Using the Spotlight

The Spotlight page contains the latest games for Windows Phone that Microsoft is promoting. You can install a game that is featured on the Spotlight page by opening the Games hub and completing these steps:

1. Flick to the Spotlight screen.

2. Tap the game you are interested in.

3. Tap either Try or Buy.

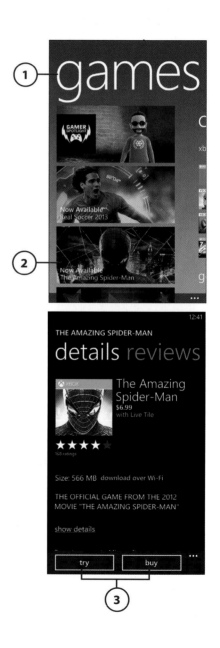

Browsing for New Games

Many games are available for Windows Phone 8, and you can shop for them directly through the Games hub. To do so, open the Games hub and, at the bottom of the Collection screen, tap Get More Games.

**Tap Get More Games to
search for new games.**

The Games screen contains the following items:

A. Top Free: The highest rated free games

B. Xbox: A catch all category containing links to various types of games.

C. Collections: Apps that have been grouped together into collections (navigation apps, photo apps, essential apps, etc.). A variety of apps are presented, not just games.

D. New+Rising: The newest games that are receiving favorable ratings.

E. Best Rated: The top games as rated by other users.

F. Picks for You: Game recommendations based on your previous usage history.

G. Search: Search for games.

Finding Games by Genre

Windows Phone 8 enables you to browse games by genre. To do so, open the Games hub and complete the following task:

1. Tap Get More Games.

2. Flick to the Genres screen.

3. Tap the Genre that you want to browse.

Searching for a Game

If you have a specific game in mind that you want to install, you can search for the game instead of having to browse the store to find it. To search for a game by title, open the Games hub and complete these steps:

1. Tap Get More Games.

2. Tap the Search icon.

3. Enter the name of the game you want to search for.

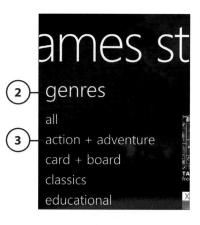

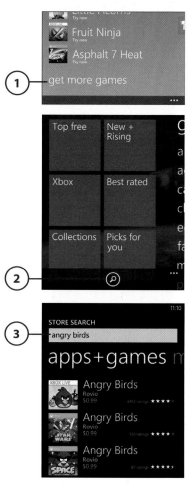

Installing a Game

After you have located a game that you want to install, the installation process is simple. You can install a game by completing these steps:

1. Tap the tile representing the game that you want to install.

2. Tap Install (for free games) or Try or Buy (for paid games).

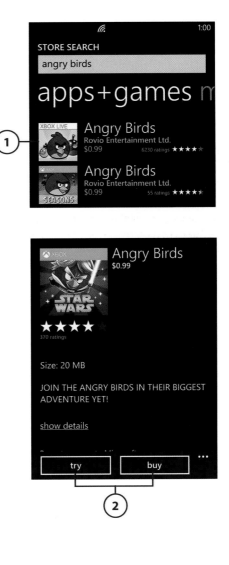

GAMING CONSISTENCY

As you shop for games, all the available games are displayed in a consistent manner. Microsoft requires game developers to provide a full description and a set of screen captures for every game that is available in the Marketplace. You'll also find a free trial version of most, if not all, games. The instructions here demonstrate the process of downloading the trial version. After you have played the trial, you always have an option to upgrade from within the game.

Playing a Game

After you have installed a game, it is available through the Games hub. Unlike other types of apps, games are not listed on the phone's main App List screen. To access a game, open the Games hub and follow these steps:

1. Flick to the Collection screen, if necessary.

2. Tap the icon for the game you want to play.

3. The game loads and you can begin to play.

Easy Access

You can pin a game to the phone's Start screen for easy access to the game. To do so, just tap and hold the game's icon and then choose the Pin to Start option from the shortcut menu.

Rating and Reviewing a Game

Just as you can read the reviews for a game, you have the option to rate and review games yourself directly through the phone. You can even rate and review the Xbox Extras software, if you want. To rate and review a game, open the Games hub and locate the game you want to review. Then follow these steps:

1. Tap and hold the icon for the game you want to rate.

2. Choose Rate and Review from the resulting menu.

3. Assign a rating to the game by tapping a star.

4. Tap the text box and enter a review for the game.

5. Tap Submit.

Default Games
Some Windows Phone 8 devices list games within the Collection by default. Often these default games are not actually installed, but are simply game installation shortcuts. You can identify such a shortcut because it includes a Try Now link beneath the game's title. Default links such as these also offer a Remove link instead of an Uninstall link and lack the option to rate and review the game.

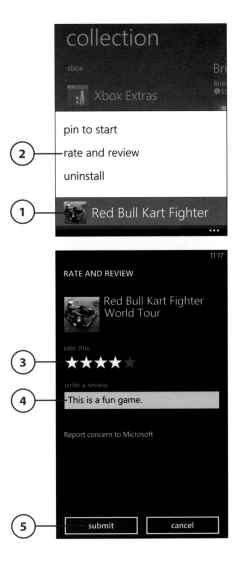

Uninstalling a Game

If you want to remove a game from your phone, go to the Games hub and complete these steps:

1. Flick the screen, if necessary, to access your game collection.

2. Tap and hold the icon for the game you want to remove.

3. Tap the Uninstall option.

Confirmation

Some games are removed at this point; others display a confirmation screen asking if you really want to remove the game.

Xbox SmartGlass

Xbox SmartGlass is a feature that enables Windows Phone 8 devices to act as a second screen for the Xbox 360 gaming console. You can use Xbox SmartGlass to control your Xbox dashboard, display information about the game or media that is currently being played on the Xbox 360 console, and even allow a Windows Phone 8 device to act as an Xbox 360 controller for titles and applications that support it.

Installing Xbox SmartGlass

Before you can use Xbox SmartGlass, you need to install it. To do so, open the Games hub and complete these steps:

1. Flick the display to access the secondary Xbox screen.

2. Tap the Xbox SmartGlass tile.

3. Tap Install.

4. When the Get Started Screen display, you can tap any of the tiles to view introductory videos, or tap OK to access SmartGlass.

Where Did the SmartGlass Tile Go?

If you are signed into your Xbox 360 console at the time you install SmartGlass, you might not see a SmartGlass tile. The tile might be replaced by a tile with the name of the game that you are playing. For example, if you are playing Leisure Suit Larry, the SmartGlass tile would be temporarily renamed to Leisure Suit Larry on Your Xbox.

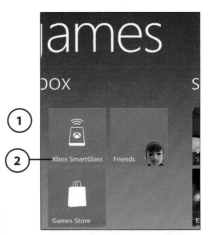

Interacting with the SmartGlass Interface

SmartGlass consists of several screens, which you can access by flicking your phone's display to the left or right. The actual screens you see vary, depending on whether you're using your console's primary dashboard interface or what game you're running on your Xbox 360 console. Some of the more common screens include these:

Smart Glass consists of several screens.

This icon indicates there is currently a game running on your Xbox 360 console.

- **Home:** The Home screen tells you which game you're currently playing.
- **Discover:** The Discover screen lists other Xbox games and media that you might enjoy, based on the game you are currently playing.
- **Bing:** You can use the Bing screen to search Xbox for music and games.

If you're currently running a game on your Xbox console, the SmartGlass interface contains an icon in the lower-left corner. Tapping this icon causes SmartGlass to display a series of game-specific screens:

**There are a several screens
displayed for each game.**

The game
title is
displayed
here.

- **Details:** The Details screen displays the game you are currently playing and enables you to set or update game beacons.

- **Friends:** The Friends screen enables you to see your friends' activity for the game.

- **Achievements:** The Achievements screen lists your achievements for the game.

- **Images:** The Images screen displays pictures related to the game.

- **Related:** The Related screen displays other games that you might enjoy, based on the game you are currently playing.

Accessing the Xbox Guide

The Xbox Guide is the interface that controls your Xbox 360 console. You can use your Windows Phone 8 device to display the Xbox Guide on your TV screen. To do so, open the SmartGlass app from the Games hub and complete the following steps:

1. Tap the Menu icon.

2. Tap Remote.

Power On Your Console

If your Xbox isn't powered on when you attempt these steps, you won't be able to access the Xbox Guide. Instead of seeing the Remote menu option shown here, you'll see one that reads Connect to Your Xbox. Turn on your Xbox console and then tap this menu item to connect to it.

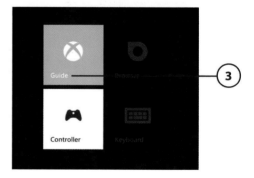

3. Tap Guide.

Using Your Phone as an Xbox Controller

SmartGlass enables you to use your phone as an Xbox controller. By doing so, you can navigate the Xbox Guide and even use your phone to control some games. Open SmartGlass from the Games hub and complete these steps:

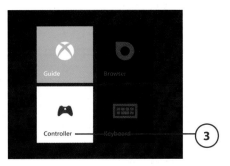

1. Tap the Menu icon.

2. Tap Remote.

3. Tap Controller.

4. Use the buttons on the screen as if you were using them from a regular Xbox 360 game controller.

Invisible Controls

Microsoft did not create an onscreen A button. You can emulate the A button by tapping any empty area of the phone's screen. Likewise, you can flick the screen left, right, up, and down to control movement on your Xbox 360 console.

Close button

Swipe to move and hold to move faster

Tap anywhere to select (A)

Tap anywhere for the A button.

Tap here to reveal Guide and Controller tiles.

It's Not All Good

Although SmartGlass allows a Windows Phone to be used as an Xbox controller, the phone is not an ideal game controller and doesn't work with all Xbox 360 games. Furthermore, certain buttons on the Xbox 360 controller are not duplicated on the phone. On the other hand, your Windows Phone makes for a great controller in other nongaming Xbox 360 apps, including the Internet Explorer web browser and the Netflix video-streaming app.

Believe it or not, your Windows Phone also works as a phone.

In this chapter, you will learn how to use the Windows Phone 8 device. Some of the topics covered in this chapter include:

→ Making and taking phone calls
→ Working with your call settings
→ SMS text messaging

The Phone

Cellphones have undergone amazing progress over the years. Smartphones have become so packed with features that having the capability to make a phone call has become something of an afterthought. After all, this chapter is near the end of the book, and I'm just now getting around to talking about using Windows Phone 8 devices as a phone. Rest assured, your Windows Phone functions just fine as an actual phone. This chapter helps you use its telephonic features to their fullest.

Making and Taking Phone Calls

Windows Phone 8 makes it easy to make or accept phone calls. In this section, you learn how to place a call as well as how to receive calls.

Making a Phone Call

As you probably expect, Windows Phone 8 makes it simple to place a phone call. To do so, go to the Start screen and follow these steps:

1. Tap the Phone icon. (Each carrier assigns a different name to this icon.)

2. When you reach the Call History screen, tap the Keypad icon.

3. Dial the phone number.

4. Tap call.

CALL HISTORY

The Call History screen, shown here, displays your most recent phone calls, along with the date and time of each call. Tapping a name within your Call History list brings up the contact information for that person. Tapping the phone icon next to an item on the history list places a call to that person.

Occasionally, you may want to clear your call history. You can do this by tapping open the Call History menu and selecting the Delete All menu option.

Calling Your Contacts

You can call one of your contacts by going to the Start screen and following these steps:

1. Tap the People tile.

Taking a Shortcut

Windows Phone 8 is designed so that you can also access your contact list directly through the Phone app. From the History screen, just tap the People icon at the bottom of the screen.

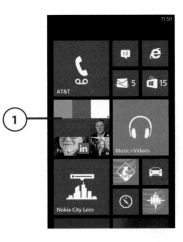

2. Tap the contact you want to call.

3. Tap the number you want to call.

Ending a Call

When you finish a call, you might not have to do anything to end the call. If the person you are talking to hangs up first, the call terminates automatically. However, if you want to end the call yourself, you can do so from the phone screen by completing this step:

1. Tap the End Call button.

The Speaker Phone

Similar to most cellphones on the market, Windows Phone 8 devices have a speaker phone. To turn on the speaker while you are on a call, activate your phone's screen and perform these steps:

1. Tap the Speaker icon.

2. Verify that the On Speaker status is displayed.

Turning Off the Speaker Phone

If you want to turn off speaker phone mode, simply tap the Speaker icon again.

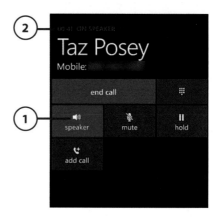

Muting a Call

If you need to mute a call, you can do so on the phone screen by performing these steps:

1. Tap the Mute icon.

2. Verify that the On Mute status is displayed.

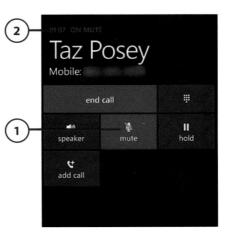

Unmuting a Call

When you mute a call, the Mute icon illuminates to indicate that the call is muted. The words On Mute also appear next to the timer. You can tap the Mute icon again to unmute the call.

Accessing the Keypad

Whether you are checking your answering machine at home or calling your cellular provider with a question about your account, you are bound to occasionally run into menus that require you to press specific buttons on your keypad. If you encounter such a menu during a call, you can access the keypad from the phone screen by performing this step:

1. Tap the keypad icon.

2. The keypad is displayed on the screen.

Getting Back to the Phone Screen

If you need to return to the screen containing the Speaker and Mute icons, you can do so by tapping the keypad icon again.

Returning a Missed Call

When you miss a call, the Phone icon on the Start screen displays a number reflecting how many calls you have missed. When you tap the Phone icon, the History screen displays all your recent calls. Missed calls are highlighted and flagged as missed. You can return a call by performing these steps:

1. Tap the Phone icon.

2. Tap the missed call in the History list.

3. Tap the option to call the person (Call Home, Call Mobile, and so on).

Accessing Voicemail

When someone leaves you a voice message, the Phone tile on the Start screen displays the voicemail icon to indicate that you have a message waiting. To retrieve a voice message, follow these steps:

1. Tap the Phone icon.

2. Flick to the Voicemail screen.

3. Tap the voicemail message.

4. Tap Play to play the voicemail message.

5. Tap the Delete icon to delete the message.

6. Tap the Call icon to return the call.

7. Tap the Profile icon to view the caller's profile.

The number of calls you've missed

You have a voicemail message

Visual Voicemail

These steps require support for Visual
Voicemail on your phone. If your calling
plan doesn't include that feature, you
must instead dial in to your voicemail by
tapping the voicemail button at the bottom of the call History screen.

Configuring Your Voicemail

Most cell providers design their phones
to access voicemail without requiring
any configuration changes. However,
it is possible to manually provision
your phone with a voicemail phone
number in case the default voicemail
configuration isn't working. To do so, go
to the Start screen, tap the Phone icon,
and follow these steps:

1. Tap the Menu icon.

2. Tap Settings.

3. Move the Use Default Voicemail
   Number slide bar to the Off
   position.

4. Tap the New Voicemail Number
   field and enter a voicemail
   number.

5. Tap an empty area of the screen.
   Your changes are automatically
   saved.

Conference Calling

Assuming that your cellular provider offers the service, you can use Windows Phone 8 for conference calling. To place a conference call, start by making a regular phone call to one person. After that, you can add another person to the call by completing these steps:

1. Tap the Add Call icon.

2. Your previous call is placed on hold.

3. Use either the keypad or the address book to place a call to the third person.

4. When the recipient answers the call, tap the Merge Calls icon.

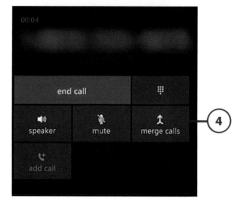

5. The phone screen displays the word Conference, indicating that you are on a conference call. The names or numbers of the people you are talking to display beneath the Conference indicator.

Answering a Call

When you receive a call, the device displays the caller ID information for the person who is calling, along with a picture (if you have a picture associated with the caller's contact information). You can answer the call by following these steps:

1. Flick the screen upward.

2. Tap the Answer icon.

Ignoring a Call
If you prefer, you can tap the Ignore tile. Ignoring a call silences the ringer.

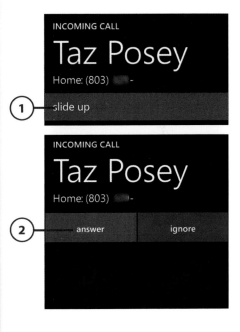

Call Waiting

If another call comes in while you're on the phone, the device's screen displays the caller ID information for the caller. Windows Phone 8 gives you three options for dealing with the incoming call:

A. Answer: Tap this tile to answer the call. Your original call is placed on hold.

B. Ignore: The inbound call is ignored, and your original call continues.

C. End Call+Answer: Tapping this tile causes your original call to be terminated and the inbound call to be answered.

Call Settings

Although it is easy to think of a telephone as being rather simplistic, the Windows Phone 8 Phone app is fully customizable. In this section, you learn how to create custom ring tones, enable talking caller ID, and much more.

Changing Your Ringtones

You can change the phone's ringtone by going to the phone's Settings screen and following these steps:

1. Tap Ringtones+Sounds.

2. Tap the Ringtone box.

3. Tap the ringtone you want to use.

Sampling a Ringtone

You can sample a ringtone by tapping the Play button located to the left of it.

Enabling Vibrate

As with most cellphones, Windows Phone 8 devices include a vibrate option. Vibration can serve as an alternative to the ringer (so as not to disturb those around you), or it can be used with the ringer. Combining the ringer with vibration is useful in noisy environments where you might not hear the ringer. To enable vibration, go to the phone's Settings screen and complete these steps:

1. Tap Ringtones+Sounds.

2. If you want to use vibration while the ringer is turned on, slide the Ringer slide bar to the On position. Otherwise, place the Ringer slide bar in the Off position.

3. Set the Vibrate slide bar to the On position.

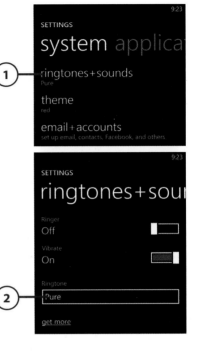

Using Custom Ringtones

Windows Phone 8 enables you to use an audio file as a ringtone. The easiest way to accomplish this is to use File Explorer (or Windows Explorer) to copy the audio file to your phone's Ringtones folder. The exact method you use to accomplish this varies, depending on the version of Windows you are using and the ringtone's file location. The following are general instructions based on Windows 8.

1. With your phone attached to your computer via USB cable, open File Explorer.

2. Locate the audio file you want to use as a ringtone.

3. Right-click the audio file and choose the Copy command from the shortcut menu.

4. Navigate through the file system to Computer\Windows Phone\Phone Ringtones.

5. Right-click an empty area within the Ringtones folder and choose the Paste command from the shortcut menu.

6. Go to your phone's Settings screen and tap Ringtones+Sounds.

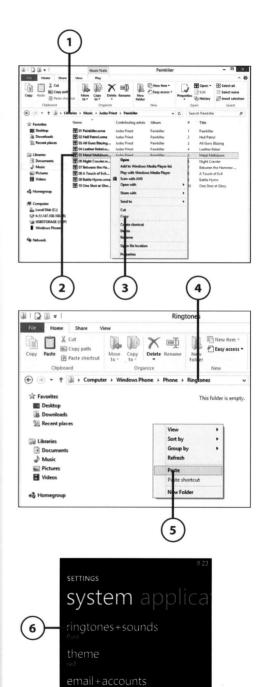

7. Tap Ringtone.

8. Tap your custom ringtone.

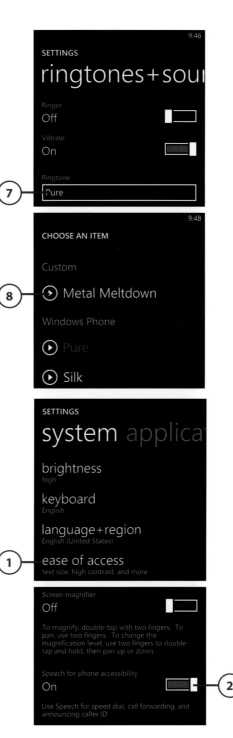

Enabling Talking Caller ID

Windows Phone 8 enables you to configure the phone's caller ID to verbally announce the person who is calling. When a call comes in, the ringtone initially plays at the normal volume. After a couple seconds, the ringtone volume is reduced and the caller is verbally announced. You can enable the talking caller ID feature by going to the phone's Settings screen and following these steps:

1. Tap Ease of Access.

2. Scroll to the bottom of the screen and set the Speech for Phone Accessibility slide bar to the On position.

Using International Assist

The International Assist option, which is enabled by default, is designed to automatically correct the most common errors that are made when dialing international numbers. You can enable or disable the International Assist feature by going to the Start screen, tapping the phone tile, and following these steps:

1. Flick the menu icon upward.

2. Tap Settings.

3. Scroll the screen upward and then slide the International Assist slide bar to either the On or the Off position.

Enhancing SIM Security

Some, but not all, Windows Phone 8 devices use a SIM card to link the phone to the owner's account with the cell provider. Because SIM cards can be moved from one cellular device to another, it is possible to protect a SIM card with a PIN by activating the Phone tile and following these steps:

1. Tap the Menu icon.

2. Tap Settings.

3. Scroll to the bottom of the screen and set the SIM Security option to On.

UNDERSTANDING SIM SECURITY

Enable SIM Security only if you know your SIM PIN. As you can see in the figure, you have only three attempts to enter the PIN correctly.

If you enter your PIN incorrectly three times in a row, you are locked out of the phone. The only way to regain access is to contact your cell provider and get the service provider key (SPK), which you then have 10 attempts to enter correctly.

It's Not All Good

Exercise extreme caution when using the SIM Security feature. It is possible to permanently disable your SIM card, rendering it useless!

Enabling Airplane Mode

Due to FAA regulations, if you want to take a Windows Phone 8 device on an airplane, you must either do a full device shutdown or put the phone into Airplane Mode. Airplane Mode disables the radios used for cellular, Wi-Fi, and Bluetooth communications, while allowing you to continue to use the device's other features. To put the phone into airplane mode, go to the device's Settings screen and follow these steps:

1. Tap Airplane Mode.

2. Set the slide bar to On. An airplane icon indicates the phone is in Airplane Mode.

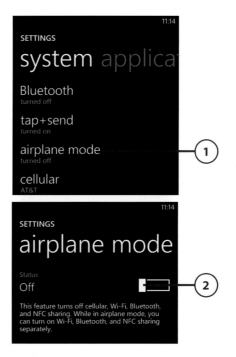

Disable Airplane Mode

When you arrive at your destination, you can disable Airplane Mode by going back to the Airplane Mode screen and setting the slide bar to the Off position.

Enabling Bluetooth

The exact method you use to pair your Windows Phone 8 with a Bluetooth device varies, depending on the device type you are using. You usually can complete the process by putting your Bluetooth device in pairing mode, going to the phone's Settings screen, and completing these steps:

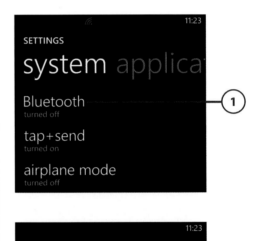

1. Tap Bluetooth.

2. Move the slide bar to the On position.

3. Tap the device that you want to pair the phone to. It is worth noting that the device might initially be listed as a headset, regardless of what the device actually is.

Entering a PIN

If prompted, enter a PIN to complete the pairing process.

BLUETOOTH COMPATIBILITY

For Windows Phone 8 to use a Bluetooth device, it must be connected to the Bluetooth device through a procedure known as pairing. Simple devices such as a Bluetooth headset, can often be paired simply by pressing a button. More complex devices, such as hands-free systems that are integrated into vehicles, often require you to enter a PIN into your phone before the phone can be paired with the vehicle.

The functionality that can be achieved through a Bluetooth connection varies widely, depending on the type of Bluetooth device that is being connected. In some cases, though, the phone can interact with the Bluetooth device in ways you might not expect.

I own a 2011 Ford Fusion that is equipped with Microsoft Sync. When my Windows Phone is connected to the car, the LCD display in my dash shows the current signal strength and the amount of battery remaining.

Perhaps the most impressive feature is that I can text while I am driving! When a new text message comes in, the car verbally reads it to me. I can verbally compose and send a response without ever taking my hands off the wheel. The speech recognition engine isn't perfect, but it seems to work pretty well, and the phone confirms what it thinks I said before it sends the text.

SMS Text Messaging

Similar to any other cellphone, Windows Phone 8 enables you to send and receive SMS text messages. The Messaging tile on the Start screen provides access to the text messaging client. When you receive a text message, the Messaging tile on the Start screen changes to indicate that a new message has arrived.

The tile's icon also might change to reflect the text messaging status. For example, if a text message failed to send properly, the tile looks like this:

Text messages are grouped into conversations. When you tap the Messaging tile, you see a list of everyone you have recently had a conversation with. Each person's name is listed along with an excerpt from the most recent message in the conversation. The excerpt can be from a message that the other person sent or that you sent.

You can view a conversation by tapping on the thread.

You can view a conversation by tapping it. Windows then shows you all the messages within the conversation. You can scroll through the messages by flicking the screen up or down.

This is what a text conversation looks like.

It's Not All Good

Windows Phone 8 groups conversations based on who the conversation was with, not when the conversation took place. This can lead to some potentially confusing conversations. If you send a message to someone (or receive a message from someone) and a conversation already exists, the message is added to the previously existing conversation, regardless of when the original conversation actually took place. This can lead to confusion if you go back and read a conversation later. Thankfully, Windows displays a date and time stamp for each message. You can also delete the entire conversation when it's complete, as I discuss later in the section "Deleting a Conversation."

Reading a New Text Message

You can read a new message by completing these steps:

1. Tap the Messaging tile.

2. Tap the conversation that contains the message you want to read.

Identifying New Text Messages

Windows Phone displays conversations with new messages at the top of the screen, along with the first part of the message. This text is displayed in color, to indicate that the message is new.

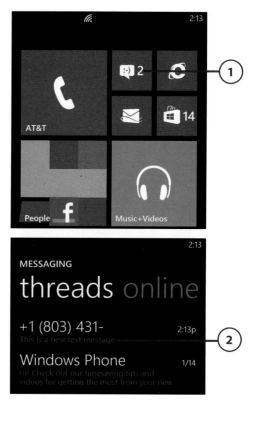

Replying to a Text Message

When you open a new text message, the message appears in conversation view. The original message is listed within a speech bubble, and Windows places an empty speech bubble beneath the most recent message. To reply to the message, follow these steps:

1. Enter your response into this speech bubble.

2. Tap the Send icon.

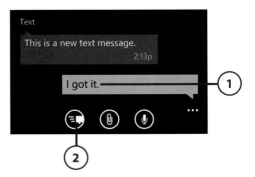

Sending a Text Message

If you want to send a text message to one of your contacts, you can do so by going to the Start screen, tapping the messaging icon, and following these steps:

1. Tap the New icon.

Entering a Mobile Number
If the intended recipient of your text isn't in your contact list, you can manually enter the person's phone number on this line instead of tapping the + icon.

2. Tap the + icon, to the right of the To field.

3. Tap the name of the contact to whom you want to send the message. If multiple phone numbers are listed for the contact, you are prompted to choose the number you want to send the message to.

4. Tap the speech bubble.

5. Compose your message.

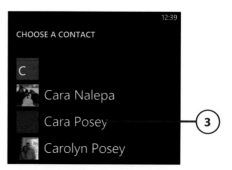

Typing Suggestions

When typing a message, Windows displays a series of suggestions beneath the speech bubble. If you see the word you are typing, you can tap it to have Windows automatically add it to the speech bubble.

6. Tap Send.

SENDING MESSAGES TO MULTIPLE RECIPIENTS

You can also send a single text message to multiple recipients. The procedure for doing so is nearly identical to that of sending a message to a single recipient. All you have to do is press the + icon again and choose another recipient. Continue doing so until you see everyone you want included on the message listed in the To field.

Sending Long Text Messages

Because of the SMS messaging standards, text messages cannot exceed 160 characters. As you compose a text message, Windows keeps track of the number of characters you have entered. When your message reaches 130 characters, Windows displays a counter showing you the number of characters you have typed.

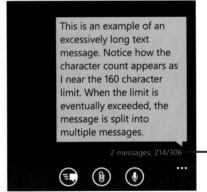

A character counter displays your message length.

If your message exceeds 160 characters, Windows splits your message into two separate messages that are sent together in sequence. The character counter also changes to reflect that two messages will be used and that the maximum length of the two messages is 306 characters. If you exceed 306 characters, Windows splits the text into three separate text messages. Many smartphones can reassemble text messages into a single text message, although it depends on the carrier they're using and the type of phone.

Sending an Attachment with a Text Message

It's possible to send a variety of attachment types along with a text message. For example, if you have pictures stored on your phone, you can easily send a copy of a picture to a friend through a text message. To do so, go to the Messaging app and follow these steps:

1. Tap the New icon.

2. Add a recipient to the message.

3. Enter your message in the speech bubble.

4. Tap the Attach icon.

5. Tap the type of attachment you want to use. For this example, we use Picture, but you can also send videos, voice notes, contact information, and even a map image of your current location.

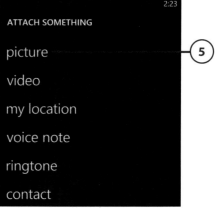

6. Locate the specific item you want to attach. When choosing a picture, for example, you can select from any image stored on your phone, your Facebook account, or your SkyDrive. (If you're sending a voice note, you're asked to start recording it.)

Snapping a Photo

Instead of choosing an existing photo, after tapping Picture, you can tap the Camera icon at the bottom of the screen and snap a fresh picture to attach to your text message.

7. Tap Send.

Removing an Image

If you change your mind about sending an attachment, you can tap and hold the attachment and select Remove from the menu that appears.

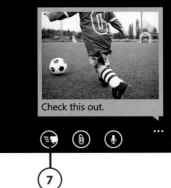

It's Not All Good

Rejected Messages

Occasionally, you might receive a notification that an attachment sent to a contact was not delivered successfully. This problem usually is related not to Windows Phone 8, but rather to the recipient's cellular service. Some cell providers limit the size of text message attachments and might reject a message containing an image or video that exceeds the size limit. Large attachments can also fail to be sent if you do not have adequate signal strength.

Deleting a Conversation

If you want to delete an entire
conversation thread, you can do so
by going to the Messaging app and
completing these steps:

1. Tap and hold the conversation
   thread you want to delete.

2. Tap Delete.

3. Tap Delete again to confirm that
   you want to erase the conversation thread.

Another Way to Delete

Windows Phone 8 provides an alternative method for deleting a conversation
thread: Open the conversation you want
to delete, tap the Menu icon, and tap
Delete Thread.

Deleting a Message

Occasionally, you might need to delete
a single message without deleting
an entire conversation thread. To do
so, open an existing message in the
Messaging app and complete these
steps:

1. Tap and hold the message you
   want to delete.

2. Tap Delete.

3. Tap Delete again to confirm that
   you want to delete the message.

Forwarding a Text Message

Windows Phone 8 enables you to forward a text message to someone else. To do so, open an existing message in the Messaging app and complete the following steps:

1. Tap and hold the message you want to forward.

2. Tap Forward. The forwarded message is displayed within a new text message.

3. Enter the recipient for your message.

4. Tap the Send icon.

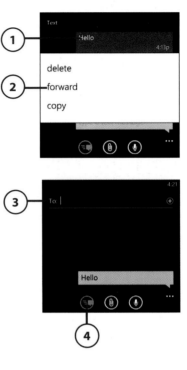

Copying a Text Message

Sometimes it's handy to be able to copy the contents of a text message so that you can use the information in another app. For example, if someone texts you a phone number or an address, you might want to add it to your contacts. Likewise, if someone sends you an important text, it might be helpful to copy the contents to OneNote. To do so, open an existing message in the Messaging app and complete the following steps:

1. Tap and hold the message you want to copy.

2. Tap Copy.

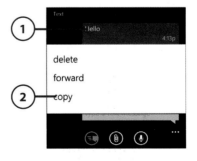

Pasting a Text Message's Contents into an App

Copying a text message only copies the message's contents to the phone's Clipboard. The other half of the operation involves pasting the message into an app. The method for doing this varies from one app to another, but it generally involves tapping a text area (a place where you would normally type) and then tapping the Paste icon.

Text Messaging Backup

Windows Phone 8 provides automatic backup for text messages, but the backup feature is not enabled by default. To enable text message backup, open the Messaging app and complete these steps:

1. Tap the Menu icon.

2. Tap Settings.

3. Set the Text Message Backup slide bar to the On position.

Group Text

If you are sending a text message to multiple recipients, it might be better to group all the replies into a single conversation thread instead of grouping each person's response into a separate thread. You can accomplish this by enabling the Group Text feature. To do so, open the Messaging app and follow these steps:

1. Tap the Menu icon.

2. Tap Settings.

3. Set the Group Text slide bar to On to enable the Group Text feature.

Press the Search button
to access Bing search

This chapter discusses all the different ways you can use the phone's built-in search feature. Some of the topics covered in this chapter include:

→ Searching with Bing
→ Searching by voice
→ Searching with Internet Explorer
→ Using Maps
→ Finding locations with Local Scout
→ Additional ways to search

Search

Although it might seem a bit unusual for a phone, Windows Phone 8 devices can accumulate a lot of data. Many devices include 16GB or more of storage, which can be used for storing apps, messages, photos, videos, music, Microsoft Office documents, and more. The built-in search function makes it easy to locate specific items, regardless of how much data your phone accumulates. The phone is also designed to perform Internet searches when appropriate, and it can even take your location into account when compiling the search results.

Bing and the Search Button

As discussed in Chapter 1, "Getting Started with Windows Phone 8," Windows Phone 8 devices come equipped with a dedicated hardware search button. You can press this button at any time to access Bing search.

Bing is an Internet search engine that is similar to Google. Depending on what you are looking for, Bing sometimes delivers better search results than Google, but sometimes Google fares better. There is a web page (www.bing-vs-google.com/) that enables you to compare Bing and Google search results side by side.

In a recent comparison, I entered my own name into both Bing and Google. Google returned results related primarily to my bio and to books and articles that I had written. Bing returned that too, but also returned a news story explaining that someone with my name (but spelled differently) had been charged with murder!

Searching with Bing

In most cases, pressing the Search button causes the phone to open Bing. To see how a Bing search works, follow these steps:

1. Press the Start button. You can do a Bing search from almost anywhere, but for the sake of example, I use the Start screen to ensure a consistent experience.

2. Press the Search button.

Locations

The first time you perform a Bing search, you see a screen asking if you want to allow Search to use your location. If you see this screen, tap Allow.

3. Enter your search criteria.

4. Bing displays search results across three different category tabs. You can access the various tabs by flicking the screen to the left or to the right. The tabs include the following:

   Web: Websites related to the search phrase

   Local: Relevant search results from your immediate area

   Media: Images related to your search query

   Shopping: Online shopping results related to your search

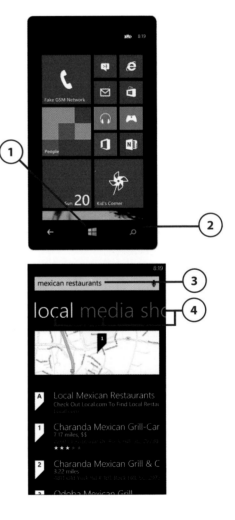

>>>Go Further

USING CATEGORIES

If search on the phrase "Mexican restaurants," the Web tab probably will link you to websites for the big national chains. The Local tab will show you nearby Mexican restaurants. The Media tab might contain photos of various restaurants or video restaurant reviews. Finally, the Shopping tab might offer Mexican cookbooks or Mexican seasonings. These category tabs are a fantastic way to filter your search results according to this criteria that's most useful to you.

The Bing Interface

Although it's easy to think of Bing as a typical search engine, Bing actually spans several screens. You can access these screens by pressing the phone's Search button and flicking the screen left or right. These screens make up the Bing interface:

- **Bing:** You see this screen when you press the Search button. It allows you to perform search queries.

- **Top Videos:** This screen displays the top viral videos.

- **Top Headlines:** This screen provides the latest news headlines.

- **In Theaters:** This screen displays the latest movie releases.

- **Local Deals:** This screen displays coupons from local retailers and service providers.

- **Local Events:** This screen lists events taking place nearby.

You can flick the Bing screen to the left or right to access additional screens.

Configuring Bing Settings

You can configure various settings to control the way Bing searches behave. You can access the search settings by opening Bing search and completing the following steps:

1. Tap the Menu icon.

2. Tap Settings.

3. Tap the Use My Location slide bar to control whether Bing uses your location in determining search results.

4. Enable the Send Location Info for Microsoft Tags check box if you want to help Microsoft make Bing better.

5. Tap Suggestions if you want Bing to generate personalized suggestions based on your past usage. When you tap this button, you see a screen that allows you to enable this feature.

6. Tap SafeSearch to control whether the search results include adult material and other questionable content. Settings include Off, Moderate, and Strict.

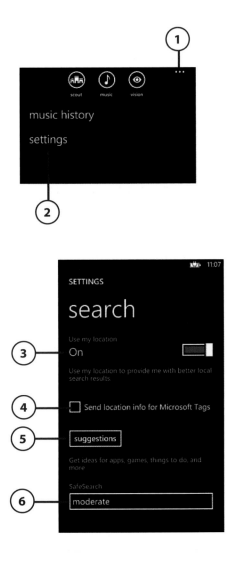

Where Are My Suggestions?

When you enable suggestions, the personalized suggestions are provided through the Store and the Local Scout app's For You screen. I discuss Scout later in this chapter, in the section "Finding Locations with Local Scout."

7. Enable the Allow Search Button from Lock Screen checkbox to allow searches to be performed without first unlocking the phone.

8. Enable the Get Suggestions from Bing as I Type checkbox to get search suggestions based on the text you've entered.

9. Enable the Allow Microsoft to Store and Use Images from Vision Searches checkbox to control whether images used in Bing Vision searches are sent to Microsoft to help improve future searches.

10. Tap the Delete History button to delete your search history.

7 ──── ☑ Allow search button from lock screen

8 ──── ☑ Get suggestions from Bing as I type

9 ──── ☑ Allow Microsoft to store and use images from vision searches

When you allow us to store and use images from vision searches, it helps us provide better search results.

10 ──── delete history

Deletes previously-typed search terms, vision searches, and music searches from your phone.

Searching by Voice

Although you might be inclined to enter your search criteria into the phone's search box, you can also perform verbal searches. To do so, go to the Start screen and press and hold the Start button on your phone. You see a screen that looks like this:

Say "Find" followed by whatever you are looking for.

Location Acceptance

The first time you perform a verbal search, you are asked whether you want to allow the phone to use your location. Some types of searches require location information to deliver accurate results. For example, using a search phrase such as "Find a coffee shop" would be pointless if Bing didn't know your location.

At this point, you can tell your phone what you want Bing to search for. Start by saying "Find" and then stating what you want found. When you are done speaking a command, you can tap Go to launch the search, but doing so is almost never necessary.

Including Find, Windows Phone 8 understands six main commands:

What Can I Say: The What Can I Say command tells the phone to display a few example commands. After doing so, you tap the Speak button and then speak your command.

Saying "What Can I Say" gives you a list of common voice commands.

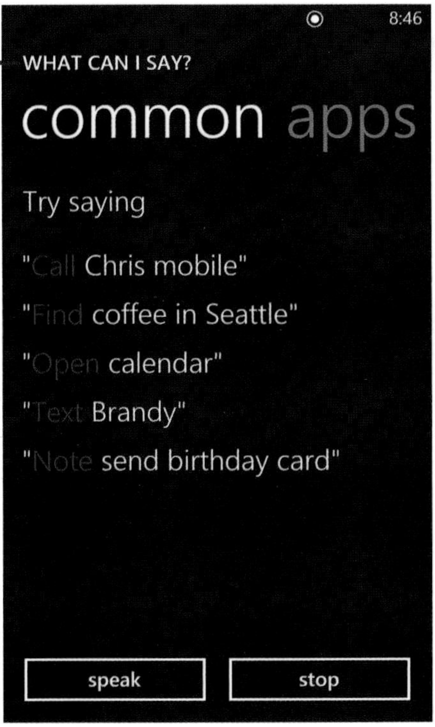

⊙   8:46

WHAT CAN I SAY?

common apps

Try saying

"Call Chris mobile"

"Find coffee in Seattle"

"Open calendar"

"Text Brandy"

"Note send birthday card"

| speak | stop |

Call: The Call command places a phone call. To use this command, combine it with a name from your contacts. For example, you could say, "Call Brien Posey."

Open: The Open command launches an application. An example of this command is "Open Pac-Man."

Find: The Find command performs a Bing search. At its simplest, you can just say "Find" followed by whatever you are looking for. For instance, you could say, "Find Fast Food." If necessary, you can also append a location, such as, "Find Mexican food in Redmond."

Text: The Text command sends a text message. For example, you might say, "Text Brien," followed by your text message.

Note: The Note command makes a note of something you want to remember.

MORE COMMANDS

The voice commands listed are not the only voice commands you can use—they are simply the most common. Some apps also support the use of voice commands. After activating voice input, if you flick the screen to the left, you go to the Apps page, which lists any voice-enabled apps and the supported command set.

If you flick the screen once again, you go to the More screen. This screen lists some additional voice commands you can use:

- **Press:** Presses a number on the phone keypad
- **Save Speed Dial:** Saves a number to speed dial
- **Turn Call Forwarding On or Off:** Turns call forwarding on or off

Searching with Bing Music

Bing Music is a new feature that enables you to search the Marketplace for music based on a song that is playing. The phone listens to the song, identifies it, and then retrieves a listing for the song from the Marketplace.

To use Bing Music, make sure that the music that you want to sample is at an adequate volume. You can sample only the original recording. Singing or humming a song doesn't return a valid result. Then from the Bing Search screen, tap the Music icon and place the phone where it can hear the music.

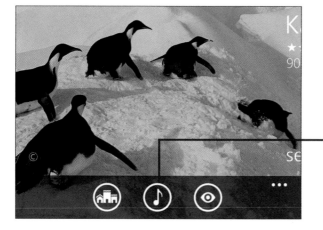

Tap this button to have Bing Music attempt to identify a song.

If Bing Music can identify the song, it displays it in the search results. If your only goal is to identify the song playing, you can tap Close after Bing Music identifies the song. If you want to purchase the song, tap the Store button.

Bing Music identifies the song and the album.

Music History
Windows Phone 8 maintains a history of the music Bing Music has identified. If you want to retrieve the list of previously identified songs, you can do so by opening the menu in Bing Search and tapping Music History.

It's Not All Good

Although Bing Music normally works pretty well, it isn't perfect. The previous version of Bing Music occasionally misidentified songs. Microsoft seems to have corrected that problem, but some songs aren't in Bing's song library. For example, I tried several times to get Bing Music to identify Keel's "The Right to Rock," but I only got the "No Matching Songs" error.

Searching with Bing Vision

Bing Vision is a Windows Phone 8 function that allows the phone to perform searches using the phone's camera. A basic Bing Vision search can be performed against bar codes, QR codes, Microsoft tags, CD covers, DVD covers, and book covers. You can initiate a Bing Vision search by tapping the Vision icon on the Bing Search screen.

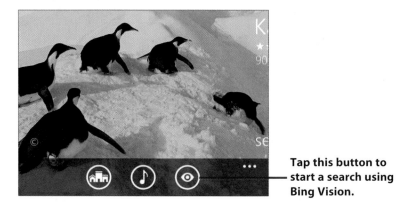

Tap this button to start a search using Bing Vision.

At this point, hold the phone near the item (using its camera) that you want to search until it is displayed clearly on the screen. The phone searches for the item and returns the best search results it can find.

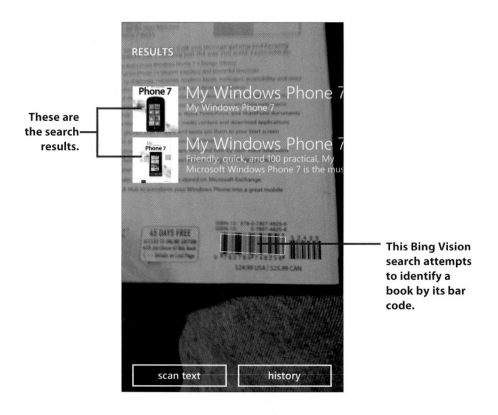

These are the search results.

This Bing Vision search attempts to identify a book by its bar code.

TRANSLATING AND SEARCHING TEXT

In addition to being able to scan things like bar codes and album covers, Bing Vision can scan plain text. After the scan, it is possible to search on the text or translate it to English (if the text is in a foreign language). To perform a text scan, activate Bing Vision, hold the phone in front of the text you want to scan so that the text displays on screen, and tap the Scan Text button.

Windows draws a rectangle around the text that it identifies. If you want to work with specific blocks of text, tap the rectangles containing the text you want to work with. When you're done, tap either the Translate or Search buttons to generate your results.

Searching with Internet Explorer

Being able to search the Internet is an important function for any smartphone. Although you can certainly use Bing for web searches, you also can perform various types of searches through Internet Explorer.

Internet Explorer is configured to use Bing as its search provider, and Microsoft does not give you a way to change that. If you begin typing something other than a URL, Internet Explorer uses the Bing search engine to pull relevant matches from your web browsing history, as well as from Bing's suggested sites. Items from your history display at the top of the list.

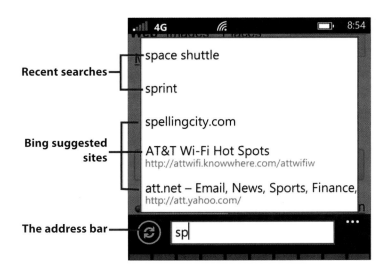

Context-Sensitive Searches

In some cases, Bing is even smart enough to interpret what you have typed. For example, if you enter a street address into Internet Explorer's address bar, Bing automatically shows you a map of the address.

If you choose to enter a phrase into Internet Explorer's address bar instead of choosing one of the suggestions, Internet Explorer performs a full-blown Bing search on the phrase you entered.

If you don't want to use Bing, however, you still have the option of browsing to a search engine home page to use search engines such as Yahoo! and Google.

You can use Google, Yahoo, etc.
You aren't limited to using Bing.

Pinning a Search Engine to the Start Screen

If you tend to use a certain search engine on a regular basis, you always have the option to pin the search engine to the start screen. To do so, open Internet Explorer and follow these steps:

1. Go to your preferred search engine.

2. Tap the Menu icon.

3. Tap Pin to Start.

4. The Search engine is made available on the device's Start screen.

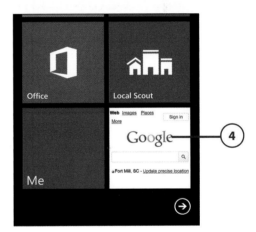

Turning Suggested Sites On and Off

Site suggestions are enabled by default, but you can disable or re-enable this feature by opening Internet Explorer and following these steps:

1. Tap the Menu icon.

2. Scroll to and tap Settings.

3. Tap Advanced Settings.

4. Use the check box titled Get Suggestions from Bing as I Type to enable or disable search suggestions.

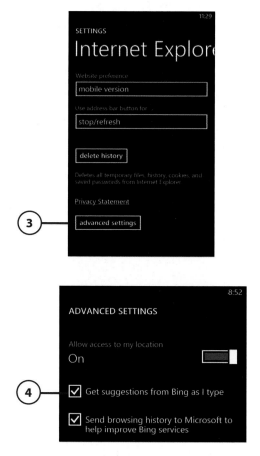

Maps

All Windows Phone 8 devices have built-in GPS functionality. Although a number of built-in and third-party apps make use of the phone's GPS, the primary application for GPS mapping is known simply as Maps. You can access Maps by going to the apps screen and tapping its tile. If this is the first time you've used the app, it asks if it can use your current location. Tap Allow. After it opens, it immediately zooms in on your current location.

The Maps interface contains several elements:

A. The last known target location. This could be your current location or the last-known destination you used with Maps.

B. The Scout Icon. Use this icon to find things like nearby restaurants and shopping.

C. The Directions icon. Get directions from your current location.

D. The Me icon. Find your present location on the map.

E. The Search icon. Search for a place.

F. The Menu icon. Get access to various mapping options.

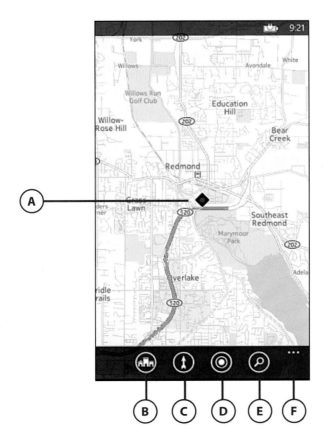

It's Not All Good

Some device manufacturers replace the Maps app with a proprietary mapping application. For example, the Nokia 920 does not list Maps on the Apps screen, but it provides an app called Nokia Maps in its place.

This doesn't mean that you can't use the mapping features discussed in this chapter. Even though there's no listing for the Maps app on the Apps screen, Nokia phones contain a Local Scout tile on the Start screen. You can access most of the mapping functions in a roundabout way, through the Local Scout feature.

Getting Directions

The Maps app is primarily designed to give you driving directions to a location. To get directions from your current location to a specific destination, follow these steps:

1. Tap the Directions icon.

2. Enter your destination (such as Miami, FL) and tap Enter.

3. Maps generates directions to your target location

Walking Directions

Windows Phone 8 is designed to provide driving directions by default, but you also can get walking directions. To do so, just tap the Walking icon near the top of the screen.

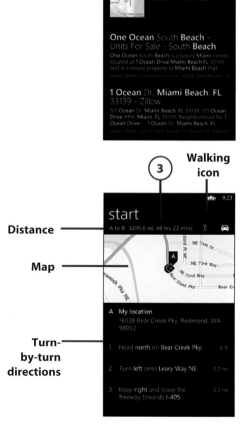

Walking icon

Distance

Map

Turn-by-turn directions

>>>Go Further

CONTROLLING THE MAP

When you bring up directions, Maps shows a split-screen view of your route. The top half of the screen shows a map, and the bottom half of the screen displays driving directions. If you need to alter the view, you must bring the map back to a full-screen view by tapping on it. From there, you can interact with it in the following ways:

- You can use the pinching gesture to zoom in and out of the map.

- You can use the flicking gesture to scroll the map in any direction.

- You can display the map full screen by tapping the map.

- You can go back to a split-screen view by tapping the Menu icon and choosing the Directions List option.

Clearing a Map

After you have used the phone to get directions, you might want to clear the map and start fresh. You can clear the map at any time by following these steps:

1. Tap the Menu icon.

2. Tap Clear Map.

Displaying Aerial View

You can switch from Map view to Aerial view by completing these steps:

1. Tap the Menu icon.

2. Tap Aerial View On.

3. The map displays a view that uses satellite imagery.

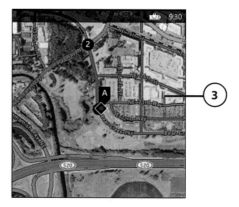

Turning Aerial View Off

You can switch back to Map view by going to the menu and tapping Aerial View Off.

Showing Traffic Patterns

When available, Windows Phone 8 can give you information about the traffic conditions along your route. After you have specified a route, you can get traffic information by completing these steps:

1. Tap the Menu icon.

2. Tap Show Traffic. Streets with traffic information are highlighted in green, yellow, or red to indicate density.

Missing Traffic Information

Keep in mind that traffic information is available only in some areas.

Searching for a Destination

Sometimes you need to search for a destination before you can ask the phone for driving directions. For instance, you might know that you are supposed to meet some friends at a McDonald's in Charleston, South Carolina, but you might not know the exact address. This is where the Search function comes into play. To perform a search, open the Maps app and follow these steps:

1. Tap the Search icon.

2. Enter the name of the place you want to search for.

3. The search results display on top of the map as a series of numbered flags. Lower-numbered flags represent results that are closer to your location, and flags with higher numbers are farther away.

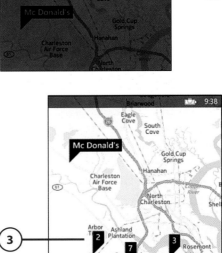

>>>Go Further

WORKING WITH THE SEARCH RESULTS

You can change how you view these results. If you want more information about a specific result, tap the flag. Doing so takes you to a screen that displays information such as the location's address, phone number, and website. If you want to see more information on all the search results, tap the Menu icon and select Search Results. Doing so displays the address and distance for each search result.

Finding Locations with Local Scout

Without a doubt, my personal favorite part of Maps is the Local Scout (or Scout, for short). Local Scout helps you find out what restaurants, shopping centers, and attractions are nearby. I travel almost constantly and often find myself staying in unfamiliar areas, which makes Scout a real lifesaver.

You can access Scout from a couple places. Your phone probably includes a Local Scout tile, by default, that you can tap. Scout is also available from the Maps app and the Search app by tapping the Scout icon.

Local Scout tile

Local Scout contains several pages that you can swipe through:

- **Eat+Drink:** A list of bars and restaurants in the area around your search result.

- **See+Do:** A list of attractions in the area.

- **Shop:** A list of nearby stores

- **For You:** Suggestions based on your tastes. The suggestions are populated when you enable Bing search suggestions, as described earlier in this chapter.

Swipe left or right across these headings to see Scout's other pages.

Quick cards represent a location or an event.

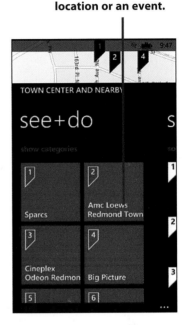

Events quick cards may offer venue information or the option to purchase tickets.

When possible, Windows Phone 8 displays scouting results as quick cards. A quick card is an icon representing a location.

When tapped, the quick card displays information such as the address, phone number, and website for the selected search result. Depending on the individual quick card, there might be one or more additional pieces of information, such as options to display event information, buy tickets for an event, and get information about the surrounding area.

ADDITIONAL INFORMATION

>>>Go Further

When you tap a quick card for a location or an event, you go to a results screen that displays on an About screen one or more of the pieces of information discussed on this page. However, depending on the location or event, you might be able to access some additional information by flicking the screen to the left or right. Some pages that might exist for certain locations and events include these:

- **About:** The About screen provides basic information (such as address and phone number) for the location or event.

- **Directory:** The Directory screen provides a directory of the location. For example, in the case of a shopping mall, the Directory screen might list the mall's stores and restaurants.

- **Buzz:** The Buzz screen provides ratings and reviews of a location.

- **Upcoming:** Some locations, such as museums, provide a list of upcoming events.

- **Apps:** The Apps screen lists apps related to the event or location.

Pinning a Local Scout Result

Windows Phone 8 enables you to pin a Local Scout result to the Start screen. To do so, follow these steps:

1. Tap the quick card for the result you are interested in.

2. Tap the Pin icon.

3. Tapping a pinned Scout tile takes you to its About page.

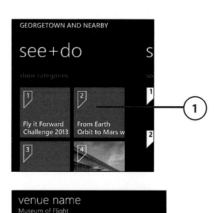

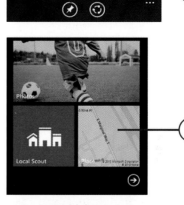

Tapping on a pinned result takes you to the Local Scout screen.

Adding a Local Scout Result to Your Map

If you have a favorite location, you might want to mark it on your phone's map for future reference. To do so, complete these steps:

1. Tap the quick card for the location you are interested in.

2. Tap the Add icon.

3. Local Scout adds a pin to your map that is marked with a star icon.

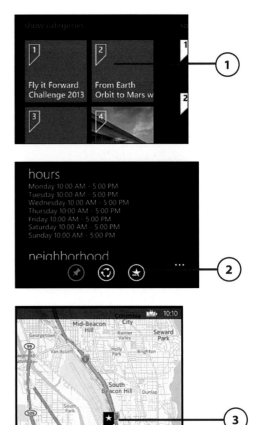

Sharing a Local Scout Result

If you want to share a Local Scout result with a friend, you can do so by completing these steps:

1. Tap the quick card for the result you want to share.

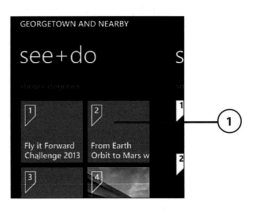

2. Tap the Share icon.

3. Choose the mechanism you want to use to send the quick card.

Sharing Options

The options available for sharing a location or event vary depending on how your phone is configured. Generally, you can share a Local Scout result using email, text, or Tap+Send.

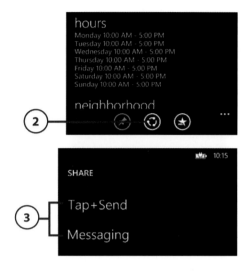

It's Not All Good

Local Scout does not always display all the venues that are nearby. Through my travels, I have noticed that Local Scout tends to display "real" restaurants but often omits fast food restaurants. Then again, sometimes Local Scout doesn't know about other "real" restaurants.

Once in a great while, the results list contains something inappropriate. One particularly amusing example recently occurred while I was in downtown Denver, Colorado. Windows Phone 8 listed a strip club among the list of restaurant results (in all fairness, the place did serve food). Even funnier was the fact that, when I tapped the listing for the club, Local Scout provided reviews. I will leave the contents of these reviews to your imagination, but they were as lude as you might expect.

Clearing Map History

If you sometimes share your phone with others, you might want to protect your privacy by clearing your mapping history. You can clear the map history at any time by opening Maps and following these steps:

1. Tap the Menu icon.

2. Scroll to and tap Settings.

3. Tap Delete History.

4. Tap Delete.

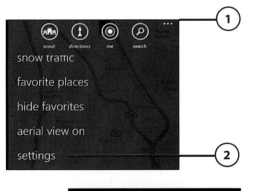

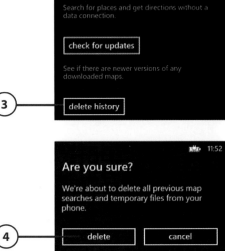

Downloading Maps

Unlike Windows Phone 7, Windows Phone 8 enables you to download maps ahead of time so that you can use the maps even if you don't have Internet access. To download maps, complete these steps:

1. Tap the Menu icon.

2. Scroll to and tap Settings.

3. Tap Download Maps.

4. Tap the Add icon.

5. Tap the map you want to download.

6. Tap Download.

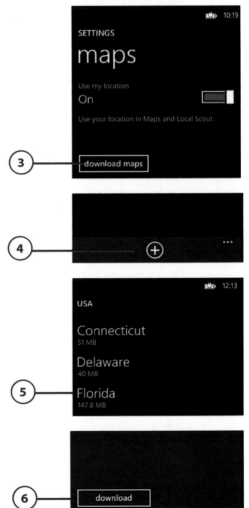

Updating Downloaded Maps

The maps that you download can eventually become outdated. Fortunately, you can periodically check for updates to downloaded maps. To do so, complete these steps:

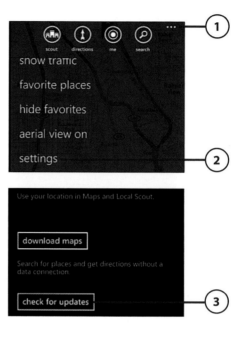

1. Tap the Menu icon.

2. Scroll to and tap Settings.

3. Tap Check for Updates.

More Ways to Search

In addition to Windows Phone 8's major search features such as Bing and map searches, there are also a few minor, but useful, search types. For example, you can search your call history or your contact list.

Call History

If you tend to make or receive a lot of phone calls, it can be frustrating to try to manually scroll through your call history in search of a specific phone number. You can make this process easier by searching your call history. To perform a search, tap the Phone tile and follow these steps:

1. Tap the Search icon.

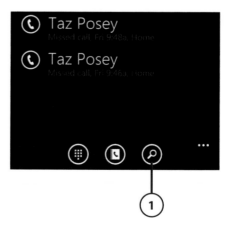

2. Enter your search criteria.

How Search Works

The search interface enables you to search based on the first or last name or on the phone number. The search results display instantly as you type each letter of your query, so you don't need to enter an entire name in most cases.

SEARCHING PHONE NUMBERS

The Call History search enables you to search by phone number, but only if a call was made to or received from someone who is not in your contacts list. For example, suppose that you need to call someone you haven't previously called. You remember that this person lives in the 803 area code, but you can't remember the phone number. In this situation, you can search the call history for 803. However, the search will not return any results for contacts who also happen to be in the 803 area code.

>>>Go Further

Contact Search

You can search your contacts in much the same way you can search your call history, except that contact list searches do not filter the results based on whether you have talked to a person recently. You can search your contacts by tapping the People tile and following these steps:

1. Tap the Search icon.

2. Enter your search criteria.

Searching Your Contacts

As was the case with the call history search, you can search your contacts by both first and last name.

Searching for OneNote Notes

Windows Phone 8 includes a search function for finding OneNote notes. To search for a note, open OneNote and follow these steps:

1. Tap the Search icon.

2. Enter your search criteria.

Titles and Contents

When you enter your search criteria, Windows Phone 8 searches both the titles of all your notes and their contents.

Searching for Microsoft Office Documents

Windows Phone 8 includes a search function for finding Microsoft Office documents. To search for an Office document, open Office and follow these steps:

1. Tap the Search icon.

2. Enter your search criteria.

Titles Only

When you enter your search criteria, Windows Phone 8 searches only the document titles. Unlike OneNote searches, Microsoft Office document searches do not analyze the document contents.

Searching Email

Windows Phone 8 makes it easy to locate specific items within your email. To do so, open your mailbox and complete the following steps:

1. Tap the Search icon.

2. Enter your search criteria.

Searching Your Email

When you perform an Email search, Windows Phone checks the sender line, the subject line, and the message body for occurrences of the search phrase.

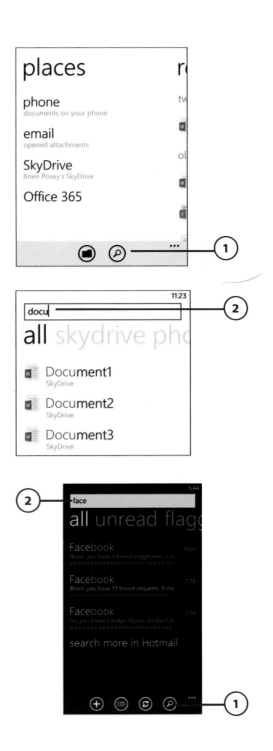

Setting the Search Language

When you enter a search phrase into your phone, the phrase you enter is searched based on the language you have configured the phone to use. If necessary, you can configure the phone to use a different language by going to the phone's Settings screen and following these steps:

1. Tap Language+Region.

2. Tap the Browser and Search Language box, and select the language you want to use.

Deleting Search History

In some situations, you want to protect your privacy by clearing your search history. You can accomplish this by going to the Settings screen and following these steps:

1. Flick the Settings screen to the right or left to access the Applications page.

2. Tap Search.

3. Scroll to the bottom of the screen and tap Delete History.

4. When prompted, tap Delete.

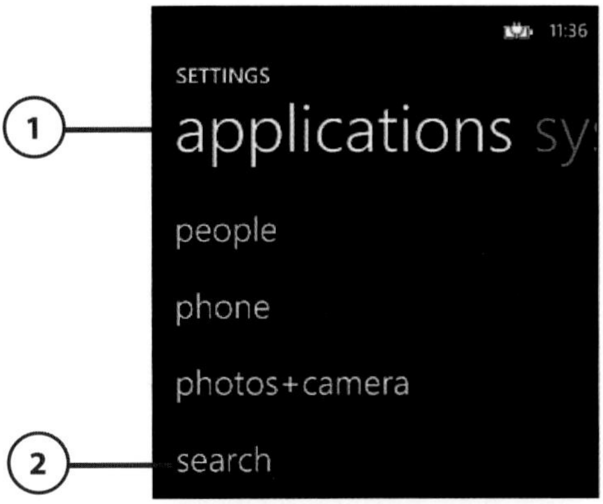

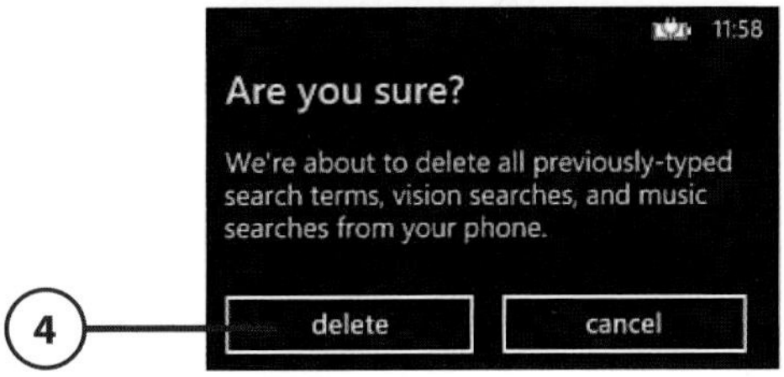

11:36

SETTINGS

applications sy

people

phone

photos+camera

search

search

☑ Allow Microsoft to store and use images from vision searches

When you allow us to store and use images from vision searches, it helps us provide better search results.

delete history

11:58

Are you sure?

We're about to delete all previously-typed search terms, vision searches, and music searches from your phone.

delete   cancel

Access your favorite social
media services directly
through your phone!

ME
Hotmail, Facebook, Twitter, LinkedIn

share notificatio

post an update

check in

set chat status
available

In this chapter, you learn how to use Windows Phone 8 social networking features, including the People Hub, organizing contacts, accessing Facebook, Twitter, LinkedIn, and more. Some of the topics discussed in this chapter include:

- → Using the People Hub for contacts
- → Working with groups
- → Creating and using rooms
- → Integrating Facebook
- → Using the Me tile for your social networks
- → Tweeting
- → Using LinkedIn

Working with People

Over the last several years, social networking has become all the rage. Windows Phone 8 was designed with social networking in mind. The phone offers native Facebook, Twitter, and LinkedIn integration so that you can access your social networks without ever having to directly visit the individual social networking sites. This integration enables you to interact more efficiently with the various social networking sites through the People Hub, which can provide an aggregate view of your social networking contacts. Likewise, the Me tile provides a centralized location for posting status updates or checking feeds from your social networks. Windows Phone 8 even allows you to create rooms that act as private collaboration environments for you and your friends, family, or co-workers.

The People Hub

The People hub is the Windows Phone 8 contact list. You access it by tapping the People tile on your Start screen or by using your phone's Apps list. Unlike a normal contact list, however, the People hub displays contacts from multiple sources. For example, it can simultaneously display contacts from Outlook, Gmail, Facebook, and more.

The People hub contains four screens.:

All: The All screen lists all your contacts from all your accounts.

Recent: The Recent screen displays contacts with whom you have recently been in contact. The Recent page remains hidden until the first time you interact with one of your contacts.

What's New: The What's New screen displays the most recent posts from your connected social networks.

Together: The Together screen provides access to the new Rooms and Groups features.

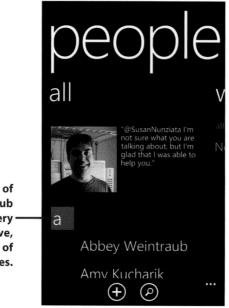

The All page of the People Hub shows every contact you have, across a variety of connected services.

Windows Phone 8 displays the profile information for all your contacts in a single place, regardless of whether the contacts are from a Microsoft account, Hotmail, Twitter, or somewhere else. The profile information for a person contains basic contact information, but it also can contain additional information, such as birthdays and children's names. As you see later in this chapter, a profile can also act as a direct link to the person's Facebook Wall.

Whenever you connect your phone to a social networking site, your "friends" on that site are automatically synchronized to the phone's People hub. The same holds true for any email accounts that you set up on the phone. When you connect Windows Phone 8 to a mailbox, the contacts associated with that mailbox are added to your phone's People hub.

Viewing a Profile

If you want to view the profile information for one of your contacts, you can do so by opening the People hub and following these steps:

1. Scroll through the list of contacts and tap the person whose profile you want to view.

2. Any information about the contact you selected appears on the Profile screen.

Adding a Contact

If you want to add a contact not already linked to an email account or social network, you can manually add that person. When you do, the contact that you add is synchronized to the mailbox of your choice. To add someone to your list of contacts, open the People hub and follow these steps:

1. Flick the display to the All page.

2. Tap the + icon to add a new contact.

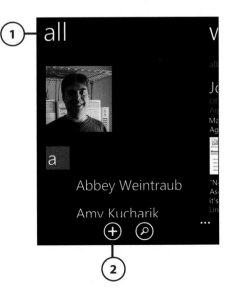

3. Tap the + icon next to the Name option.

Choosing a Mailbox

If you have more than one email account configured for your phone, it asks you to specify the account where you want to store your new contact.

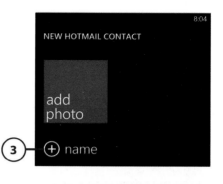

4. Enter the contact's name and any other relevant information, such as a nickname or the company the person works for.

5. Tap the Save icon.

6. Provide any additional profile information you want to add, such as a phone number, an email address, or a custom ringtone.

7. When you are done, tap the Save icon.

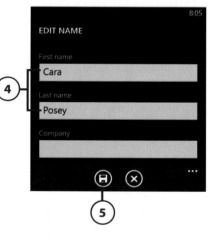

Syncing in New Contacts

Windows Phone automatically syncs in any new contacts you add directly to your email provider. For example, if you use your PC web browser to add someone to your Yahoo! email account, that contact automatically is added to your phone's People list the next time it syncs.

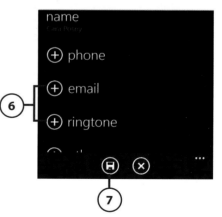

Editing a Profile

Windows Phone 8 enables you to add or modify a contact's profile information at any time. Any changes you make here sync back to the email service with which it's associated. To edit a contact, open the People hub and follow these steps:

1. Tap the name of the person whose information you want to modify.

2. Tap the Edit icon.

Editing Restrictions

You cannot edit contact details provided from a social network such as Facebook or Twitter.

3. Make any desired modifications.

4. Tap the Save icon.

Adding Pictures

Windows Phone 8 automatically displays profile pictures for Outlook and Facebook contacts (assuming that a profile picture exists). However, you can also add a profile picture manually. To do so, just tap the Add Photo icon when you create or edit a contact and then choose a picture from the camera roll.

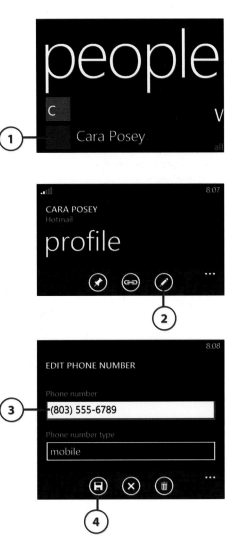

Deleting a Contact

If you want to remove a contact from your phone, you can do so by pressing the Start button, tapping the People tile, and completing the following steps:

1. Tap and hold the contact you want to remove.

2. Choose the Delete option from the pop-up menu.

3. When Windows asks if you really want to delete the contact, tap Delete.

Synchronized Deletes

When you delete a contact, the contact is also removed from any synchronized sources. For example, if you delete an Outlook contact, the contact is also removed from the Contacts list associated with your Microsoft Exchange mailbox.

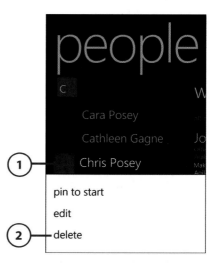

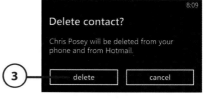

Searching for a Contact

As you begin linking multiple accounts to your phone, there's a good chance that you will accumulate a rather long list of contacts. Thankfully, you don't have to scroll through the full list of contacts every time you need to find someone specific. Instead, you can do a search. To search for a contact, open the People hub and follow these steps:

1. Tap the Search icon.

2. Enter the name you want to search for. You can search for the first or last name.

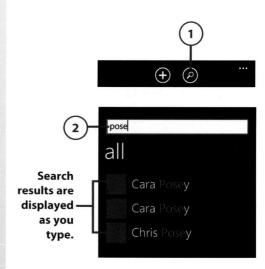

Search results are displayed as you type.

Using Jump Lists to Find a Contact

Another way of quickly locating contacts is to browse for contacts using jump lists. Jump lists let you jump to a specific letter of the alphabet in the alphabetical list of contacts. To use a jump list, open the People hub and complete these steps:

1. Tap a letter of the alphabet. You can tap any letter, regardless of what you are searching for.

2. Tap the letter you want to jump to. This letter should correspond to the first or last name of the person you want to search for.

3. Tap the contact you want to view.

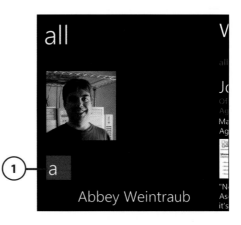

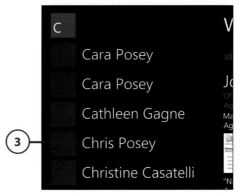

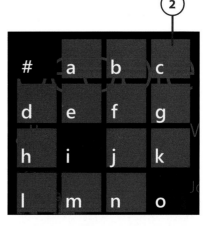

Pinning a Contact to the Start Screen

If you like to frequently check on certain friends or family members, you can pin someone's profile to the start screen. Doing so gives you one-touch access to the person's profile so that you can easily call, send an email message or a text message, or view that person's Facebook Wall. To do so, open the People hub and follow these steps:

1. Tap and hold the contact you want to pin to the Start screen.

2. Tap Pin to Start.

3. The contact now appears in a separate tile on the Start screen.

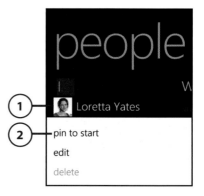

Linking Contacts

Because the People hub aggregates your contacts from multiple sources, you might end up with multiple entries for the same person. Although Windows automatically attempts to find and merge all the profile information for that person and display it as a single contact, sometimes it misses and a contact appears in your list more than once. Fortunately, Windows Phone 8 enables you to manually merge contacts by linking them. To do so, open the People hub and follow these steps:

1. Tap the contact you want to link.

2. Tap the Link icon.

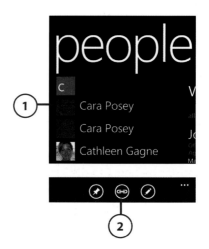

3. Tap the profile you want to add to this contact's Linked Profiles, and then press your phone's Back button.

Manually Choosing

If the contact you want to link doesn't appear in the Suggested Links list, you can tap the Choose a Contact link and manually select someone from your entire contacts list.

4. Verify that the Link icon displays a number 2, indicating that there are two linked profiles. If necessary, you can link more than two profiles.

5. Tap the Back button and verify that there is only one listing for the linked profile.

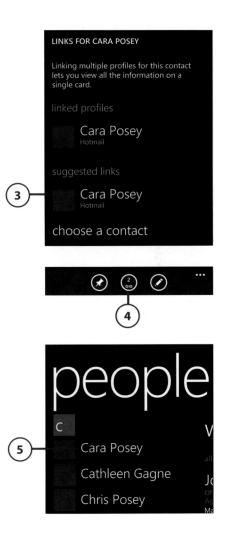

LINKS FOR CARA POSEY

Linking multiple profiles for this contact lets you view all the information on a single card.

linked profiles

Cara Posey
Hotmail

suggested links

Cara Posey
Hotmail

choose a contact

people

C

Cara Posey

Cathleen Gagne

Chris Posey

Configuring Social Network Settings

The People hub provides access to a Settings page that enables you to customize your phone's behavior. Some of these settings are Facebook specific and others relate solely to the People hub. (I talk more about Facebook later, in the section "Facebook Integration.") You can access these settings by opening the People hub, tapping the Menu icon, and selecting Settings.

The Settings screen contains these settings:

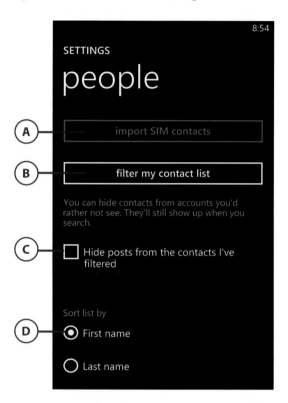

A. **Import SIM Contacts:** This option does not exist on every Windows Phone 8 device. On devices that accept SIM cards, this option can import contacts.

B. **Filter My Contact List:** You can tap the Filter My Contacts List button and then choose which account's contacts show up in the People hub. All contacts remain searchable, regardless of whether you choose to filter them.

C. **Hide Posts from the Contacts I've Filtered:** You can use this setting, which applies to feeds incoming from social networks to which you're connected, to prevent uninteresting posts from cluttering your profile.

D. **Sort List By:** You can choose to sort your contacts by either first name or last name.

E. **Display Names By:** The People hub displays your contact's names in alphabetical order. This setting controls whether the list is organized according to first name or last name.

F. **Use My Location:** This setting controls whether your phone is allowed to use your GPS information when you check in at a location.

G. **Save Check-In Searches and Locations with My Microsoft Account to Improve Search Results:** You can choose whether your check-in history is saved with your Microsoft account.

Groups

Just as you can add a new contact to your phone, you can also add a new group. Groups make it easy to send a single message to multiple recipients. For instance, suppose that you frequently send email messages to several friends. Instead of manually adding each of your friends to each message you send, you can create a group called Friends and add your friends to it. That way, you can send future email messages to the group rather than to individual contacts.

Creating a New Group

To create a group, open the People hub and complete these steps:

1. Flick to the Together screen, if necessary.

2. Tap the New icon.

3. Tap Group.

4. When prompted, enter a name for the group you want to create.

5. Tap Save.

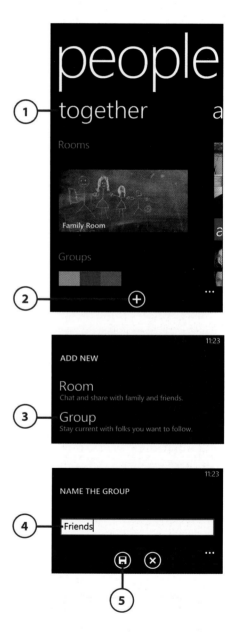

Adding a Contact to a Group

After creating a group, you need to add some contacts to it. To do so, open the People hub and complete these steps:

1. Flick the screen to access the Together page, if necessary.

2. Tap the group name.

3. Tap the Members icon.

4. Tap the Add icon.

5. Tap the name of a contact you want to add to the group.

6. Tap the Done icon.

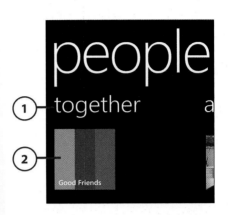

Removing a Group Member

If you use the Groups feature, at some point, you will need to remove a contact from a group. You can accomplish this by opening the People hub and following these steps:

1. Go to the Together screen and tap the name of the group you want to modify.

2. Tap the Members icon.

3. Tap the name of the group member you want to remove.

4. Tap Remove from Group.

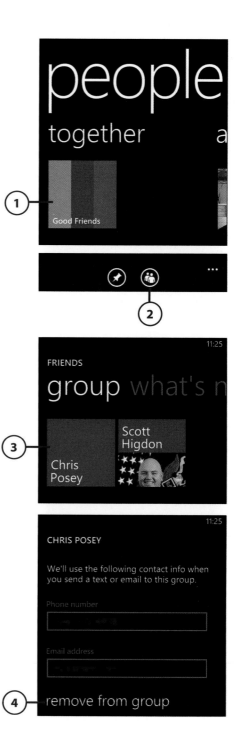

Renaming a Group

Occasionally, you might create a group and then later decide that you want to call it something different. You can rename a group by opening the People Hub and following these steps:

1. Flick to the Together screen.

2. Tap the name of the group you want to rename.

3. Tap the Menu icon.

4. Tap Rename.

5. Provide a new name for the group.

6. Tap the Save icon.

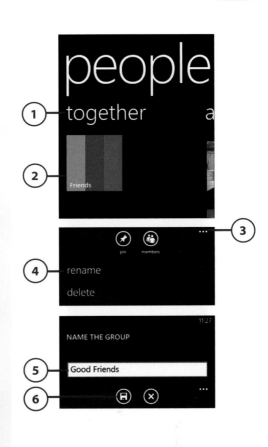

Pinning a Group to the Start Screen

If you have a group that you use frequently, you might benefit from pinning the group to the Start screen. You can accomplish this task by opening the People hub and following these steps:

1. Tap and hold the name of the group you want to pin to the Start screen.

2. Tap Pin to Start.

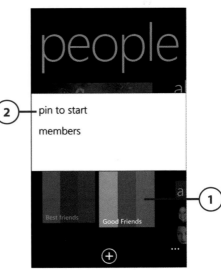

Deleting a Group

If it becomes necessary, you can delete a group. Deleting a group deletes only the group structure, not the contacts within the group. You can delete a group by going to the Start screen, tapping the People tile, and following these steps:

1. Flick to the Together screen, if necessary.

2. Tap the name of the group you want to delete.

3. Tap the Menu icon.

4. Tap Delete.

5. When prompted for confirmation, tap Delete.

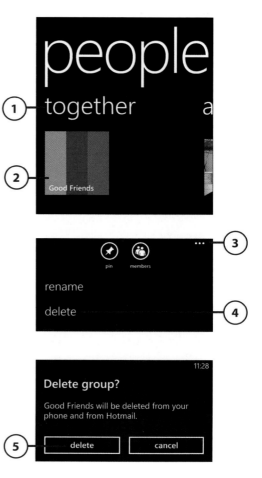

Sending an Email Message to Group Members

One of the main reasons for creating groups is that doing so makes it easy to send email messages to everyone in the group at once. To send an email to group members, open the People hub and follow these steps:

1. Flick to the Together screen, if necessary.

2. Tap the group to which you want to send the email message.

3. Tap Send Email.

4. Select the account from which you want to send the message.

5. Compose your message.

6. Tap Send.

Missing Recipients

The Send Email option (step 3 in this task) lists the group members to which an email will be sent. If you don't have email addresses for one or more group members, the Send Email option provides a list of the people to whom you can send the message.

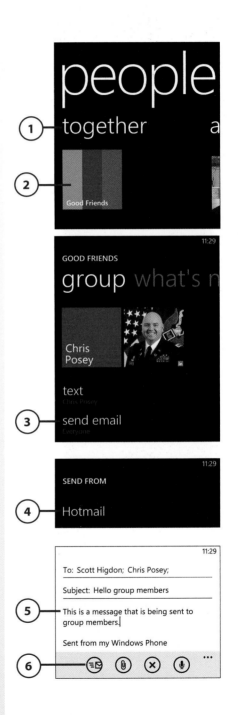

Sending a Text Message to Group Members

One of the main reasons for creating groups is that doing so makes it easy to send messages to everyone in the group at once. To send a text message to group members, go to the Start screen, tap the People tile, and follow these steps:

1. Flick to the Together screen, if necessary.

2. Tap the group to which you want to send the text message.

3. Tap Text.

4. Compose your message.

5. Tap Send.

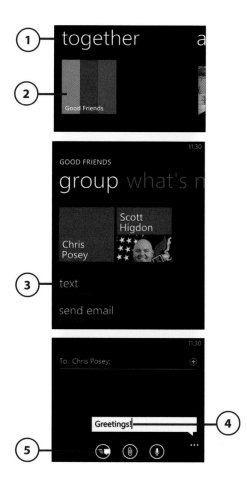

Rooms

Rooms are a new feature on Windows Phone 8. Rooms are a private environment where you can interact with specific people without having to worry about publicly exposing things that should be kept private. For example, you might create a room for a group of friends, a room for family, or a room for coworkers.

Although rooms are a Windows Phone 8 feature, the participants do not necessarily need to have Windows Phone 8. People can join rooms that you create if they have Windows Phone 7 or the iPhone. However, they cannot use the Group Chat feature. Likewise, some of the other room features might not be quite as full-featured as they would be on Windows Phone 8. Regardless of whether or not participants have a Windows Phone 8 device, a Microsoft account is required.

Creating a Room

The first step in using the Rooms feature is usually to create a room. Windows Phone 8 devices include a predefined room called Family Room, but you can delete this room, if necessary. You can create a room by opening the People hub and completing these steps:

1. Flick the screen to access the Together page, if necessary.

2. Tap the New icon.

3. Tap Room.

4. Specify a name for the room you want to create. This is the name that is displayed on each member's phone.

5. Tap Save.

6. Tap the Done icon.

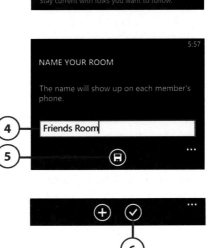

Accessing a Room

After you have created a room, you can access it by opening the People hub and following these steps:

1. Flick the screen to access the Together page, if necessary.

2. Tap the name of the room you want to enter.

Adding Members to a Room

After creating a room, you can add members by going into the room and completing these steps:

1. Tap the Members icon.

2. Tap the Invite icon.

3. Choose the contact you want to invite to the room.

4. Tap Send to send the invite.

The Recipient Experience

When you invite someone to a room, that person receives two text messages. The first test message says, "Hey, I set up a room on my phone called <room name>. Join it, then we can privately share a calendar, photos, group chat, and notes." The second text message contains a URL that the recipient can tap to accept the invitation. The URL takes the recipient to a web page that prompts the person to sign in using a Microsoft account.

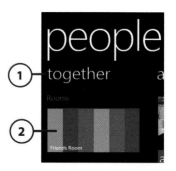

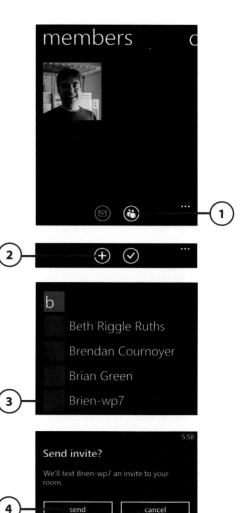

Deleting a Room Member

If you need to remove a member from a room, you can do so by opening the room and completing these steps:

1. Tap the Members icon.

2. Tap the member you want to remove.

3. Tap Remove.

Choosing a Room Background

Windows Phone 8 enables you to change a room's background. Doing so causes the selected image to display as wallpaper while you are in the room. The image is also used within the room's Live Tile. You can change a room's background image by going into the room and completing these steps:

1. Tap the Menu icon.

2. Tap Choose Background.

3. Locate and select the image you want to use for the room background.

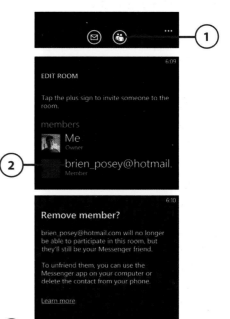

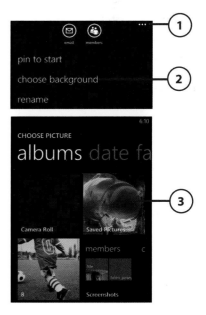

4. Adjust the picture's position and tap the Crop icon.

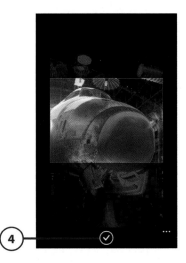

Pinning a Room to the Start Screen

If you use a room often, it can be handy to pin the room to the start screen. You can accomplish this by going into the room and completing these steps:

1. Tap the Menu icon.

2. Tap Pin to Start.

3. The room now appears in a tile on the start screen.

Renaming a Room

Windows Phone 8 gives you the option to rename a room. You can rename a room by going into the room and completing these steps:

1. Tap the Menu icon.

2. Tap Rename.

3. Enter a new name for the room.

4. Tap the Save icon.

Deleting a Room

If you no longer need a room, you can delete it by going into the room and completing the following steps:

1. Tap the Menu icon.

2. Tap Delete Room.

3. When prompted for confirmation, tap Delete.

Using Group Chat

One of the nice things about rooms is that they enable you to have private chats with the members of the room. You can engage in a group chat by going into the room and completing these steps:

1. Flick the screen to the Chat page.

2. Enter the text that you want to send to the other room members.

3. Tap the Send icon.

Other Group Chat Features

Using the Group Chat feature is similar to sending a text message to members of the room. As with a text message, you simply compose your message and tap Send. However, the Group Chat screen also contains two other icons: the Speak icon and the Location icon. You can use the Speak icon to verbally compose a message. Tapping the Location icon causes Windows to create a map of your current location. This map can be sent to room members as a part of the group chat.

It's Not All Good

Windows Phone 7

The Group Chat feature works only on Windows Phone 8 devices. It is not supported for members accessing the room from Windows Phone 7 or iPhone devices.

Sharing Photos and Videos

To share a photo with other room members, go into the room and complete the following steps:

1. Flick the screen to the Photos page.

2. Tap the Add button.

3. Tap Photo or Video.

4. Choose the photo or video you want to share.

5. Tap the Done icon.

Viewing Shared Photos and Videos

Rooms enable members to privately share photos and videos with one another. To view photos or videos that you or others have shared, open the room and complete these steps:

1. Flick the screen to the photos page.

2. Tap the photo or video you want to view.

Refreshing the Screen

If you don't see the photo or video you are looking for, but you know it's there, tap the Menu icon and tap Refresh.

Viewing the Shared Calendar

When you create a room, Windows automatically creates a calendar that is shared among room members. You can view the shared calendar by going into the room and completing these steps:

1. Flick the screen to access the Calendar page.

2. Any appointments from the shared calendar appear on the Calendar page.

Viewing Multiple Calendars

If you go to the phone's Start screen and tap the Calendar tile, Windows Phone 8 displays appointments from all your calendars (including shared calendars). As an alternative, you can go into a room, go to the Calendar page, tap the Menu icon, and tap Show All Calendars.

Adding an Appointment to the Shared Calendar

If you want to add an appointment to a shared calendar, you can do so by going into the room and completing these steps:

1. Flick the screen to access the Calendar page.

2. Tap the New icon.

3. Enter the details of your appointment.

4. Tap the Save icon.

Creating a New Shared Note

You can create a new OneNote document from within a room to share with room members. To do so, go into the room and complete these steps:

1. Flick the screen to access the Notes page.

2. Tap the Add icon.

3. Assign a title to your note.

4. Compose the note.

5. Press the phone's Back button twice. The note appears on the Notes page.

Viewing Shared Notes

Windows Phone 8 also enables you to use rooms as a way of sharing OneNote notes with room members. To view a shared note, open the room and complete these steps:

1. Flick the screen to access the Notes page.

2. Tap the note you want to view.

Facebook Integration

Windows Phone 8 offers built-in Facebook integration. This means that you can access your friend's Facebook Wall (as well as your own) without actually having to go to the Facebook website. Instead, Facebook information is automatically made available through the People hub. Of course, before you can access anyone's Facebook Wall, you have to connect your phone to your Facebook account.

Connecting to Facebook

You can link your Windows Phone 8 device directly to your Facebook account. To do so, go to the Settings screen, tap Email+Accounts, and follow these steps:

1. Tap Add an Account.

2. Tap Facebook.

3. Enter your email address and password.

4. Tap Sign In.

5. Tap Connect.

Viewing a Wall Post

After you have added a Facebook account to your phone, you can access a friend's Facebook Wall directly through the People hub. To view a friend's Wall posts, open the People hub and follow these steps:

1. Tap on the name of a contact.

2. When the phone displays the contact's profile, flick the screen to the right to access the What's New page.

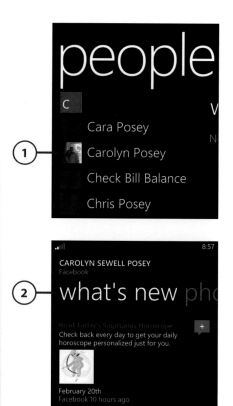

Viewing Comments to Wall Posts

Windows Phone 8 displays a speech bubble to the right of each Wall post. If the speech bubble contains a plus sign, it means that nobody has commented on the post. If you tap the + icon, you can read the full post and also see how many people like the post.

If the speech bubble contains a number, that number reflects the number of comments that have been made regarding the post. Tapping the speech bubble causes Windows to display the full post, the comment threat for the post, and the number of people who like the post.

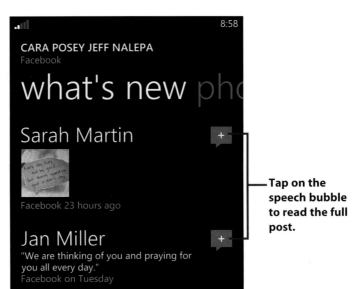

Tap on the speech bubble to read the full post.

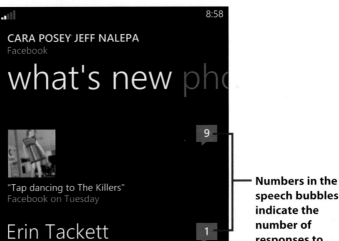

Numbers in the speech bubbles indicate the number of responses to the post.

Commenting on a Wall Post

If you want to comment on someone's Facebook Wall post, you can do so by following these steps:

1. Tap the speech bubble next to the post.

2. Tap the comment bubble and enter your comment.

3. Tap the Post icon.

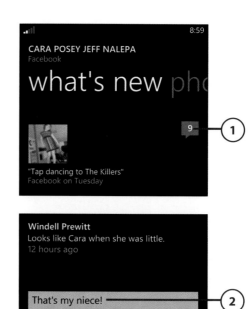

Liking a Post

Windows Phone 8 also enables you to like someone's Facebook post. To like a post, follow these steps:

1. Tap the speech bubble next to the post you like.

2. Tap the Like icon.

Unliking

If you accidentally like a post, you can undo your mistake by tapping the Unlike icon.

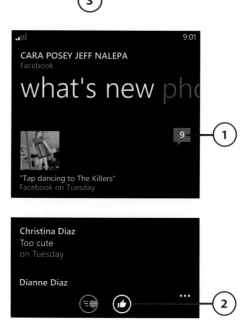

Writing on a Friend's Facebook Wall

Windows Phone 8 enables you to write on a friend's Facebook Wall. To do so, open the People hub and follow these steps:

1. Tap the name of a contact.

2. Flick to the Profile screen, if necessary.

3. Tap Write on Wall.

4. Write your post in the space provided.

5. Tap the Post icon.

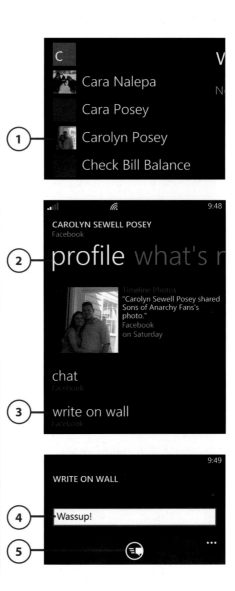

Viewing Facebook Photos

Windows Phone 8 enables you to view and comment on pictures that your friends have posted on Facebook. You have several different methods for viewing Facebook photos, but here I focus on viewing Wall photos and albums.

Viewing Facebook Wall Photos

To see the photos that your friends have uploaded to their Facebook Walls, open the People hub and follow these steps:

1. Tap the name of the person whose photos you want to view.

2. Flick the screen to access the What's New page. If the person has recently uploaded any photos, they are displayed on the What's New page as thumbnails.

3. Tap the thumbnail for the photo you want to view.

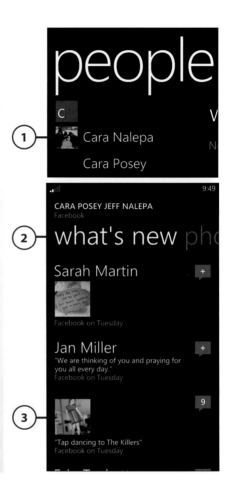

>>>Go Further

VIEWING ALL RECENT FACEBOOK PHOTOS

Windows Phone 8 makes it easy to view all the pictures that your Facebook friends have recently uploaded. To do so, instead of going to the People hub, open the Photos app and flick the What's New page. The What's New page displays all the pictures that your friends have recently uploaded.

Viewing a Friend's Facebook Albums

You can also view your friends' Facebook albums through Windows Phone 8. To do so, open the People hub and follow these steps:

1. Tap the name of the person whose albums you want to view.

2. When the person's profile is displayed, flick the screen to access the Photos page.

3. Tap the tile representing the person's albums.

4. Tap the individual album you want to view.

ACCESSING FACEBOOK ALBUMS THROUGH THE PHOTOS HUB

Facebook albums are also accessible through the Pictures hub. To access Facebook albums this way open the Photos app and, from the People page, select a contact whose albums you want to view. You can then choose from any album that person has added to the Facebook account.

The Me Tile

The Me tile is a central location where it is possible to access feeds from your social networks. Through the Me tile, you can post status updates to any of your social networks, view social network feeds, or check out update notifications.

Viewing Your Own Social Networking Wall

Just as Windows Phone 8 enables you to view your friend's Facebook Walls, you can also view your own Wall (which can include feeds from Facebook or any other social network that is connected to your phone). To do so, go to the Start screen and follow these steps:

1. Tap the Me tile.

2. Flick to the What's New page to view your Wall.

Non-Facebook Content

If Facebook is the only social network you have configured, the What's New page acts as your Facebook Wall. However, if you have accounts with Twitter or LinkedIn, content from those networks also appears on the What's New page.

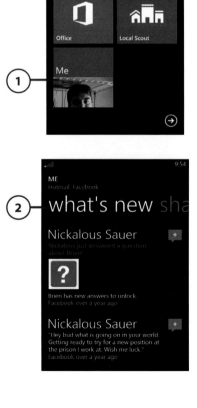

It's Not All Good

Don't Delete Me Tile

Be careful not to delete the Me tile from the Start screen. Unlike the other default Start screen tiles, it's not obvious how to get it back: Me isn't an app that appears on the App screen. If you intentionally or accidentally remove it and want it back, you can do so by opening the People hub and tapping your own photo at the top of the All screen. On your profile page is a Pin icon that you can tap to put the Me tile back on the Start screen. This icon appears only if the Me app isn't already on the Start screen.

Posting Status Updates

You can perform a status update directly from your phone. To do so, go to the Start screen, tap the Me tile, and follow these steps:

1. Flick the screen to the Share page, if necessary.

2. Tap the Post an Update link.

3. Choose the social networking site where the post should appear.

4. Choose who to share the post with.

5. Type your message.

6. Tap the Post icon.

Checking In

Windows Phone 8 enables you to check in at a location. To perform a Facebook check-in, open the Me tile and follow these steps:

1. Flick the screen to the Share page.

2. Tap Check-In.

3. Windows uses your location information to retrieve a list of nearby locations. Tap your desired location.

Custom Locations

Although being able to choose from a list of locations is handy, it might not work so well in dense urban areas. If you find that your location isn't on the list (or if the list is too long to sort through), you can use a different method. At the bottom of the locations list are two icons. One is a Search icon, which lets you search the locations for the one you want to check in at. The other is an Add icon that lets you define your own locations.

ME
Hotmail, Facebook

share notificati

post an update

check in

set chat status
available

PICK A PLACE

Pier 51 Seafood
0.53 mi

Lake Club Marina LLC
0.43 mi

Museum of York County
0.64 mi

Howard's Automotive
0.59 mi

Uploading a Photo

Windows Phone 8 enables you to upload a photo from your photo roll directly to Facebook. To do so, open the Photos app and follow these steps:

1. Tap the picture you want to upload (as an alternative, you can also post a picture directly from the camera).

2. Tap the Menu icon.

3. Tap Share.

4. Tap Facebook.

5. Enter a caption for your picture.

6. Optionally, tag people who appear in the photo.

7. Tap the Upload icon.

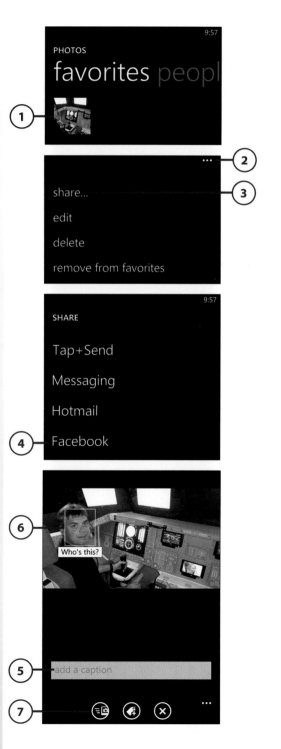

>>Go Further

FACEBOOK TAGGING

When you get ready to upload a photo to Facebook, it is possible to tag the people shown in the photo. If the photo contains one or more people, the phone automatically draws a rectangle around each face. Just beneath the rectangle is a tag that reads "Who's This." If you tap this tag, you have the choice of either typing a name or selecting a name from your Facebook contacts.

Every once in a while, Windows Phone 8 devices might not properly detect that there are faces shown in a photo. In this situation, you can tap the Add Tag icon and then tap the face in the photo. Windows then allows you to either manually enter a name or choose a name from your Facebook contacts.

Chatting with Friends

Windows Phone 8 devices enable you to chat with your social networking friends (Facebook and Messenger) directly through your phone. To do so, open the Messaging tile and follow these steps:

1. Flick the screen to access the Online page.

2. Tap the person you want to chat with.

3. Enter your message.

4. Tap the Send icon.

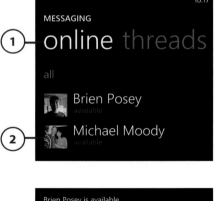

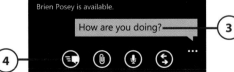

Setting Your Chat Status

You can manually set your chat status at any time by opening the Messaging app and following these steps:

1. Flick the screen to the Online page.

2. Tap the Status icon.

3. Tap your desired status.

MESSAGING

10:18

online threads

all

Brien Posey
available

Michael Moody
available

10:30

SET CHAT STATUS

available

busy

away

invisible

offline

Notifications

You can use Windows Phone 8 to view notifications from your social networks. To do so, open the Me tile and complete the following steps:

1. Flick the screen to the Notifications screen.

2. This screen lists any recent notifications you've received. Tap the notification you want to view.

Mixed Updates

The Notifications screen contains notifications from Facebook, Twitter, and any other social networking sites you have configured through your phone.

ME
Hotmail, Facebook, Twitter

10:55

notifications wh

BTG mentioned you in a tweet
Twitter last Thursday

SearchCIO.com mentioned you in a tweet
Twitter last Thursday

VT Technology mentioned you in a tweet
Twitter last Thursday

>>>Go Further

THE FACEBOOK APP

By now, you have probably noticed that various Facebook elements are scattered throughout the phone. Wall posts are in the People hub, chat is in the Messaging area, and photos are accessed through the Pictures hub. If you prefer to have everything in one place, a number of free Facebook apps for Windows Phone 8 can accomplish this. These apps, which include an official Facebook app that you can download through the Store, enable you to access your Facebook account through a single interface.

Twitter

Windows Phone 8 devices include full Twitter integration. You can send and receive tweets directly through the phone without installing any extra software.

Configuring Your Twitter Account

Before you can use Twitter from your phone, you must link the phone to your Twitter account. You can do so by going to the Settings screen and following these steps:

1. Tap Email+Accounts.

2. Tap Add an Account.

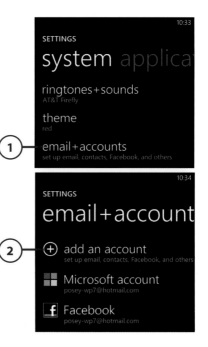

3. Tap Twitter.

4. Tap Connect.

5. When prompted, enter the email address and password for your Twitter account.

6. Tap Authorize App.

Sending a Tweet

Using the Me tile, you send a tweet in essentially the same way you post a message to Facebook (see "Posting Status Updates"). However, tweets must be 140 characters or less in length.

Checking for Tweets

You can access the tweets of Twitter users that you follow by opening the People hub and following these steps:

1. Flick the screen to access the What's New page.

Responding to a Tweet

If you want to respond to tweet, you can do so by following these steps:

1. Tap the tweet to which you want to respond.

2. Enter your comment.

3. Tap the Post icon.

Checking Twitter Notifications

Windows Phone 8 enables you to check your Twitter notifications. To do so, open the Me tile and complete these steps:

1. Flick to the Notifications screen.

2. Click the tweet that you want to view.

THE TWITTER APP

As was the case for Facebook data, elements related to Twitter are scattered throughout the phone. If you are interested in centralizing the Twitter experience then you might consider downloading a Twitter app. The Store contains an official Twitter app, and there are also unofficial Twitter apps from independent developers.

LinkedIn

Windows Phone 8 devices are capable of connecting to LinkedIn without the aid of any additional software.

Configuring Your LinkedIn Account

To connect a phone to LinkedIn, go to the Settings screen and follow these steps:

1. Tap Email+Accounts.

2. Tap Add an Account.

3. Tap LinkedIn

4. Tap Connect.

5. Enter the email address and password that are connected to your LinkedIn account.

6. Tap OK, I'll Allow It.

Accessing LinkedIn Content

Content from LinkedIn is shown in the same place as Facebook and Twitter content. You can view content from LinkedIn by opening the People hub and following these steps:

1. Flick the screen to access the What's New page.

Responding to a LinkedIn Post

You can respond to a LinkedIn post by following these steps:

1. Tap the speech bubble for the post you want to respond to.

2. Enter your response in the Add a Comment field.

3. Tap the Post icon.

Liking a LinkedIn Post

You can like a LinkedIn post by tapping the Like (heart-shaped) icon instead of the Post icon.

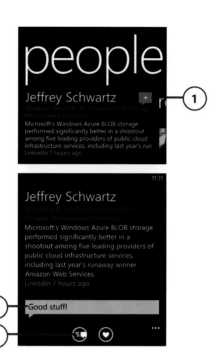

Posting a Message

You can post a message to LinkedIn by going to the Me tile and following these steps:

1. Tap Post an Update.

2. Tap the Post To field.

3. Clear all the check boxes except for the LinkedIn box.

4. Tap the Done icon.

5. Enter your message.

6. Tap the Post icon.

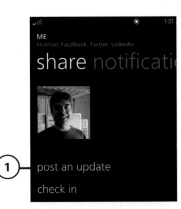

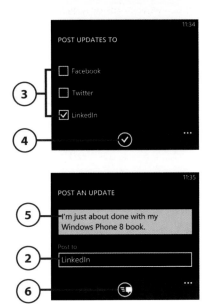

The Feeds Filter

Because Windows Live, Facebook, Twitter, and LinkedIn content is all aggregated and displayed on the What's New page, the page might become so cluttered that you can no longer easily find what you are looking for. If this happens, you can use the Feeds Filter to cut through the clutter.

To use the Feeds filter, open the People hub and complete the following steps:

1. Flick the screen to the What's New page.

2. Tap All Accounts.

3. Choose the account for which you want to view status updates.

Feeds are currently being displayed from Facebook, Twitter, and LinkedIn.

Feeds are now being displayed for Facebook only.

Index

X-Y-Z

My Windows® Phone 8

Brien Posey

FREE · Online Edition

Safari Books Online